THE NATIONAL SOCIETY FOR PERFORMANCE AND INSTRUCTION (NSPI)

The National Society for Performance and Instruction (NSPI) is the leading international association dedicated to improving productivity and performance in the workplace. Founded in 1962, NSPI represents over ten thousand members throughout the United States and Canada and in thirty-three other countries. NSPI members work in over three thousand businesses, governmental agencies, academic institutions, and other organizations. Monthly meetings of over sixty different chapters provide professional development, services, and information exchange.

NSPI members include performance technologists, training directors, human resource managers, instructional technologists, human factors practitioners, and organizational development consultants. They are business executives, professors, line managers, government leaders, and military commanders. They work in a variety of areas: the armed forces, financial services, government agencies, health services, high technology, manufacturing, telecommunications, travel and hospitality, and universities. NSPI members are leaders in their fields and work settings. They are strategy-oriented, quality-focused, and results-centered.

The mission of NSPI is to improve the performance of individuals and organizations through the application of Human Performance Technology (HPT). NSPI's vision for itself is to be the preferred source of information, education, and advocacy for enhancing individual and organizational effectiveness, and to be respected for the tangible and enduring impact it is having on people, organizations, and the field of performance technology.

NSPI makes a difference to people by helping them grow into skilled professionals who use integrated and systematic approaches to add value to their organizations and the profession. Whether designing training programs, building selection or incentive systems, assisting organizations in their own redesign, or performing myriad other interventions, NSPI members produce results.

NSPI makes a difference to organizations by increasing professional competence and confidence. NSPI members help organizations anticipate opportunities and challenges and develop powerful solutions that contribute to productivity and satisfaction.

NSPI makes a difference to the field of performance technology by expanding the boundaries of what we know about defining, teaching, supporting, and maintaining skilled human performance. With a healthy respect for research and development, a variety of technologies, and collegial interaction, NSPI members use approaches and systems that ensure improved productivity and a better world.

For additional information, contact:

National Society for Performance and Instruction
1300 L Street, N.W., Suite 1250
Washington, DC 20005
Telephone: (202) 408-7969
Fax: (202) 408-7972

MAKING COMPUTERS PEOPLE-LITERATE

Other Titles in the Series

Set I:
*DESIGNING THE WORK ENVIRONMENT
FOR OPTIMUM PERFORMANCE*

*CREATING THE ERGONOMICALLY
SOUND WORKPLACE*
Lee T. Ostrom

*CREATING WORKPLACES
WHERE PEOPLE CAN THINK*
Phyl Smith
Lynn Kearny

MAKING COMPUTERS PEOPLE-LITERATE

Elaine Weiss

 JOSSEY-BASS PUBLISHERS AUG 8 1995
SAN FRANCISCO

The excerpt from "Farewell My Lovely!" by E. B. White on page xix is from
Essays of E. B. White (Harper & Row); © 1936, 1964 The New Yorker
Magazine, Inc. Originally published in *The New Yorker* in 1936 over the
pseudonym "Lee Strout White." Richard L. Strout had submitted a manuscript
on the Ford, and White, with his collaboration, rewrote it.

The excerpt from *The Nurnberg Funnel* by J. M. Carroll on page 48 is
reprinted with the permission of MIT Press.

The User Satisfaction Survey described in Chapter Two is adapted with the
permission of Ben Shneiderman and Kent Norman.

Substantial discounts on bulk quantities of Jossey-Bass books are available to
corporations, professional associations, and other organizations. For details
and discount information, contact the special sales department at Jossey-Bass
Inc., Publishers. (415) 433-1740; Fax (415) 433-0499.

For sales outside the United States, contact Maxwell Macmillan
International Publishing Group, 866 Third Avenue, New York,
New York 10022.

Manufactured in the United States of America. Nearly all Jossey-Bass
books and jackets are printed on recycled paper that contains at least
50 percent recycled waste, including 10 percent postconsumer waste. Many of
our materials are also printed with vegetable-based inks; during the printing
process these inks emit fewer volatile organic compounds (VOCs) than
petroleum-based inks. VOCs contribute to the formation of smog.

Library of Congress Cataloging-in-Publication Data

Weiss, Elaine.
    Making computers people-literate / Elaine Weiss.—1st ed.
      p.   cm.—(The Jossey-Bass management series)
    Includes bibliographical references and index.
    ISBN 1-55542-622-0
    1. Human-computer interaction.   2. User interfaces (Computer
systems) I. Title. II. Series.
    QA76.9.H85W45   1994   93-41613
    004′.01′9—dc20   CIP

FIRST EDITION
PB Printing   *10 9 8 7 6 5 4 3 2 1*   *Code 9418*

THE JOSSEY-BASS
MANAGEMENT SERIES

CONTENTS

This book is dedicated to my father,
Bernard W. Weiss, M.D.
1922-1993

From Training to Performance in the Twenty-First Century: Introduction to the Book Series

For most trainers and instructional developers, the following request from a client sounds familiar: "I have a problem. Give me some training to solve it." We are taught to think that training is the answer to most human performance problems. But those of us who are veterans in the field have learned from our own experience and from others' research and theories that most of the problems our clients bring us are *not* best solved by training, or require some other solution in addition to training. What do we do in the face of this contradictory evidence?

We change our view of the world, our paradigm for thinking about how to solve our customers' problems. We look at practitioners in other fields and see how they recommend solving problems, and we try to incorporate their ideas and interventions into our own "bag of tricks."

We have heard and read about a wide array of such interventions: human-computer interface and workplace design; work process reengineering and sociotechnical systems; job aids, expert systems, and performance support systems; motivation, incentive, and feedback systems; organizational design, cultural change, and change management; measurement of results to demonstrate bottom-line savings. How do all these interventions fit together? Is there a field that incorporates and relates them? Yes. It is called Human Performance Technology (HPT).

What is human performance technology?

What makes HPT different from training, management consulting, and other practices aimed at improving the performance of people and organizations? According to Foshay and Moller (1992, p. 702), HPT is unique because it is "an applied field, not a discipline. It is structured primarily by the real world problem of human performance (in the workplace). It draws from any discipline that has prescriptive power in solving any human performance problem." Stolovich and Keeps (1992a, p.7) have incorporated a variety of definitions of the field into their descriptions of HPT's unique approach to synthesizing ideas borrowed from other disciplines:

HPT, therefore, is an engineering approach to attaining desired accomplishments from human performers. HP technologists are those who adopt a systems view of performance gaps, systematically analyze both gap and system, and design cost-effective and efficient interventions that are based on analysis data, scientific knowledge, and documented precedents, in order to close the gap in the most desirable manner.

Rummler and Brache (1992, p. 34) explain that the view HP technologists have of "what is going on . . . in organizations" is "fundamentally different" from views held by practitioners in other disciplines. HP technologists conceptualize "what is going on" by looking at and assessing three levels of variables that affect individual and organizational performance: the organization level, the work process level, and the job/worker level.

An HP technologist looks first at the total organization and at such variables as strategy and goals, structure, measurements, and management (see Figure P.1). Next, an HP technologist looks at work processes carried out across functions within the organization and analyzes the goals, design, measurement, and management of those processes to determine their effectiveness (see Figure P.2). Finally, an HP technologist looks at the job and the performer, focusing on five variables (Rummler and Brache, 1992, pp. 35–41):

1. *The performer.* Does the person have the physical, mental, and emotional ability as well as the skills and knowledge needed to perform?

2. *Inputs to the performer.* Are the available job procedures and work flow, information, money, tools, and the work environment adequate to support the desired performance?

3. *Outputs of the performer.* Do performance specifications for the outputs exist and is the performer aware of them?

4. *Consequences of the performer's actions.* Are consequences designed to support the performance and delivered in a timely manner?

5. *Feedback the performer receives about the performance.* Does the performer receive feedback, and if so, is it relevant, timely, accurate, and specific?

Figure P.1. The Organization View of Work.

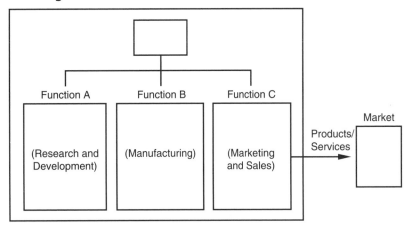

Source: Rummler and Brache, 1992, p. 35.

Figure P.2. The Cross-Functional View of Work Process.

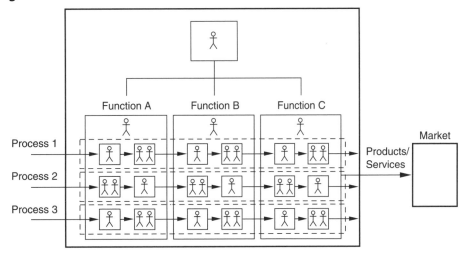

Source: Rummler and Brache, 1992, p. 37.

Figure P.3. The Job/Performer View of Work.

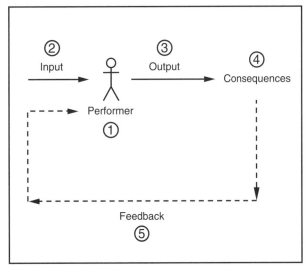

Source: Rummler and Brache, 1992, p. 38.

Purpose of the series

Once we have changed our worldview and accepted the notion of HPT interventions into our paradigm of how to approach the resolution of clients' problems, we would really like to try to implement some of them. But how?

1. Instruction is not the answer to every challenge in the workplace.

2. There are a wide array of interventions that can be used to enhance performance.

3. The HP technologist cannot be expected to be an expert in every intervention [Rossett, 1992, p. 98].

As Rossett points out, it is not feasible for us to be experts in all these interventions. First, because the fields from which the interventions come are so diverse and constantly changing, it is virtually impossible for any of us to learn everything about and keep current in all fields. Second, there are very few resources out there to help us design and implement performance-enhancing interventions. Most books on the subject focus on what the inteventions are and why they are important, but contain precious few specific guidelines, procedures, or rules for how to actually carry out the interventions.

So, as practitioners we face several gaps: between our grounding in the "training" field and the recognition that we need to expand our worldview to include other performance-enhancing interventions; between our desire to learn about the other interventions and the difficulty of keeping current in all the fields from which they derive; and between the desire to try performance-enhancing interventions and the last of specific, practical guidance on how to do so.

The series "From Training to Performance in the Twenty-First Century" tries to bridge these gaps. First, the series is based on two assumptions: (1) that training/instructional design/HPT practitioners are, for the most part, currently limited to implementing training interventions in the workplace, and (2) that most practitioners recognize the need to broaden their worldview and range of interventions to embrace the approach described above. The series is designed to serve as a bridge from training to other areas of HPT.

Second, the series is a *translation/how-to-do-it* series that tracks down and summarizes the knowledgebase of the fields from which the performance-enhancing interventions are derived and focuses on specific, practical *how-to* techniques for implementing performance-enhancing interventions in real job situations.

Organization of the series

To accomplish our purpose, we have organized the series into manageable chunks called Topics, each comprising three to five books that address a related set of performance-enhancing interventions. Each book covers one performance-enhancing intervention completely.

To implement the translation/how-to-do-it approach, maintain consistency across the series, and make the procedures as easy as possible to learn and use, each book makes extensive use of procedure and decision tables, forms, examples (both successful and unsuccessful), and case studies. Each book begins with a brief synthesis of the theoretical foundations of the intervention, acknowledging different points of view where they exist. This introductory material is followed by chapters containing a wide variety of procedures that show how to implement each intervention step by step. Many job aids and forms are provided. The book presents one or more real-world case studies showing the entire intervention in practice, complete with filled-out forms. It also provides a resource section that contains blank forms for reproduction and a glossary. Finally, an extensive bibliography covers almost all the current thinking about the intervention.

Audience

The "From Training to Performance" series is designed for three audiences. The primary audience is trainers, training managers, and novice HPT practitioners, who will use the books as an on-the-job reference and work tool as they move from applying training solutions to using performance improvement interventions. The second audience is longtime instructional design and HPT practitioners, who will use the books for continuing education in performance improvement interventions that have evolved since they joined the field. The third audience is graduate students in training, instructional design, performance technology, organizational development, human resource development, and management, who will use the books to learn HPT techniques.

Each audience will use the series slightly differently. Trainers and training managers might want to begin with the case studies to see how the intervention really works, then go to the procedures and forms to try out the interventions. Graduate students will almost certainly begin with the theoretical material and integrate it into their schema of HPT before moving on to apply the procedures and forms to real-world or simulated performance problems. Veteran HPT practitioners might use either of the approaches, jumping back and forth between the procedures, case study, and theory, or focusing on the design and usability of the procedures and forms that are of particular professional interest to them.

It is the fervent hope of the National Society for Performance and Instruction (NSPI) that readers will use the books in this series as a continuing source of self-development, training for others, and, most important, on-the-job reference tools, to provide clients with the most cost-effective and efficient interventions for solving their business problems.

Acknowledgments

This series would not exist without the help and support of the following people, who helped create and nurture it: the late Paul Tremper, NSPI's executive director from 1985 to 1993, who provided vision and emotional support for the series and expert handling of the seemingly infinite details associated with the series at NSPI; Maurice Coleman, vice president of research and development at NSPI in 1991, and the 1991 publications committee, whose idea it was to create the series: Esther Powers (1991 NSPI president), Roger Addison (1992 NSPI president), William Coscarelli (1992 vice president of publications and president-elect), and Kathleen Whiteside (1993 NSPI president)—who led their boards of directors in providing emotional and financial support for the series from the beginning to the present; the topic editors and authors of the series, who through vision, intelligence, and perseverance transformed the idea of the series into the book you are now reading; Sarah Polster, editor of the management series at Jossey-Bass, who taught us what the business of publishing was all about, helped formulate the final look, feel, and chapter structure, negotiated the sometimes rough waters between our dreams about the series and what could actually be done, and coordinated the learning everyone at both NSPI and Jossey-Bass did about working together and producing a state-of-the-art series using state-of-the-art technology; Barbara Hill at Jossey-Bass, who coordinated all the deadlines, manuscripts, authors, reviewers, and many other things we're glad not to have to know about; James Jackson, manager of information technology training at Amoco Corporation, who saw the value of the series and my involvement in it and continually and generously supported my efforts.

Dedication

This series is dedicated to a forgotten leader in the HPT field and in NSPI: the 1963 "Man of the Year in Programming," whose ideas formed the early basis for HPT's processes and interventions; a visionary who challenged the status quo, always with logic, reason, and passion; a teacher, guide, and friend who pushed his students to exemplary performance, encouraged them also to challenge the status quo, assisted them in their journey, and then rewarded their successes lavishly; the series is dedicated to the late James D. Finn, with respect and thanks for all he gave to me personally as my mentor, to those (too numerous to mention) who knew and worked with him, and to the field and profession of Human Performance Technology.

Chicago, Illinois
January 1994

Kenneth H. Silber
Series editor

Designing the Work Environment for Optimum Performance: About This Group of Books

What is the purpose of these books?

- "Ever since I moved to this new office, I go home with a backache every night."

- "The only way I can get any work done around here is to hide in the cafeteria."

- "I suppose the new computer system would save us time—if anyone around here could figure out how to use it."

Have you ever heard statements like these in your workplace? Have you been known to make some of them yourself? Complaints about too much noise, too little light, uncomfortable chairs, cramped storage, or perplexing equipment may be a cue that the work environment is getting in the way of good performance.

What exactly is a "work environment"? It includes the resources that are available to perform the work, the design of the work, the tools in the environment, and how well the tools match human capabilities. Performance can suffer if any of these environmental factors are unavailable, inaccessible, or inadequate (Bullock, 1981; Rummler and Brache, 1990).

Improving the work environment has rich potential for improving human performance. This topic, which we explore in three books that discuss designing the work environment for optimum performance, is grounded in the philosophical belief that it is both easier and more effective to manipulate a problematic work environment than to change the people who must function in that environment. To put it simply, this approach says, *Don't fix the worker, fix the workplace.* The three books in this group tell you how to use the approach to create work environments that support rather than hinder performance.

How do these books fit in the series?

The books in this group are a subset of the series From Training to Performance in the Twenty-First Century. They focus on the input that a performer receives while doing work (see Figure P.4). They help readers discover whether the work environment, which is an essential component of this input, is adequate to support the desired performance. They then offer strategies for redesigning inadequate work environments.

Figure P.4. Work Environment as an Element of Input in the Human Performance System.

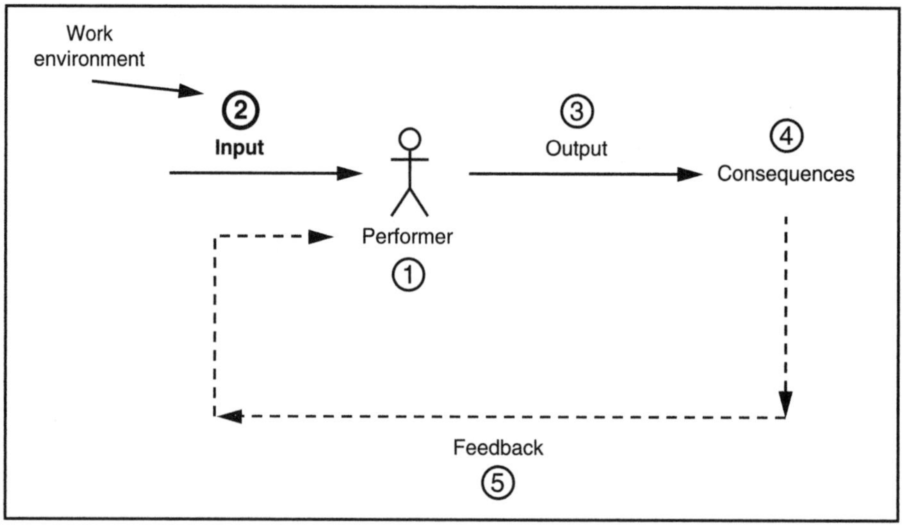

Source: Rummler and Brache, 1992, p. 38.

Creating the Ergonomically Sound Workplace, by Lee Ostrom, provides a basic understanding of the principles and methods of ergonomics. The procedures in the book will help you prevent worker injury by implementing such strategies as redesigning workstation layout, simplifying repetitive tasks, improving lifting tasks, and adjusting lighting.

Whereas Ostrom's book deals with the impact of the workplace on the body, *Creating Workplaces Where People Can Think,* by Phyl Smith and Lynn Kearny, is concerned with the impact of workplace design on the mind. The procedures in this book will help you identify attention-demanding features of the workplace that interfere with mental processing and then redesign work areas to meet individual and group needs for privacy, stimulation, and communication.

Ostrom's and Smith and Kearny's books take a general view of work environment problems and solutions. *Making Computers People-Literate,* by Elaine Weiss, zeroes in on a specific tool that is increasingly present in work environments: the computer. The procedures in the book will help you improve the performance of computer users by conducting a targeted review of the computer system, identifying flaws in its user interface, and recommending redesigns to improve the interface.

Salt Lake City, Utah   Elaine Weiss
January 1994   Topic editor

Preface

Why I wrote this book

This book crystallizes the methodology I have developed over the years as I have worked to improve interactions between people and computers. I entered the computer arena through a side door, as an instructional design consultant: clients hired me to develop training courses, job aids, and user guides to improve the performance of computer users. The more systems I saw, however, the clearer it became that these strategies were aimed at only half the problem. My interventions made people computer-literate, but they couldn't make computers "people-literate." I concluded that if a system's user interface (screens, error messages, menus, and so on) is poorly designed, it is bound to interfere with performance; hours of training and pounds of user guides won't save it. So I broadened my scope to include the other half of the equation: making the user interface accessible to users. Enormous strides have been made in user interfaces over the years, but in many ways, computers are just as esoteric and enigmatic as were automobiles in the early part of the twentieth century. The era of the Model-T Ford was best recalled by E. B. White in "Farewell, My Lovely!" (1977, p. 167):

A Ford owner had Number One Bearing constantly in mind. This bearing, being at the front end of the motor, was the one that always burned out, because the oil didn't reach it when the car was climbing hills. (That's what I was told, anyway.) The oil used to recede and leave Number One dry as a clam flat; you had to watch that bearing like a hawk. It was like a weak heart—you could hear it start knocking, and that was when you stopped to let her cool off. Try as you would to keep the oil supply right, in the end Number One always went out. "Number One Bearing burned out on me and I had to have her replaced," you would say, wisely; and your companions always had a lot to tell about how to protect and pamper Number One to keep her alive.

Nearly a century later, this sounds much like my behavior at social gatherings. Another computer enthusiast and I will find each other, and my husband's eyes will glaze over as the conversation moves from spreadsheet macros to graphics format conversions, with side excursions to the joys of hard disk defragmentation. But just as cars eventually became standardized and relatively straightforward, so too must computers. This book is about how to make that happen.

Who should read this book

This book is intended for anyone who is responsible for the performance of computer users, including trainers, training managers, human factors practitioners, developers of computer-based training, technical writers, and systems analysts. It is about what you can do to make computers people-literate, by identifying and redesigning the user interface flaws that get in the way of performance. It contains specific procedures developed in the real world that you can use immediately within a systems-related project. For example:

- You are developing a course to support a new in-house system. You have a vague feeling that the system will be time-consuming to learn, and you need an orderly way of communicating your concerns to the programmers.

- You have been hired to develop an on-line help system. You want to target the help system to the parts of the software that are most likely to cause problems for users.

- You are designing a computer-based training course. You want to ensure that learners focus on the content of the training material, not on the user interface that delivers the material.

- You are the training manager in charge of course development for end-user computing. You want to identify the parts of a system that are contributing most to user performance problems.

- You are an internal or external consultant. You want to add to the repertoire of services you can offer your clients.

How the book is organized

Section One briefly describes the theoretical foundations that support the methodology of the book. It seeks to answer the question, "What is the context for the procedures in this book?" Chapter One describes the problems caused by flawed user interfaces and explains how the problems affect you, the reader. It establishes research-based heuristics for designing easy-to-learn and easy-to-use user interfaces. It identifies the measurable results of applying the heuristics to interface redesign.

Section Two is the heart of the book. It is designed to answer the question, "What can I do to make computers people-literate?" Think of this section as a "procedural cookbook"; it is not meant to be read from beginning to end, but to be picked up and used whenever you determine that a poorly designed user interface is contributing to a performance problem.

Section Two contains six chapters. Chapter Two presents procedures that will help you decide which aspects of the user interface are most in need of review, and target your evaluation to critical system tasks. The next four chapters offer procedures to help you review and recommend redesign of a system's presentation (Chapter Three), conversation (Chapter Four), navigation (Chapter Five), and explanation (Chapter Six) interfaces. These terms are explained fully in Section One. Chapter Seven provides procedures that will help you communicate your interface design recommendations and evaluate their impact, once they are implemented, on user performance.

Section Three contains a case study, presented in Chapter Eight. The chapter aims to answer the question, "How can I pull these individual procedures together to solve a problem?" It applies a representative sample of the detailed procedures presented in Section Two to a real-world business case.

Section Four contains reproducible copies of all the forms and checklists you will need to perform the procedures. Feel free to copy and use them.

Acknowledgments

The novelist Isabelle Allende claims that she does not own her stories. She says they belong to everyone; she simply writes them down. What I have been able to write down in this book is due, in large part, to the many colleagues and clients who have contributed to my understanding of interactions between people and computers. I am especially thankful to David Bakkom and Mark Zuckerman, talented and creative programmers who listen patiently to my always-exuberant, frequently unrealistic recommendations on interface design—and implement a surprising number of them. I have been fortunate to find a friend and colleague in Nicki Mertes, who since 1977 has pushed my thinking to new heights whenever we collaborate. Thanks also go to Carolyn Conner, Michael Horowitz, Cheryl Hurst, Suzy Johnson, Richard Lentz, William Robinson, Jan Sanfilipo, Bruce Stowell, and Michael Venn.

Many people read all or part of my manuscript and took time to give me comments. Sarah Polster, editor of the Management Series at Jossey-Bass, provided a potent combination of moral support and critical observation. I also appreciate the special efforts of Gilbert Baehr, Steve Burkholder, Grant Richard, and Lee Ostrom. This book would never have been possible without the support of the National Society for Performance and Instruction and the NSPI Publications Committee. I am particularly grateful to Roger Addison, Maurice Coleman, and William Coscarelli. Special thanks go to Kenneth Silber, editor of the series, for giving me the opportunity to be both topic editor and author.

Finally, I thank my husband, Neal Whitman, for his understanding and support during the past year as I thrashed around in a sea of doubt, despair, and deadlines. He has been my lifeboat.

Salt Lake City, Utah   Elaine Weiss
January 1994

The Author

Elaine Weiss has been a performance technology consultant since 1975. In 1979, she formed Educational Dimensions, a firm that specializes in the design of training and nontraining solutions to performance problems in automated work environments. Weiss earned her B.A. degree (1969) in education from Boston University, and both her M.Ed. degree (1977) in supervision and leadership and her Ed.D. degree (1979) in instructional design from Columbia University. In her consulting practice, she has analyzed user requirements, redesigned user interfaces, created documentation, designed performance aids, and developed end-user training for more than fifty computer systems. Her clients have come from such industries as banking, communication, insurance, health care, financial services, manufacturing, and electronics. Her training and experience allow her to offer clients comprehensive service on a system development project from beginning to end.

MAKING COMPUTERS
PEOPLE-LITERATE

SECTION ONE:

HOW THE INTERFACE BETWEEN USER AND COMPUTER AFFECTS PERFORMANCE

Overview

What is this section about?

There are two parts to solving any problem: what you want to accomplish and how you want to do it. Even the most creative people attack issues by leaping over what they want to do and going on to how they will do it. There are many hows but only one what. The what drives the hows. You must always ask the question "What is?" before you ask the question "How to?" (Wurman, 1989, p. 81).

This book is basically about "how to's": how to improve interactions between people and computers by identifying and redesigning the user interface flaws that affect a person's performance. This section of *Making Computers People-Literate* is the "what" of the book: the context and theoretical foundations for user interface design.

How is this section organized?

## CHAPTER 1

What Makes Systems Easy to Learn and Easy to Use?

Why Should I Read This Book?

Dealing with computers

The novelist and social commentator Gregory Mcdonald (1985) tells of a Kansas gentleman who received a bill from a department store for $00.00. When he ignored the bill, he received another the next month for $00.00. The third month the bill for $00.00 was marked Past Due. The fourth month the bill arrived with a nasty note threatening civil suit if he did not pay $00.00 immediately. Not to be outdone, he sent the department store a check for $00.00—and heard no more about it, "which was the first proof we had that anyone can communicate with a computer, if you just take your time and think about it" (p. 114).

Where we were

This century has seen exponential growth in the use of automated systems to support work. While the "technology" of office work in 1850 consisted of no more than a steel-nib pen on paper, by 1900 mechanical devices in use included the telegraph, telephone, dictating machine, and typewriter. The first half of the twentieth century saw the development of automatic telephone switching, duplicating machines, and data-processing equipment operated with punch cards. And since World War II, computers have evolved from behemoths that were tended by an elect few to equipment that is standard in every office and, frequently, on every desk.

Where we are today

Computers have become an integral part of doing business. Computing technology and related services account for about 5 percent of the gross national product (Hartmanis, 1992).

While there were ten office workers to every display terminal in the early 1980s, today the ratio has dropped dramatically to 2:1 (Galitz, 1993). More than 80 percent of all office workers use computers. One survey showed that office, technical, and professional workers spent an average of 3.8 hours a day at a terminal or PC, and one-third of the workers used the equipment 5 or more hours a day. Managers averaged 2.9 hours, with 50 percent of executives having computers in their offices ("Office Computer Use . . . ," 1988).

So what's the problem?

The problem is that organizations spend billions of dollars a year to install computer systems, with the expectation that this investment will result in improved productivity and quality. In practice, however, such investments frequently hold more promise than substance. Efficiency and effectiveness may even decrease when automated systems are installed (Bowen, 1989). The systems may be too complex, the learning curve too long, or the design unsuitable for the needs of the organization.

Computers are tools that get introduced into the workplace to do something better than it was done before: to increase information processing efficiency, to improve the quality of work, or to accomplish new tasks that were not previously possible (Weiss, 1989). But any tool, no matter how powerful, is only effective if people can use it. If people can't use a tool, they either won't use it effectively or won't use it at all.

What this problem means to you

Sheer economics is forcing companies to recognize that they must refocus their system-design emphasis onto users. This has led to an increasing interest in designing people-literate systems to facilitate interactions between people and computers. For example, in 1991 the Association for Computing Machinery had more than 5,000 members in its Special Interest Group in Computer Human Interaction (SIGCHI) (Shneiderman, 1992). The Human Factors Society also devotes attention to human-computer interaction.

This book is intended for trainers, training managers, human factors practitioners, developers of computer-based training, technical writers, systems analysts, and others who work to improve the performance of people who use computers to do their jobs. Generally, however, this charge does not come in the form of a request to redesign the system to make it more usable. More likely, the conversation goes something like this:

> **Manager:** I need a course.
>
> **You:** What kind of a course?
>
> **Manager:** Well, they installed this new billing system, and the data entry clerks have done nothing but complain ever since.
>
> **You:** What are they complaining about?
>
> **Manager:** They say they liked the old system better. So can you make me a course to motivate them to like the new system?
>
> **You:** Well . . .

If part of your job is to improve the performance of people who use computers, these are some of the issues that may keep you awake at night:

- The company spent $700,000 to install a computer on every manager's desk last year and an additional $240,000 to send those managers to a five-day course in computer literacy. You designed and taught that course. In a follow-up survey, you learn that 75 percent of the computers are now living in closets.

- You are gathering data to write a user guide for an in-house payroll system. After an hour talking to the programmers about how the system works, you suspect that the user guide will weigh more than the computer.

- You have been told that employees won't need training in how to use the company's new E-mail system because the system has on-line help. When you interview users they respond "What's on-line help?" or "Yeah, I tried that . . . once."

What's going on here? People need to use computers to do their jobs. Yet training and documentation, once considered the only strategies for improving the performance of computer-users, don't always work. If a system is poorly designed, hours of training and pounds of user guides can't save it.

Why training is necessary but not sufficient

People in training organizations typically get called in to solve the performance problems of computer-users after the system is up and running (Pipe, 1992). By then, it may seem that the only solution is to design end-user training courses and other support materials, such as user guides and job aids. But your own experiences have probably demonstrated that these are not the ideal solutions to such problems. If you try to train users without removing basic flaws in the system, you can expect performance problems to persist. I am *not* saying that if a system is designed well enough, training won't be necessary. But I *am* saying that if a system is designed badly, training will not be adequate. Why? Because if the goal is to improve interactions between people and computers, training addresses only half the interaction. In other words, training, user guides, and job aids can make people computer-literate, but they can't make a computer people-literate.

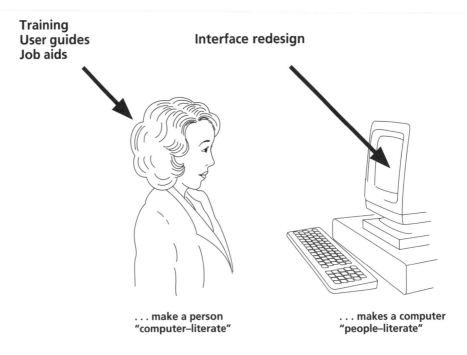

Training
User guides
Job aids

Interface redesign

. . . make a person
"computer–literate"

. . . makes a computer
"people–literate"

Moving from training to performance

This book challenges you to view training as only one of the strategies available to improve interactions between people and computers by applying principles of "performance technology." Performance technology uses an engineering-like approach to systematically identify performance gaps, identify factors contributing to these gaps, and design cost-effective and efficient interventions to close the gaps (Stolovitch and Keeps, 1992a). Instruction is not the only answer to every challenge in the workplace (Rossett, 1992); careful analysis is required to determine the source of performance problems and discover the appropriate combinations of interventions to close the gap between desired and actual performance (Rummler, 1992). Examples of interventions are

- Feedback systems

- Motivation and incentive systems

- Organizational design

- Process engineering

- Job and workflow design

- Performance aids

To improve interactions between people and computers, taking the engineering approach of performance technology means that you must pay attention to the system itself, as well as to the people who use it. "We often blame human error for disasters and near-disasters, from nuclear near-meltdowns to bank errors in checking account balances. Equally often, we blame "the computer" for some ill fate that befalls us. Seldom do we recognize that neither man nor machine alone is completely responsible. In today's complex world, man and machine work together interactively. The 'system' is the combination of both" (Simpson 1982, p. 108).

Following the principles of performance technology, you must be able to

- Determine which components of the user interface are most likely to be the source of performance problems.

- Isolate the specific interface design flaws that are contributing to performance deficiencies.

- Recommend intelligent, explicit, research-based techniques to improve the interface, if such improvement is within the organization's control.

If user interface redesign is not an option, either because of cost factors or because the system cannot be modified, you must be able to recommend alternative solutions to support performance, such as the following:

- Improve the fit between manual and mechanized procedures. For example, if a new data entry system is installed, existing paper forms often must be revised.

- Improve organizational support to users. For example, establish a technical support hotline to handle common user problems.

- Provide performance and instructional aids to bridge the gap between system flaws and user needs. For example, if the system requires users to type complex commands, a list of these commands could be designed to fit over the computer keyboard.

Specific strategies for implementing these alternative solutions do not fall within the scope of this book; such strategies have been well addressed elsewhere (Duncan and Powers, 1992; Jackson and Addison, 1992; McConnell and Koch, 1990; Rossett and Gautier-Downes, 1990; Rummler, 1990; Silber, 1992; Swanson, 1992; Tosti and Jackson, 1992; Wilson, 1991). However, this book does suggest ways you can design targeted performance aids and documentation if interface redesign is not under your control.

Why Is a User Interface So Important?

What is the user interface?

Effective interactions between people and computers require that the computer be usable, and a critical factor in the usability of a computer is its *user interface.* The user interface is the part of a system the user interacts with directly: the "Janus-faced structure with connections in one direction to the rest of the computational system and connections in the other direction to the human system" (Foss and DeRidder, 1987, p. 165). A user interface might include

- The commands users type when they want to perform a task
- The wording and sequence of options on a menu
- The layout of information on a data entry screen
- The use of color on the screen to highlight important information
- The error messages given when incorrect data are entered

The current buzzword in user interface design is "intuitive." This descriptor supersedes my former pet peeve, "user-friendly," a phrase which sounded like marketing hype at best and a patronizing put-down at worst. Then, once this term become trivialized (ads tout user-friendly dishwashers!), it was replaced by "intuitive." But should we expect a computer system to be intuitive—obvious at first glance? I don't think so. Clock radios should be "intuitive." So should VCRs (although they're not there yet . . . I want a dollar for every VCR in America that's flashing 12:00). Computers, however, are complex tools. For computers to be usable, they must be not intuitive but accessible. What is the difference between an intuitive and an accessible user interface?

Why not an intuitive user interface?

Let's start with the parts of an interface that are generally considered to be intuitive: the keyboard and the monitor. A computer keyboard is a lot like a typewriter, and a monitor is a lot like a TV set. We know that when our fingers perform actions on the keyboard the results will appear on the monitor. But this design is intuitive only if it falls within the framework of a person's prior experience. For example, in the movie *Star Trek IV,* Scotty is confronted with a Macintosh computer when the crew travels back in time to 1988. Holding the mouse to his mouth, he cheerfully says, "Hallo, computer." When he is advised that he will have better luck if he types his requests on the keyboard, he wrinkles his nose in disgust and responds, "How quaint." To this starship chief engineer, the keyboard was not an intuitive interface.

Thus, interfaces are intuitive only if they attempt to exploit the user's prior knowledge of other domains. For example, the introduction of the Graphical User Interface (GUI) in the early 1980s was an attempt to use the metaphor of a "desktop" to make interfaces more intuitive. However, this focus on an intuitive interface can lead to such nonsensical instructions as "close the window and place it on your desktop" (Carroll, 1990, p. 64). Comparing the computer system to something the users were already familiar with (in this case, their physical desks) solved some performance problems, but it caused others.

Thus, while I am certainly not arguing that we should deliberately make user interfaces counter-intuitive, performance problems will not necessarily be solved by intuitive interfaces. Instead of trying for *intuitive* interfaces, we should be trying for *accessible* ones.

Why an accessible user interface?

So let's think about accessibility. Computer columnist John Dvorak tells of an employee who was found at the photocopy machine with a stack of floppy disks, carrying out the supervisor's instructions to "make backup copies." Nothing in that employee's prior experience would have made the backup process intuitive. But that process *can* be made accessible. In the olden days (the Dark Ages of 1978), the task might have involved typing pip b:*.* a:. Now, on some systems, users just use a mouse to click on a picture of a disk, drag it over another picture of a disk, and the job is done. The skill still has to be learned ("Why click? Why drag? What's that a picture of?"), but arcane commands don't have to be memorized. Richard Saul Wurman defines accessibility as "the ability to do what everybody else can do and to make use of what everybody else can use . . . the liberty to take advantage of resources" (Wurman, 1989, p. 45). An accessible interface allows users to take advantage of the resources provided by the computer system. Characteristics of accessible interfaces include:

- *They are consistent:* actions, terms, and appearance are the same throughout the system.

- *They offer informative feedback:* every user action is followed by information about the success or failure of that action.

- *They handle errors easily:* user errors are prevented whenever possible and explained clearly when they occur.

- *They reduce short-term memory load:* users need not memorize complex commands and procedures to use the system.

The impact of an accessible user interface on performance

Still, is it really worth the effort required to replace pip b:*.* a: with a picture of a disk? It seems reasonable to assume that an accessible user interface will improve interactions between people and computers. But well-designed interfaces, like well-designed training programs, take time to develop. How can you justify the time and cost required to develop accessible interfaces?

One justification is the elimination of performance problems caused by poor interface design. According to Shneiderman (1992), these problems include

- Increased time to learn the system
- Increased time to perform tasks
- Decreased retention of learned skills over time
- Higher rate of errors during system use
- User dissatisfaction with the system

A second justification is the cost savings that can accrue when interfaces are made more accessible. Galitz (1993) established that, in a large system that processed 4.8 million screens per year, if poor design forced users to spend twenty extra seconds per screen, the cost to the organization would be more than fourteen additional person-years.

Even small productivity improvements in individual system tasks can add up to significant cost savings (Mayhew, 1992). For example, consider a small system with 250 users who have an average salary of $15 an hour. They interact with the system via data entry screens, which are used an average of 60 times a day, 230 days a year by each user. If the user interface is redesigned to increase the efficiency of each interaction by three seconds per screen, the estimated benefit can be calculated as follows:

- 250 x 60 x 230 = 3,450,000 interactions per year
- multiplied by 3 unnecessary seconds per interaction = 10,350,000 superfluous seconds
- Divided by 3,600 seconds saved by interface redesign = 2,875 hours
- multiplied by $15/hour = $43,125 saving per year

The "Computer" Side of People-Computer Interactions

Reviewing interfaces to target performance interventions

Okay . . . you're convinced. You agree that performance can suffer if a user interface is poorly designed and that training won't always solve the problem. So what do you do when you encounter a performance problem that is caused by a system's user interface? First, here's what *not* to do:

> **Manager:** Nobody can use the new billing system. I need a course.
>
> **You:** No, you don't.
>
> **Manager:** I don't?
>
> **You:** Nope. I just took a look at the user interface . . .
>
> **Manager:** The user who???
>
> **You:** The user interface. And it's terrible. All of it. The only solution is to throw it away and start from scratch.
>
> **Manager:** Listen, bozo . . . that system took the company two years and $2 million to build. It stays. You go.

To be effective, you must do more than wave your arms around and mumble vaguely about a bad interface. You need a structured approach. The approach described in this book provides a structure for targeting your recommendations to address explicit interface flaws. The structure includes

- *A user interface model* that splits the user interface into four major categories, and

- *Explicit criteria* to help you identify interface design flaws in each category

The interface model used in this book

The user interface model on which this book is based splits user interface characteristics into four major categories. Figure 1.1 shows the four categories of the model, including the general design guidelines for ease of learning (see pages 21 to 23) and ease of use (see pages 25 to 26) that support each.

- The *presentation interface* controls the way users are shown information. It includes screen design, graphics, menu layout, attention-getting devices, and color.

- The *conversation interface* controls the method of communication, both system-to-user (prompts, feedback, and menus) and user-to-system (locus of control, commands, and data input).

- The *navigation interface* controls the ways users make their way from one part of the system to another, including moving from menu to menu, moving within a single screen, moving from screen to screen, and direct manipulation (GUI). It also controls the design of input devices.

- The *explanation interface* controls the way the system teaches users about itself, including error-handling, performance support, and on-line help.

Figure 1.1. The User Interface Model.

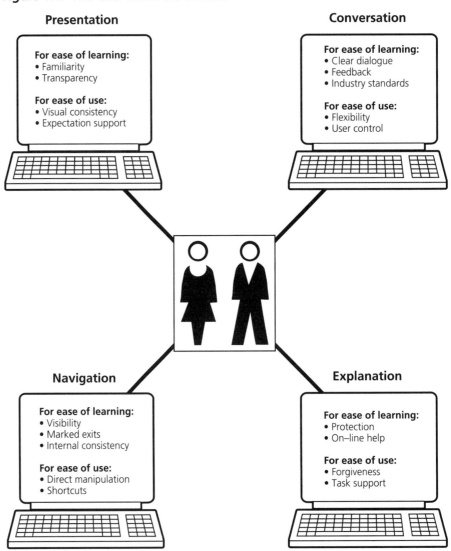

Explicit criteria: The interface review method used in this book

There are four standard methods for evaluating user interfaces:

Method	How it works
Explicit criteria (the method used in this book)	A reviewer critiques the interface using a checklist that contains distinct, well-understood attributes of a good user interface.
Heuristic evaluation	A group of reviewers look at a system and try to come up with an opinion about what is good or bad about the interface.
Usability testing	An expert tester uses specialized recording equipment to study a test population of users operating the application in a controlled setting, such as a usability lab.
Cognitive walkthroughs	A reviewer walks users through each step of each procedure required to run an application, keeping detailed records of each case where there is a discrepancy between how the user thought the application should work and how it actually worked.

Although any of these can be effective under the right circumstances, this book uses the explicit criteria method to evaluate the user interface because it is easy, inexpensive, and effective. Explicit criteria allow those who are not interface experts to critique an interface by using a checklist that contains distinct, well-understood attributes of a good interface. The procedures in Section Two use twenty detailed checklists to direct the interface review process.

Although one disadvantage of explicit criteria is that they identify relatively few severe problems (Miller and Jeffries, 1992), such problems are typically identified during the testing process before software is released. In contrast, advantages of this method include the following:

- It identifies recurring and general software problems.
- It is less expensive than other methods.
- It is less time-consuming than other methods.
- It can be performed by reviewers who are not experts in user interface design.
- It can be performed by a single reviewer.

The other methods—heuristic evaluation, usability testing, and cognitive walkthroughs—take time, equipment, and resources that are probably unavailable to you. For example, heuristic evaluation involves a group of people looking at a system and trying to come up with an opinion about what is good or bad about the interface. A disadvantage of this method is that the results are best when there are five to ten evaluators (Nielsen and Molich, 1990; Nielsen, 1992). You generally work alone. Usability testing uses an expert tester and specialized recording equipment to study the application in a controlled setting, such as a usability lab. Disadvantages of usability testing include that it requires special equipment, is expensive, and is time-consuming (Downton, 1991a). You generally do not have access to a usability lab. Cognitive walkthroughs use standard methods of software walkthroughs (Freedman and Weinberg, 1990) and a formal record-keeping methodology (Polson, 1992; Wharton, Bradford, Jeffries, and Franzke, 1992) to evaluate discrepancies between users' expectations and the steps an application actually requires. A disadvantage of cognitive walkthroughs is that they are perceived by users to be tedious and time-consuming (Rowley and Rhoades, 1992). You are generally under time constraints.

The "People" Side of People-Computer Interactions

The design challenge: Balancing the needs of novice and experienced users

By categorizing the many elements of a user interface into four categories, you can target your review and redesign recommendations to just those parts of the interface that are causing users problems. Keep in mind, however, that users come in many flavors! Just as training courses must accommodate learners of varying backgrounds, the presentation, conversation, navigation, and explanation interfaces must support the entire range of user proficiency, from novice to expert (see Figure 1.2). Designing an effective user interface is a balancing act between ease of learning and ease of use. The next part of this chapter describes the range of user abilities and the differing needs of each.

In general, the more powerful a system is, the more difficult it is to use (Jong, 1982). However, since new users eventually become experienced users, the interface design challenge is to create an interface simple enough that novices can get up to speed quickly, yet powerful enough that experts don't outgrow it (Grudin, 1989).

Types of novice users

The term *novice*—when used to describe new users of a system—is somewhat misleading because it implies that all novices have the same entry-level skills. I prefer to use the distinguishing terms *true novice, task-savvy novice,* and *system-savvy novice.*

- True novices are new to the world of computers and have no experience in the work they want to accomplish on the computer. For example, Steffi is a psychologist. She has volunteered to take over the editorship of her church newsletter, which is produced with desktop publishing software on a personal computer. Because she has never done page layouts and never used a computer, she is a true novice.

- Task-savvy novices are also new to the world of computers. However, they already know how to do the work . . . they have simply never done this work on a computer. For example, Juan is a high school student who goes to the same church as Steffi. He has volunteered to work with her on the production of the newsletter. Although he has no computer experience either, he is a talented mechanical illustrator and his work on the school newspaper includes doing hand paste-ups of artwork and text.

- System-savvy novices have used computers. They are novices in the sense that when they encounter a new system, they need to master its specific rules. For example, at Norman's last job, he wrote all his memos with FastWrite word processing software running on an Omega 632XP computer. He has just started working at a new company that uses LetterPerfect word processing software, which runs on an Alpha 327ST computer. He will have to learn new commands, but he already has word processing skills.

Figure 1.2. The Range of User Proficiency.

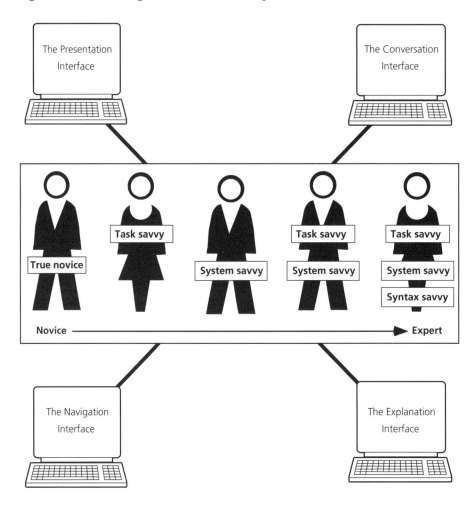

What do novice users need?

On June 12 [1982] the word processor had been sitting in my living room for a full month, and it had so far won every battle. But was I downhearted? Did I feel beaten? You bet I was, and you bet I did! (Asimov, 1982 p. 36).

Barriers of complexity and knowledge stand between novice users, whose understanding of computers is limited to what they can see and manipulate directly (Shore, 1985), and the effective use of computers. Such users need an interface to be *explorable;* they need to be able to poke around it without being penalized. To make this exploration possible, the allowable actions must be visible in each state of the system. This visibility suggests alternatives to the user and invites exploration of new system features (Norman, 1988). When the user takes an action, the result must be not only visible but easily interpreted so that users develop an accurate mental model of the system and learn relationships between actions and outcomes. To aid novice users in acquiring skills, the interface must *reduce the need to teach* (Mack, Lewis, and Carroll, 1983; Carroll, 1990) by accomplishing the following:

- Replace teaching with *knowing* by designing the interface to take advantage of the user's view of how things work.

- Replace teaching with *guessing* by providing effective feedback on the result of user actions.

- Replace teaching with *exploration* by allowing user actions to be without cost. Undesirable results should be readily reversible, and unreversable actions should be either blocked or warned about.

What do experienced users need?

Captain Kirk: Can you operate it, Spock?
Spock: Well, Jim, this computer was designed and constructed 300 million years ago by a totally alien race of methane-breathing, squidlike beings who built it using technologies unknown to us and used it for purposes we cannot conceive of and then mysteriously vanished, leaving no shred of documentation as to its operation. It may take a few moments (Jennings, 1990, p. 77).

This Star Trek lampoon, which appeared on a Bitnet electronic bulletin board, illustrates the concept of "syntax savviness." Syntax refers to the specific details required to operate a specific system (Shneiderman, 1992).

For example, in the FastWrite word processor you move a paragraph by typing (ALT) (M). In the LetterPerfect program, you select the move command from a menu. Syntax savviness comes with both length and frequency of use (Rosson, 1984). Users gain experience as they become familiar with a system. Tasks are accomplished in less time with fewer errors. Basic tasks become routine and are performed automatically. As more sophisticated tasks are attempted, the user learns complex system features (Stepich, 1991). Experienced users need the interface to be *flexible*. A flexible interface lets experienced users customize the system to fit their work patterns. For example, it allows users to bypass lengthy system prompts (Burgess, 1986) and supports user- or system-defined shortcuts for frequent and complex tasks (Powell, 1990).

Implications for user interface design

Novice users need a system that is easy to learn. Experienced users need a system that is easy to use. The next part of this chapter describes general design guidelines for navigation, conversation, presentation, and explanation interfaces that will meet the needs of both types of users.

- Pages 19 through 23 describe ten guidelines for improving interactions between novice users and computers by designing an interface that is easy to learn.
- Pages 24 through 26 describe eight guidelines for improving interactions between experienced users and computers by designing an interface that is easy to use.

Making the Interface Easy to Learn

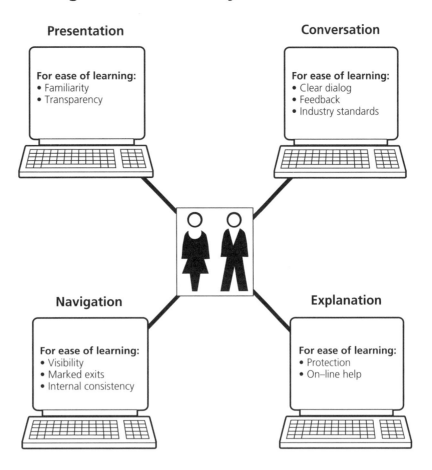

Presentation

For ease of learning:
• Familiarity
• Transparency

Conversation

For ease of learning:
• Clear dialog
• Feedback
• Industry standards

Navigation

For ease of learning:
• Visibility
• Marked exits
• Internal consistency

Explanation

For ease of learning:
• Protection
• On–line help

How do people learn a system?

Task reformulation. When people are learning a new system, they create "mappings" from external tasks (what they want to accomplish) to internal tasks (how to get it done on the computer). The ETIT (External Task-Internal Task) model was developed by Moran and colleagues (Moran, 1983) to describe this process of task reformulation. Their research indicates that the greater the degree of task reformulation required, the more time it takes to learn a system. The following is an example of ETIT mapping:

External task: I wrote this letter on my computer, but I don't have a printer. I want to print my letter on your computer.

Internal task: I must

1. Insert a floppy disk in my computer's disk drive.
2. Type cd\..
3. Type copy c: letter.doc a:.
4. Take out the floppy disk.
5. Insert it in your computer's disk drive.
6. Type copy a: letter.doc c:\DOCS (and so on).

Job-task representations. When people are learning a new system, they must learn which tasks the system can perform and how to carry them out (Polson and Kieras, 1984). The basic elements of a user's job-task representation are described by the GOMS model (Card, Moran, and Newell, 1983):

G   Users form *goals* (edit this document) and *subgoals* (move a paragraph).

O   Goals are accomplished by stringing together the *operators* that the system provides to the user (move the mouse, pull down the menu, select the find command).

M   A particular string of operators used to accomplish a goal is called a *method*. Multiple methods frequently exist for accomplishing the same goal (the "cut and paste" method, the "drag and drop" method).

S   Users follow rules to make *selections* among the different methods (this way is faster, but this way is easier to remember).

Stages of action. Norman (1988) postulates that people form a goal, execute tasks, and evaluate the success or failure of their actions as they learn to use a new system. The stages of action include these cognitive processes:

- Form the goal: "I want to center this line of text."

- Execute tasks (form the intention, specify the action, execute the action): "First I move the cursor, then I select text, then I type a command . . ."

- Evaluate success or failure (perceive the system state, interpret the system state, evaluate the outcome): "Let's see if it worked. Is the text correctly centered?"

The goal: Effective mental models

The ETIT and the GOMS model, as well as Norman's stages of action, are all basically describing a process whereby users form a mental model of the system (Rouse and Morris, 1986; Barnard, MacLean, and Hammond, 1984). Mental models allow users to predict future events, infer invisible events, and find causes for observed events. Users always form a mental model, accurate or not, as they learn to use a new system (Carroll, 1990; Mayhew, 1992).

Thus, a user interface that is easy to learn must be designed to help the user develop an accurate and effective mental model.

Does prior experience make a difference?

Transfer of knowledge. Common sense indicates that transfer of knowledge is a factor in learning: the more familiarity users have with similar systems, the easier it is for them to learn a new system. Thus, a system-savvy user with prior knowledge of Microsoft Word should take less time to learn WordPerfect than a true novice. In fact, however, the research is inconclusive (Foss and DeRidder, 1987). Prior experience correlates with shorter learning time, but there is no clear evidence that the nature of this experience is significant. For example, it seems to make little difference whether prior computer experience is with a similar system (for example, two GUI word processors), a dissimilar system with similar functions (for example, a GUI word processor and a line editor), or general computer literacy (for example, how to copy files, how to pull down menus).

In his description of the ETIT model, Moran (1983) suggests that further study is required to determine if transfer of knowledge is greater when two systems have similar external-internal task mapping rules.

Implications of savviness on learning. The previous section described three types of novice users: true novices, task-savvy novices, and system-savvy novices. What impact does savviness have on learning?

- Users who are *both system and task savvy* will probably master a new system quickly because they only need to learn the system's syntax rules.

- Users who are *only task savvy* may learn best through ETIT mapping, beginning with their existing knowledge of task objects and actions and translating this into the syntax of the new system.

- Users who are *only system savvy* will probably need preliminary training in the task domain before they attempt to learn the syntax of the new system.

- Users who are *neither system nor task savvy* will probably need the most time to master a new system because they must acquire syntactic skills, general computer skills, and knowledge of task objects and actions.

What makes an interface easy to learn?

Many learning problems are the result of interface flaws; a well-designed user interface reduces or eliminates such problems. Section Two covers specific procedures for reviewing individual features of a user interface: screen display, error messages, and the like. The ten heuristics presented here are general design guidelines to make an interface easy to learn. They are organized by the four categories already described: the *presentation interface* (screen design, graphics, menu layout, attention-getting devices, and color); the *conversation interface* (prompts, feedback, menus, locus of control, commands, and data input); the *navigation interface* (moving between menus, moving within a single screen, moving between screens, direct manipulation [GUI], and input devices); and the *explanation interface* (error-handling, performance support, and on-line help).

A presentation interface that is easy to learn has

- *Familiarity.* For example, the interface uses metaphors to describe system terms, such as file cabinets (*not* libraries), folders (*not* directories), and documents (*not* data files). (See also Apple Computer, 1992; IBM, 1989; Laurel, 1990; Mayhew, 1992.)

- *Transparency.* For example, users know that to edit a spreadsheet formula, they click on the cell containing the formula and then make the necessary changes. They do not need to understand the code that supports these actions. (See also IBM, 1989; Mayhew, 1992.)

A conversation interface that is easy to learn has

- *Clear dialogue.* For example, a data entry field is labeled Address (*not* Residence). To close an application, the user types quit (*not* terminate). A system message reads Print job canceled: printer out of paper (*not* Run aborted). (See also Apple Computer, 1992; Nielsen and Molich, 1990; van Steenis, 1990; IBM, 1991; Shneiderman, 1992.)

- *Feedback.* For example, after the user copies the files report.doc and letter.doc to a floppy disk, the system displays the message "2 files successfully copied." (See also Bailey, 1982; Norman, 1988; Nielsen and Molich, 1990; Apple Computer, 1992; van Steenis, 1990; IBM, 1991; Shneiderman, 1992; Mayhew, 1992.)

- *Industry standards.* For example, the (F1) key is rapidly becoming a standard for accessing on-line help systems in PC-based software applications. (See also Norman, 1988; IBM, 1989; Peddie, 1992.)

A navigation interface that is easy to learn has

- *Visibility.* For example, users can see the effects of their actions on the system. When the (TAB) key is pressed, the cursor moves down to the next menu item; when the mouse is dragged over a block of text, the text becomes highlighted. (See also Rubenstein and Hersh, 1984; Apple Computer, 1992; IBM, 1989; Norman, 1988; Nelson, 1990; Mayhew, 1992.)

- *Marked exits.* For example, on the bottom of a data entry screen a message reads, "To save your work, press ⟨ENTER⟩. To leave without saving, press ⟨ESC⟩." (See also Karat, Campbell, and Fiegel, 1992; Nielsen and Molich, 1990.)

- *Internal consistency.* For example, users don't have to learn different commands for different parts of the system. The (ESC) key is always used to cancel an action, whether the user is in a dialog box, a menu, or a data entry field. (See also Karat, Campbell, and Fiegel, 1992; IBM, 1989.)

An explanation interface that is easy to learn has

- *Protection.* For example, if a user attempts to exit from an application while the unsaved document 1992 Taxes is open, the system displays the message, "Save changes to 1992 Taxes before quitting? (Y,N)". (See also Bailey, 1982; Nielsen and Molich, 1990; Shneiderman, 1992.)

- *On-line help.* For example, when the user moves the cursor to a data entry field, instructions on what to type in that field are displayed at the bottom of the screen. In an error message box, pressing the (HELP) key will display information about the cause of the error and possible solutions. (See also Apple Computer, 1992; Kearsley, 1988; Nielsen and Molich, 1990; Horton, 1990; IBM, 1991; Karat, Campbell, and Fiegel, 1992; Shneiderman, 1992.)

Making the Interface Easy to Use

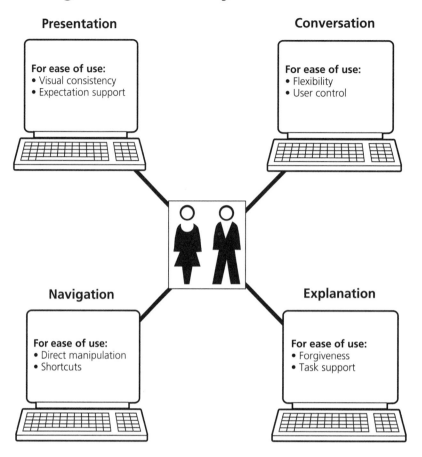

Presentation

For ease of use:
• Visual consistency
• Expectation support

Conversation

For ease of use:
• Flexibility
• User control

Navigation

For ease of use:
• Direct manipulation
• Shortcuts

Explanation

For ease of use:
• Forgiveness
• Task support

How do people use a system?

The usual concerns of interface designers—creating more legible type, designing better scroll bars, integrating color and sound and voice—are all important considerations. But they are secondary. Improving the way people can use computers to think and communicate, observe and decide, calculate and simulate, debate and design—these are primary (excerpt from an interview with Donald Norman in Rheingold, 1990, p. 7).

Pages 19 to 23 discussed the needs of novice users by investigating what happens as people learn to use a computer. Once users have acquired computer skills, they must apply these skills to their day-to-day tasks and activities. Experience is not so much innate knowledge about a system as it is understanding how to use a system to tackle and solve new problems (Downton, 1991b). Thus, the needs of experienced users revolve around using computers to accomplish tasks (Grandjean, 1980; Coe, 1980; Oborne, 1989).

The kinds of work users may need to accomplish with a computer include

- Data entry
- Editing
- Question–answer
- Information manipulation
- Information analysis
- Problem solving
- Decision making

What makes an interface easy to use?

Many performance problems are the result of interface flaws; a well-designed user interface reduces or eliminates such problems. Section Two covers specific procedures for reviewing individual features of a user interface, such as screen display, error messages, and the like. The eight heuristics presented here are general design guidelines that make an interface easy to use. Again, they are organized by the four interface categories: the *presentation interface* (screen design, graphics, menu layout, attention-getting devices, and color), the *conversation interface* (prompts, feedback, menus, locus of control, commands, and data input), the *navigation interface* (moving among menus, moving within a single screen, moving between screens, direct manipulation [GUI], and input devices), and the *explanation interface* (error handling, performance support, and on-line help).

A presentation interface that is easy to use has

- *Visual consistency.* For example, system prompts are always displayed at the top of the screen and error messages are always displayed at the bottom. In a graphical user interface (GUI), all application icons are diamond shaped and all documents are rectangular. (See also Apple Computer, 1992; Horn, 1989; Kay, 1990; Peddie, 1992; Tognazzini, 1990.)

- *Expectation support.* For example, severe error conditions are displayed in a red octagon. This design conforms to expectations of North American users because a red octagon is reminiscent of a stop sign, but it would not be an effective visual prompt for some European users. (See also van Steenis, 1990; Salomon, 1990.)

A conversation interface that is easy to use has

- *Flexibility.* For example, users can customize the word processor so that each new document they create is already set up with their preferences for margins, tabs, line spacing, and typefaces. (See also Karat, Campbell, and Fiegel, 1992; Mayhew, 1992.)

- *User control.* For example, the system command "Enter parameters" places the locus of control with the system; the preferable command, "Ready for parameters," places the locus of control with the user. (See also Bailey, 1982; Apple Computer, 1992; IBM, 1989; van Steenis, 1990; Chen and Leahy, 1990; Shneiderman, 1992; Mayhew, 1992.)

A navigation interface that is easy to use has

- *Direct manipulation.* For example, instead of typing copy c:\MYDOCS\myfile.doc a:, the user can drag a visual representation of the file (an icon) over to a visual representation of a floppy disk. (See also Apple Computer, 1992; Brennan, 1990; Mayhew, 1992.)

- *Shortcuts.* For example, to leave an application, the user can either pull down the File menu and select Quit or use the keyboard shortcut (CTRL) (Q). (See also Nielsen and Molich, 1990; Chen and Leahy, 1990; Mayhew, 1992; Shneiderman, 1992.)

An explanation interface that is easy to use has

- *Forgiveness.* For example, an ''oops'' function is always available to cancel the last action. If the user types a command to reformat the hard drive, the system displays the message, "This will erase all data from your computer. Do you really want to do this? (Y,N)." (See also Apple Computer, 1992; IBM, 1989; Shneiderman, 1992; Mayhew, 1992.)

- *Task support.* For example, choices on the main menu of a Personal Information Manager are stated in terms that match users' daily tasks: Schedule Appointments, Write Memos, Update To-Do List, and so on. (See also Bailey, 1982; van Steenis, 1990; Mayhew, 1992; Gery, 1991.)

What Are the Results of an Improved User Interface?

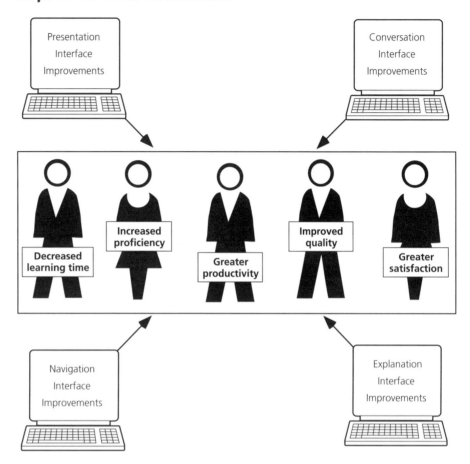

The goals of interface review and redesign

The purpose of reviewing an interface is to identify flaws that are interfering with performance; the purpose of fixing these flaws is to improve user performance. Five measurable goals of interface review and redesign are

- Learning time
- Proficiency
- Productivity
- Quality
- User satisfaction

A positive outcome in each of these areas can benefit user performance.

Goal 1: Decreased learning time

How long does it take typical members of the user population to learn how to accomplish particular tasks? Improving the user interface should decrease learning time (Shneiderman, 1992).

The length of time it takes to master system functions is frequently referred to as the system's "learning curve" (Kemerer, 1992). The terms *long* and *steep* are often used interchangeably and pejoratively; however, the two mean very different things. A *long* learning curve is one where users learn system operations gradually over time. A *steep* learning curve is one where users learn many system operations in a short time. Thus, a system with a steep learning curve is more efficient.

Goal 2: Increased proficiency

How many system functions are actually being used by a representative sample of the user population? Improving the user interface should allow more people to use more system functions (McConnell and Koch, 1990).

Different user population groups can be expected to have different levels of mastery. For example, a manager may only need to know the basic editing functions (adding and deleting text, moving paragraphs, printing a document). The manager's secretary needs to have mastered formatting functions too (changing typefaces, making text bold, adjusting margins). Some systems can automate the process of gathering these data by tracking frequency of command use, time spent on individual applications, or number of system log-ins.

Goal 3: Greater productivity

What is the comparison between time and output when using a single system function and when performing a complex set of tasks? Improving the user interface should allow users to accomplish their work more efficiently (McConnell and Koch, 1990).

According to Gilbert (1978), productivity measures include

- Rate (for example, the number of claims processed per hour)
- Timeliness (for example, the percentage of statements that are received by customers on the 20th of the month)
- Volume (for example, the total number of completed contracts)

Goal 4: Improved quality

How many and what kinds of errors are made when users perform a set of benchmarking tests? Improving the user interface should decrease the number and severity of user errors (Shneiderman, 1992).

According to Gilbert, quality measures include

- Accuracy (whether the user's accomplishments meet an established standard). Example: The number of typographical errors that need to be corrected before the letters are sent out is reduced.
- Class (whether the user's accomplishments exceed the established standard). Example: In addition to being accurate and complete, the annual report applies principles of graphical excellence to the layout, typography, and overall design to create a superlative document.

Expectations for productivity (goal 3) and quality (goal 4) are generally considered together. These expectations may be different for different user groups because their work accomplishments vary. For example, the performance requirements of a data entry claims-processing clerk might be to complete ten claims a day (rate), with only 1 percent of these claims coming back for rework (accuracy). The performance requirements of a graphics designer who develops corporate logos might be to develop creative, original designs that meet client needs (class) and to get them to the client on the date promised (timeliness).

Goal 5: Greater user satisfaction

How much do users like using various aspects of the system? Improving the user interface should make users feel comfortable with and supported by the system (Shneiderman, 1992). User satisfaction can be determined from surveys and interviews (see Chapter Two).

It is important to include user satisfaction as a goal of interface design. If users don't see the advantages of using the system, or doubt their abilities to master system functions, lack of motivation may result, which in turn may hinder learning and performance (Downton and Leedham, 1991; Rossett, 1992). For example, dissatisfaction can be high if users

- Spend their days staring at crowded screens (presentation interface, see Chapter Three)

- Must remember long sequences of complex commands (conversation interface, see Chapter Four)

- Become hopelessly lost within multiple levels of menus (navigation interface, see Chapter Five)

- Are not protected from their mistakes (explanation interface, see Chapter Six)

Summary of Key Points

☑ Although this century has seen exponential growth in the use of automated systems to support work, productivity gains are sometimes disappointing. Therefore, companies are recognizing the need to design people-literate systems.

☑ If a user interface has design flaws, training is not an adequate performance intervention. This book offers an alternative strategy: a method for reviewing and redesigning flawed interfaces to improve user performance.

☑ The user interface model on which this book is based splits the user interface into four major categories:

- The *presentation* interface
- The *conversation* interface
- The *navigation* interface
- The *explanation* interface

☑ The interface review methodology on which this book is based uses explicit guidelines, in the form of detailed checklists, to identify flaws in and target redesign of the presentation, conversation, navigation, and explanation interfaces.

☑ A major design challenge is to create a user interface that meets the needs of novice and experienced users. Novice users need a user interface that helps them develop an accurate and effective mental model; the system must be *easy to learn.* Experienced users need a user interface that supports them in accomplishing work-related tasks; the system must be *easy to use.*

Interface category	Design guidelines: Ease of learning	Design guidelines: Ease of use
Presentation	Familiarity	Visual consistency
	Transparency	Expectation support
Conversation	Clear dialog	Flexibility
	Feedback	User control
	Industry standards	
Navigation	Visibility	Direct manipulation
	Marked exits	Shortcuts
	Internal consistency	
Explanation	Protection	Forgiveness
	On-line help	Task support

☑ The results of an improved user interface include decreased learning time, increased proficiency, greater productivity, improved quality, and greater user satisfaction.

TECHNIQUES FOR IMPROVING INTERACTIONS BETWEEN PEOPLE AND COMPUTERS

Overview

What is this section about?

The computer can be the most useful tool you've ever used. Realizing its potential, however, is not automatic. It depends on the kind of partnership you form with your computer. And more than anything else, it's the user interface that determines this partnership. With the right user interface, you can waltz. With the wrong one, you'll wrestle (Shore, 1985, p. 107).

This section will show you specific procedures you can use to review and redesign a system's user interface. These procedures include

- Gathering end-user data to discover which components to review

- Identifying evaluation tasks

- Conducting a targeted review of the presentation, conversation, navigation, and explanation interfaces

- Recommending interface redesigns and alternative solutions to interface flaws

- Evaluating the impact of interface redesign on user performance

How should this section be read?

Think of Section Two as a procedural cookbook. It is composed of six chapters, each designed as a stand-alone unit. Chapter Two is meant to be read first, since it contains the procedures you will follow to identify the parts of the interface that need to be evaluated. Chapter Seven is meant to be read last, since it covers follow-up procedures. Chapters Three to Six are *not* intended to be read in their entirety, nor in any particular sequence. You need only refer to the procedures in these chapters that cover the parts of the interface you are reviewing.

For example, the results of the User Satisfaction Survey, which you'll read about in Chapter Two, indicate that the presentation interface is not causing performance problems, so you can skip Chapter Three.

Further, user interviews reveal that error-handling and performance support are satisfactory. However, some users tell you that they never use the on-line help system, while others confess that they never even knew such a system existed! Therefore, you go to Chapter Six and refer to Procedure 6.3, "Evaluating On-Line Help."

How is this section organized?

IF your goal is to . . .	AND you specifically want to know how to . . .	THEN read . . .
Decide which aspects of the interface are most in need of review and target your evaluation to critical system tasks.	1. Survey users 2. Interview users 3. Observe users 4. Identify evaluation tasks	Chapter Two
Review and recommend redesign of the *presentation interface:* how well the arrangement of information on the screen adheres to principles of graphical excellence.	Evaluate these components: 1. Screen displays 2. GUI screen displays 3. Menu displays 4. Data entry screen displays 5. Attention-getting techniques 6. Color displays	Chapter Three
Review and recommend redesign of the *conversation interface:* the adequacy of system-to-user interactions and user-to-system interactions.	Evaluate these components: 1. Prompts 2. Feedback 3. Menu language 4. Locus of control 5. Commands 6. Data input	Chapter Four
Review and recommend redesign of the *navigation interface:* how easily users can make their way in the system.	Evaluate these components: 1. Menu navigation 2. Navigation within a single screen or dialog box 3. Navigation between screens 4. Navigation by direct manipulation 5. Hardware-based navigation	Chapter Five
Review and recommend redesign of the *explanation interface:* how well the system teaches users about itself.	Evaluate these components: 1. Error-handling 2. Performance support 3. On-line help	Chapter Six
Communicate your interface design recommendations and evaluate the impact of these redesigns on user performance.	1. Document interface design recommendations 2. Evaluate the impact of interface redesign	Chapter Seven

Figure 2.1. *Using the procedures to redesign an interface.*

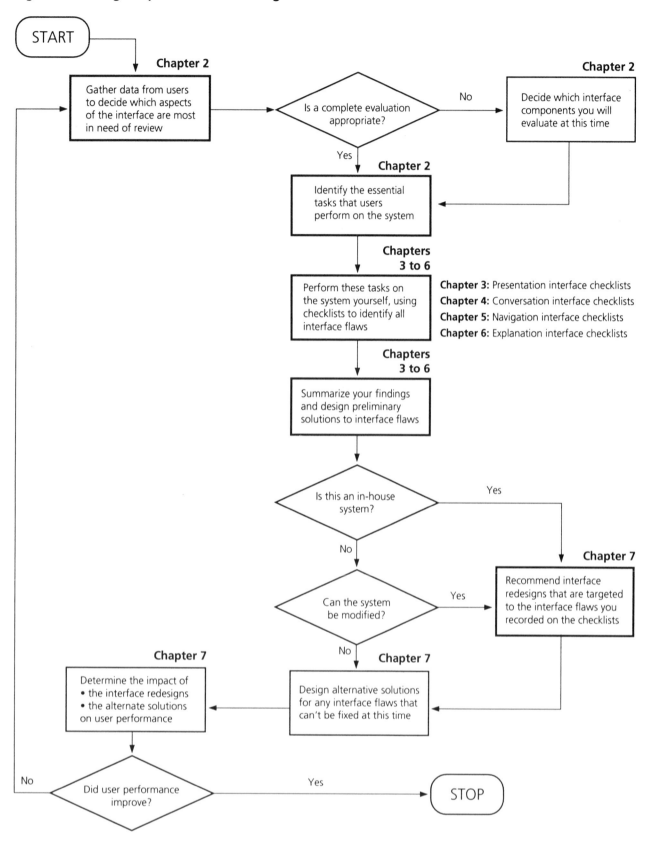

Another way to read this section

There are always choices to be made when organizing information for readers. What is the best way to present 20 interface evaluation procedures that consist of nearly 300 evaluation criteria? I created a model to group the procedures by interface category: presentation, conversation, navigation, and explanation. However, this meant splitting up some visible parts of an interface across categories. For example, menus can be evaluated in terms of their presentation, conversation, and navigation attributes, so there are three procedures for evaluating menus, and they appear in Chapters Three, Four, and Five.

This table will help you find information relating to the specific part of the interface that you want to redesign.

IF your goal is to review and redesign . . .	AND you specifically want to know how to evaluate . . .	THEN see page . . .
Menus	Menu displays	69
	Menu language	108
	Menu navigation	134
Data entry screens	Data entry screen displays	75
	Data input	124
	Navigation within a single screen or dialog box	142
	Navigation among screens	147
A GUI interface	GUI screen displays	63
	Color displays	86
	Navigation within a single screen or dialog box	142
	Navigation by direct manipulation	151
System messages	Prompts	96
	Feedback	101
	Error-handling	168
	On-line help	178

Finding the Source of Performance Problems

Introduction

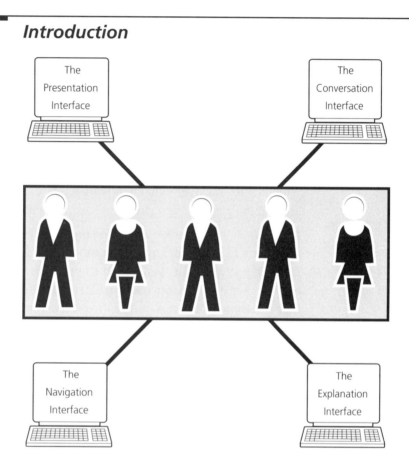

What is the purpose of this chapter?

This chapter is about getting ready. It is about the preparatory work you must do before you review the user interface, to ensure that the components you choose to review are those causing the most significant performance problems. This preparatory work ensures that your redesign recommendations will be targeted to the interface flaws that are affecting performance the most.

How do you get involved?

If you have been called in to solve performance problems experienced by users of a computer system, chances are the client organization already recognizes that the system has interface flaws. Or your client may have a vague idea that something is wrong but may not realize that the problem lies with the interface. These are some of the other ways you may become involved:

- Users are making too many data entry errors, and you are called in to design a course to "teach users to be more careful."

- Users are complaining that the old system worked better than the new system, and you are called in to design a course to "motivate users to like the new system."

- A new system is being introduced, and you are called in to develop a self-instructional course to "teach users everything about how the system works."

As you delve into these supposed training problems, it may become clear that there are significant design flaws in the system's interface. Now it's your job to discover what kinds of flaws exist and how significant they are. All interface design problems are *not* created equal.

Example 1: A complex command language (part of the conversation interface; see Chapter Four) may be cumbersome for inexperienced, infrequent users of a system but well suited to programmers who use the system for ten hours a day. If most users are programmers, this part of the interface may not be worth investigating. However, if most users are inexperienced, improving this part of the conversation interface may have a significant impact on performance.

Example 2: Inaccessible on-line help (part of the explanation interface; see Chapter Six) may not be worth investigating and redesigning if the commands and procedures required to operate a system are easily learned, relatively straightforward, and well documented. However, if users report difficulty using the system, improving this part of the explanation interface may have a significant impact on performance.

What's required to get ready?

- You need to *gather data*—to survey, interview, and observe users—to learn which parts of the interface are causing performance problems and dissatisfaction. These procedures are described on pages 39 to 48.

- You need to create a set of *evaluation tasks,* important system-based user activities that will put the system through its paces as you review individual components of the interface. This procedure is described on pages 49 to 51.

How is this chapter organized?

This chapter describes all of these procedures. The chapter is organized as follows:

Preparatory step	Procedure . . .	See page . . .
Gather usability data via surveys, interviews, and observation	How to survey users	39
	How to interview users	42
	How to observe users	46
Select interface evaluation tasks: scenarios that help guide your review	How to identify evaluation tasks	49

What are the results of following the procedures in this chapter?

Performing the four procedures in this chapter will help you identify

- The aspects of a system's user interface that are difficult to learn

- The aspects of a system's user interface that are difficult to use

- The core, frequent, and high-risk tasks that users perform on the system

You can then use this information to find and fix flaws in the presentation interface (see Chapter Three), conversation interface (Chapter Four), navigation interface (Chapter Five), and explanation interface (Chapter Six).

For more information

Andrus, G. R. "Human Interface User Analysis." *Performance & Instruction,* January 1988, *27*(1), 5–6.
Explains how to create a profile of system users to ensure that the system design meets the needs of the user population.
Bailey, R. W. *Human Performance Engineering: A Guide for System Designers.* Englewood Cliffs, N.J.: Prentice-Hall, 1982.
Chapter Eleven contains a good overview of the concept of function analysis, which can be used to identify evaluation tasks.
Bratton, B. "Getting Information from SMEs." *Performance & Instruction,* August 1984, *23*(6), 25.
Explains how to use descriptive, structured, and contrast questions to get the most important information from subject-matter experts (SMEs).

Brinkley, R. C. "Getting the Most from Client Interviews." *Performance & Instruction,* April 1989, *28*(4), 5–8.

Describes types of interview questions, methods for posing questions, and techniques for framing questions.

Burley-Allen, M. *Listening: The Forgotten Skill.* New York: Wiley, 1982.

Chapter Six contains a list of problems that can occur during an interview, accompanied by an excellent set of sample questions to solve each problem.

Campbell, R. "Will the Real Scenario Please Stand Up?" *SIGCHI Bulletin,* April 1992, *24*(2), 6–8.

Explains the use of scenarios to evaluate and design interfaces.

Carlisle, K. E. *Analyzing Jobs and Tasks.* Englewood Cliffs, N.J.: Educational Technology Publications, 1986.

Chapter One contains guidelines for developing and administering questionnaires.

Hetzel, W. *The Complete Guide to Software Testing.* Wellesley, Mass.: QED Information Sciences, 1984.

If you want to learn about formal system testing, Chapter Six describes methods for selecting functional test cases. Chapter Ten explains the role of the testing specialist.

Kemerer, R. W., and Schmid, R. F. "How to Summarize Questionnaire Data and Extract Useful Information for Revisions." *Performance & Instruction,* 1984, *23*(5), 9–10.

Describes the use of the "Adjusted Agreement Index," a technique for interpreting survey data.

Nielsen, J. "The Usability Engineering Life Cycle." *IEEE Computer,* 1992, *25*(3), 12–22.

Describes how the think-aloud methodology can be used during the usability testing process, while a system is in development.

Shneiderman, B. *Designing the User Interface: Strategies for Effective Human-Computer Interaction.* Reading, Mass.: Addison-Wesley, 1992.

The User Satisfaction Survey described in this chapter was adapted from Shneiderman's QUIS user-evaluation questionnaire (pp. 485–492). For information on the development and refinement of this instrument, see also Chin, J. P., Diehl, V. A., and Norman, K. L., "Development of an Instrument Measuring User Satisfaction of the Human-Computer Interface."

Tiemann, P. W., and Markle, S. M. "On Getting Expertise into an Expert System." *Performance & Instruction,* 1984, *23*(9), 25–29.

Presents a set of principles and guidelines for interviewing subject-matter experts.

Weinberg, G. M. *Rethinking Systems Analysis & Design.* New York: Dorset House, 1988.

Although this book is targeted to programmers, it is also helpful for anyone involved in systems design. Part IV describes specific behaviors to avoid when interviewing users.

The purpose of this procedure

Surveys allow information to be collected from many users in a short period of time. They are inexpensive to prepare and administer, and they are generally accepted by both users and managers.

The User Satisfaction Survey described in this procedure will help you identify which aspects of the interface are the greatest source of user frustration. (Section Four contains a reproducible copy of the survey.) The survey is organized by the four interface components we've already identified: presentation, conversation, navigation, and explanation.

When to use this procedure

Although most of the procedures in this book are meant to be selected only as needed, the User Satisfaction Survey should be administered for each system you are asked to review. If, for example, the system contains three applications (such as a word processor, a spreadsheet, and a graphics program), administer the survey three times. What you learn from the survey will help you target additional data-gathering efforts: interviews (see page 42) and observations (see page 46).

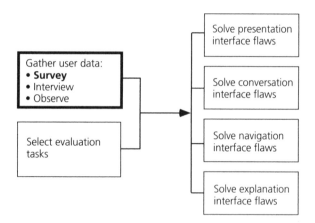

Terms you may not know

Conversation The two-way communication from the system to the user (prompts, feedback, menus) and from the user to the system (locus of control, commands, data input). For example, the wording of error messages is part of the conversation interface.

Explanation The on-line performance support provided by the system to teach itself to users. For example, an on-line help system is part of the explanation interface.

Navigation The method or methods by which users move around from one part of the system to another. For example, selecting an item from a menu is part of the navigation interface.

Presentation The design of individual screen elements and their arrangement on screens. For example, the placement of fields on a data entry screen is part of the presentation interface.

Syntax-savvy user A user who knows the specific details required to operate a specific system. For example, users of a specific word processor are syntax savvy if they know that (Ctrl) (Q) exits from this particular program and that (Ctrl) (N) opens a new file.

System-savvy novice A user who has had previous experience with computers but is new to a particular system or application. For example, a system-savvy novice may already know how to use a word processor but has never used a spreadsheet program.

Task-savvy novice A user who is new to the world of computers but already knows how to do the work that must be accomplished on the computer. For example, a task-savvy novice already knows how to balance a checkbook but has never used a computer to do this.

True novice A user who is new to the world of computers and has no prior experience with the work that must be accomplished on the computer.

Before you start

Make a copy of the User Satisfaction Survey (a reproducible copy of the survey appears in Resource A). Meet with the manager (or managers) of the people who use the system to explain the purpose of your interface review and obtain their permission to administer the survey.

Administering the User Satisfaction Survey

1. Obtain a list of names (and addresses, if necessary) of system users.

2. Distribute the survey. Include a cover letter emphasizing that the survey is being administered to evaluate the system, *not* the users.

3. Follow up with users to ensure a high response rate.

4. Tabulate the results of the survey.

5. Analyze the data from Part 1 of the survey to categorize the system users, by experience, as true novices; task-savvy novices; system-savvy novices; and syntax-savvy users.

6. Analyze the data from Parts 2 to 8 of the survey to identify potential interface flaws. Keep in mind the following:

   • Parts 2 and 8 indicate general satisfaction with the system.

   • Part 3 indicates flaws in the presentation interface.

   • Part 4 indicates flaws in the conversation interface.

   • Part 5 indicates flaws in the navigation interface.

   • Part 6 indicates flaws in the explanation interface.

   • Part 7 indicates interface flaws in systems with a graphical user interface (GUI).

7. Select a representative sample of users to interview (see Procedure 2.2 on page 42) and observe (see Procedure 2.3 on page 46). Be sure the sample reflects the range of expertise in the user population.

Example

You have been called in to evaluate the user interface of the Retail Account Management Processing system (RAMP), a database system used by a large retail chain to manage its customer accounts. You administer the User Satisfaction Survey to one hundred users located in Seattle, Portland, San Francisco, and Salt Lake City. The data seem to indicate that

- Task-savvy novices and system-savvy novices have more difficulty with the navigation interface than with the other interfaces.

- Syntax-savvy users are more frustrated by the conversation interface.

- The presentation and explanation interfaces do not pose any difficulty for users, except for a small group of true novices who have only used the system for a few hours and are having trouble with the way RAMP handles errors.

In your interviews and observations of users, you will know to concentrate on the navigation and conversation interfaces, as well as on the error-handling component of the explanation interface. If the interviews and observations confirm that these are the problematic areas, you will also focus your review and redesign efforts on this subset of interface components.

Procedure 2.2 — How to Interview Users

The purpose of this procedure

The main purposes of the user interview are *exploration* and *clarification*. Interviews with individual users, or groups of users, allow you to learn more about the parts of an interface that are causing the most significant performance problems.

Although this procedure is targeted to the people who use a system, the same techniques can be applied to interview their managers. Interviews with work center managers help pinpoint performance problems—such as a high rework rate or a low on-time delivery rate—that may be caused by the interface.

When to use this procedure

Interviews should be held after you have tabulated and analyzed the results of the User Satisfaction Survey (see page 39). The results of the interviews can be used alone or in conjunction with think-aloud observation (see Procedure 2.3 on page 46).

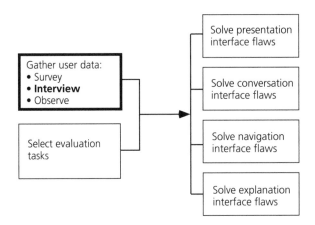

Terms you may not know

Controlling question A question that breaks into the interviewee's response (for example, "Haven't we spent enough time on error messages? I have to get back to my list of questions, or we'll never get done.").

Leading question A question phrased in a way that points to an answer (for example, "The menus seem fine . . . right?").

Loaded question A question requiring an answer that poses a potential risk for the interviewee (for example, "Do you spend more time doing your work or reading the manual?").

Syntax-savvy user A user who knows the specific details required to operate a specific system.

System-savvy novice A user who has had prior experience with computers, but is new to a particular system or application.

Task-savvy novice A user who is new to the world of computers, but already knows how to do the work that must be accomplished on the computer.

Before you start

From the group of people you surveyed with the User Satisfaction Survey, select a representative sample of people to interview. Be sure to select users in each of these categories:

- *Task-savvy novices.* Example: Noelle is a free-lance science writer. The newspaper to which she contributes most frequently has told her that to save retyping time, they need to receive her articles on disk. Although she has no computer experience, she is skilled at the tasks of writing, editing, and proofreading.

- *System-savvy novices.* Example: Alan is a college professor who has used FastWrite word processing software to write his last five books. His department has just switched over to LetterPerfect software in order to be compatible with the rest of the college. He will have to learn new commands, but he has already mastered basic word processing skills.

- *Syntax-savvy (experienced) users.* Example: Whitney is a course developer who creates her slides and overhead transparencies using TopDrawer graphics software. Because of her familiarity with the system's features and quirks, she has become a resource for other course developers in her department.

Obtain permission from the manager (or managers) to conduct individual or group interviews. Develop an initial set of interview questions aimed at discovering more about the items rated low on the survey. If possible, find a place outside the users' work areas to conduct interviews; make sure the location is private and free of distractions.

Conducting the interview

The following steps were developed for interviews with individual users but they also apply if you are meeting with a group of users. Although there are differences between individual and group interviewing techniques (for example, it may be difficult in a group interview to gather data from every group member), a discussion of such differences is not within the scope of this book. This procedure focuses on *what* to ask rather than *how* to ask it. Thus, it is not a complete interviewing description; such information can be found in any of the excellent books and articles on generic interviewing skills (see page 37 for a listing of these references).

Guidelines

- Limit the interview to one hour.
- If at all possible, do not use a tape recorder.
- Prepare a set of general interview questions, but use them only to guide, not to direct, the interview.
- Limit note-taking to critical items; fill in details after the interview.

Procedure

1. Introduce yourself to the user, and explain the goal of the interview. Be sure to emphasize that it is not the user who is being evaluated.

2. Explain that you have summarized the survey and that now you are interested in following up on specific concerns that users expressed about the system.

3. Describe what you already know about the system. For example: "The Teller Productivity Package was installed in all 300 branches about a year ago, wasn't it? And I understand that every new teller has to go through three weeks of classroom training before being allowed to use the system on the teller line. Your survey showed that you've been using TPP since March, so you were one of the early pioneers!"

4. Begin with a broad, open-ended question, and follow up with specific clarification questions. For example:

   You: "What would you like to tell me about the system?"

   User: "Well, it used to drive me crazy when they first made us use it, but it's not so bad now."

   You: "What drove you crazy?"

   User: "I guess the worst part was all those commands. You had to type them exactly right or it wouldn't understand what you were telling it. We used to joke during training that we needed a special TPP Berlitz course!"

5. Take the lead from the user, following up on each broad user statement with questions that pinpoint interface design flaws. Don't jump to conclusions: keep probing until you are sure you've dug out the "problem behind the problem." Avoid leading, loaded, or controlling questions. For example:

   You: "Tell me more about those commands."

   User: "The system has about 200 different commands."

   You (thinking the problem is a heavy memory load): "So that was a lot to learn?"

   User: "No, that wasn't really the problem. We had all worked on another system, you see, so we understood how commands work. It's just that many of the commands are similar, and it was hard to remember which one to use for which thing."

   You (still wondering if the problem is a heavy memory load, but needing more information to be sure): "Can you give me an example?"

User: "Let's see . . . oh, yeah. You type QUIT when you want to leave the calendar module, and EXIT to leave the E-mail module. That's not so bad, but if you type QUIT in the E-mail module it bumps you out of the whole system!"

You (now realizing that the problem is that the system's command structure is internally inconsistent)**:** "So QUIT means one thing in the calendar module and something else in the E-mail module?"

User: "You got it!"

6. Don't focus on interface flaws alone, also try to find out what the user finds easy or useful about the system. If there is a consensus on these features across many interviews, you may consider omitting them from your interface review. On the other hand, don't make the user feel that a positive response is required: this may be a system only a mother could love. For example:

You: "Is there any part of your job that used to be harder before they installed TPP?"

User: "The scheduling module is wonderful. I put in all my regular weekly meetings one time, and it shows them to me every week. That saves me lots of typing time. In the old system, I had to enter the same information each week, and it was easy to leave one out by mistake."

You: "Anything else?"

User: "Well . . . uh . . . uhmm . . ."

You: "If that's the only one that springs to mind, that's fine."

7. Wrap up the interview by summarizing what the user has told you. For example: "Tell me if this captures your opinion of the system. You said _____, _____, and _____. Have I left anything out?"

Procedure 2.3   *How to Observe Users*

The purpose of this procedure

The User Satisfaction Survey (see page 39) and user interviews (see page 42) are important sources of data that will help you target your interface review. However, you may find that the most problematical parts of an interface become evident only when you observe users interacting with the system. Observation allows you to learn what users *actually* do on the system rather than rely on what they *say* they do. Observation makes your data-gathering more complete because it does not rely on user self-report.

The observation procedure recommended here uses a method called "thinking aloud" to generate data. This method has the user perform a few well-chosen tasks while simultaneously articulating the mental processes required to accomplish them. This verbalization reveals the user's view of how the system works and pinpoints the parts of the interface that cause the most confusion.

When to use this procedure

Since observation is time-consuming, for you and for the people you are observing, you should perform this procedure with only a few users. The best observation candidates are novices who are both task savvy and system savvy, acquainted with the basic features of the system but not yet so comfortable with it that they fail to notice interface quirks.

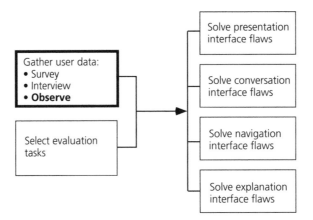

Terms you may not know

Command line A single word or an instruction string (for example, "erase myletter.doc") that is typed by the user to select a system function or object.

System-savvy novice A user who has had previous experience with computers, but is new to a particular system or application. For example, a system-savvy novice may already know how to use a word processor, but has never used a spreadsheet program.

Task-savvy novice A user who is new to the world of computers, but already knows how to do the work that must be accomplished on the computer. For example, a task-savvy novice may already know how to balance a checkbook, but has never used a computer to perform this task.

Before you start

Select several users for observation. If possible, choose people from the group you previously interviewed; the rapport you established during that interview will help users feel more comfortable about being observed. Identify users who are both task and system savvy.

Meet with the manager of the work area where the system is located. Obtain permission to spend time with several users. Be sure to confirm that the system can be made available for one or two hours per user on the day of the observation.

How to conduct a think-aloud observation

1. Set up the computer equipment outside the users' work areas. Find a location that is private and free of distractions. A think-aloud observation conducted at users' desks may not afford enough privacy for them to articulate their problems with the system.

2. Prepare a written set of tasks for the user to complete. These may be, but do not need to be, the same as the evaluation tasks you will use when you conduct a formal interface review (see Procedure 2.4 on page 49). For example, in a data entry system that uses a command-line interface for navigation, the selected tasks might include the following:

   • Change Bobbie Wickham's middle initial from G to Q.

   • Find out when Gussie Fink–Nottle's next loan payment is due.

   • Run the report that shows the Western region's year-to-date sales figures.

3. Explain the purpose of the observation. Be sure to emphasize that you are not evaluating the user; the purpose of the observation is for you (and the organization) to learn more about the system's usability.

4. Watch the user perform each task and record what he or she says during each step of the process. Be supportive: although you should not take over or give instructions, it is appropriate to encourage the user (for example, to say, "Just take your time. You're doing fine"). *Note:* Although the use of a tape recorder is not recommended for user interviews, recording a think-aloud observation generates more comprehensive data than does note-taking.

5. During the observation, users will probably stop thinking aloud, since it is unnatural for people to talk and use a system at the same time. Remind them to verbalize their thoughts by asking open-ended, nonthreatening questions. For example: "You seem confused. What are you thinking about?" or "How do you interpret what the system is telling you?"

6. Do not answer questions about how the system works, because you are trying to determine how easy the interface is to learn and use without outside help. If you want to increase a user's confidence, design the first task to be extremely easy, to ensure an early success. For example:

User: "How do I get it to print?"

You: "Tell me some of the things you think might work."

7. At the end of each observation, invite each user to make general comments about the experience, the tasks, and the system. A good open-ended question to begin this discussion is, "What do you think I should be asking you now?"

Example

This sample of a think-aloud observation appears in *The Nurnberg Funnel* (Carroll, 1990, p. 129). The learner (or user) is attempting to add a date to a letter by inserting a line of text into the existing document. Notice that the experimenter (or observer) only asks clarifying questions and does not provide guidance.

Learner: OK. Now I'll try and insert the date underneath this heading. *Moves cursor down two lines, then back up one line, then back down one line.* Now I'm just playing with the keys and trying to figure out what to do.

Experimenter: Which keys are those?

Learner: The ones on the right—the Word Return, Character Advance, Word Advance . . . *Types Word Advance three times, then Line Advance once.*

Experimenter: Does that seem to be in order?

Learner: Yeh; it seems to do what it says. I'm just figuring out what it is that it exactly does. *Presses Variable Advance (for advancing through a set of menu fields), causing a reset condition (which locks the keyboard).*
No. *Presses Reset, clearing the reset condition.*
That was Variable Advance. Umm. *Uses Space Bar to move cursor rightward, aligning the date she will insert with the return address already typed.*

Learner: OK. Now I'll add the date. *Does so.*

Experimenter: What are you thinking?

Procedure 2.4 — How to Identify Evaluation Tasks

The purpose of this procedure

Suppose you have been asked to evaluate the usability of a word processor. Where do you start? Do you sit down at the computer and start writing a letter? Do you deliberately make a typing error and attempt to correct your mistake? Do you try to figure out the mail-merge option? Do you print your document? Any or all of these might be appropriate tasks. How do you select among them? *Evaluation tasks* are scenarios that let you exercise the specific parts of the interface that you care about reviewing. In conducting an interface review, your goal is to critique the system from a user's perspective. You are not trying to test the complete system functionality; you are not even trying to test the entire interface. You simply want to evaluate, in a meaningful, reproducible way, the parts of the interface that you suspect contain design flaws. By identifying evaluation tasks, your interface review and redesign recommendations achieve greater credibility than if you simply "play around" on the system.

When to use this procedure

Chapters Three to Six describe the use of checklists to conduct an interface review and target your redesign recommendations. Evaluation tasks help guide you through the system as you use these checklists. Therefore, before you perform any of the procedures in Chapters Three to Six, *you must identify a set of evaluation tasks* that best

- Represent the major functions of the system, and
- Exercise the part of the interface you are reviewing

This procedure can be performed along with the procedures for gathering user data through surveys (page 39), interviews (page 42), and observations (page 49).

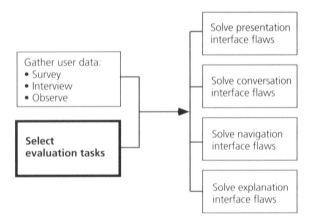

Terms you may not know

Evaluation task A core, frequent, or high-risk procedure that users perform on the system.

Functions The major activities the user can perform on a system, viewed from an external or high-level perspective.

System requirements A document, generally developed by the system analysis or design group, that uses a combination of narratives and diagrams to describe how the system will operate. The *functional requirements* are the component of the system requirements that describe the business needs being met by the system.

User guide A document, generally developed by the training or technical writing group, that describes how users interact with the system.

Before you start

Obtain a copy of the user guides and the functional system requirements to identify the main system functions and user tasks. If such documentation is not available, obtain permission to interview a subject-matter expert (SME) who is a knowledgeable member of the user group.

Selecting evaluation tasks

1. Study existing documentation, or interview a SME, to identify an initial list of tasks that users can perform on the system.

2. Interview a knowledgeable user or a member of the analysis or design group to identify just the tasks which are *core* (crucial to system operation), *frequent* (performed by most users, most of the time), and *high risk* (prone to error or serious consequences). Example: Here are seven tasks that users perform on the Environmentally Correct Catalogue Order Entry system (ECCOE). Of these, tasks 3 and 6 do not qualify as evaluation tasks because they are neither core, frequent, nor high risk.

#	Initial Task List	core	frequent	high risk	n/a
1.	Verify customer credit information	☑	☑	☐	☐
2.	Change system password	☐	☐	☑	☐
3.	Add an item to the inventory list	☐	☐	☐	☑
4.	Backorder an out-of-stock item	☐	☑	☐	☐
5.	Issue credit on a canceled order	☐	☑	☐	☐
6.	Change the price of a sale item	☐	☐	☐	☑
7.	Check item availability	☑	☑	☐	☐

3. Perform the core, frequent, and high-risk tasks identified in Step 2 as you review the interface. In the example shown here, the five tasks that are suitable for evaluation are items 1, 2, 4, 5, and 7. Each evaluation task can be used to review multiple components of the interface, but your focus will be different each time you perform the task.

Example: One evaluation task identified for the ECCOE system is #7, "Check item availability." To test the menu navigation interface (see Chapter Five), the breakdown of this task would be as follows:

- Bring up the ECCOE main menu.

- Go to the "Query" menu.

- Go to the "Inventory" menu.

- See if item 34–127 is in stock.

- Go back up to the main menu.

However, to test the error-handling interface (see Chapter Six), this task would break down as follows:

- Bring up the ECCOE main menu.

- Error condition test: Enter an invalid menu code.

- Go from the "Query" menu to the "Inventory" menu.

- Error condition test: Enter an invalid item code.

- Error condition test: Attempt to correct the invalid item code.

## CHAPTER 3

The Presentation Interface: Improving the Visual Display of Information

Introduction

Presentation

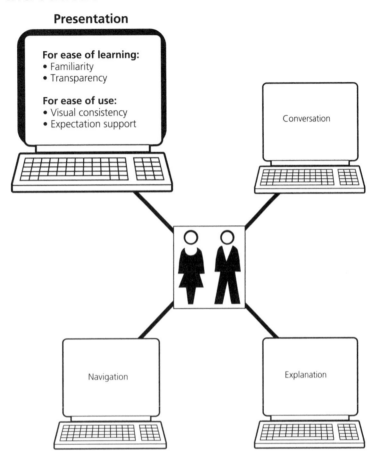

For ease of learning:
• Familiarity
• Transparency

For ease of use:
• Visual consistency
• Expectation support

Conversation

Navigation

Explanation

What is presentation?

Dictionary definitions of the verb "to present" include the following:

• To bring before the public

• To offer for observation, examination, or consideration

• To make a show or display

A system's presentation interface is its public face: the arrangement of information on the screen, including menu layout, icon design, and use of graphic elements or color to highlight important information. To be effective, it must adhere to principles of *graphical excellence*. "Graphical excellence is that which gives to the viewer the greatest number of ideas in the shortest time with the least ink in the smallest space" (Tufte, 1983, p. 51).

What is the purpose of this chapter?

This chapter shows you how to review and recommend redesign of a system's presentation interface. Many companies either already have or are in the process of developing guidelines for the display of information on screens. While these are an excellent start, they are often too general to be really useful in explicitly identifying interface flaws.

Frequently (and erroneously), user interface design is perceived as purely the design of the presentation interface. This is because the presentation interface is the most visible part of a system, but high-tech colors and snazzy graphics can often hide flawed navigation, conversation, and explanation interfaces. In contrast, a poor presentation interface can bias users against a system that is well designed in other ways.

How is this chapter organized?

This chapter contains six procedures organized around six aspects of the presentation interface.

IF you want to evaluate . . .	THEN see page . . .	Related procedures elsewhere in this book . . .
The overall presentation characteristics of any screen in the system	58	None
The system's use of icons and windows *Note:* GUI systems	63	How to evaluate navigation by direct manipulation (p. 151)
The presentation interface of the system's menus	69	How to evaluate menu language (p. 108) How to evaluate menu navigation (p. 134)
The display of information on data entry screens	75	How to evaluate data input (p. 124) How to evaluate navigation within a single screen (p. 142) How to evaluate navigation between screens (p. 147)
Special visual and auditory methods used to get people's attention	82	None
The system's use of color	86	None

What are the results of following the procedures in this chapter?

Using the procedures in this chapter to discover and correct flaws in the presentation interface can improve user performance in these ways:

Potential result . . .	For example . . .
Decreased learning time: more users can acquire more skills in less time.	*Before:* Field labels changed from one screen to another; the same person was called a "client," a "customer," and an "insuree."
	After: Because all paper forms used the single term "customer," field labels were changed to use this term consistently throughout the system.
Increased proficiency: more users can use more system functions.	*Before:* Many icons looked alike, so users were never sure which icon performed which function.
	After: Icons were redesigned to make them visually distinctive and each icon was labeled to make its purpose clear.
Increased productivity: users can accomplish a task in less time and with less effort.	*Before:* Menus were lengthy and items were arranged alphabetically, so users spent time hunting for the item they needed.
	After: Menu items were re-ordered to match the task sequence of the work.

Potential result . . .	For example . . .
Improved quality: users can produce more accurate work with less time spent correcting errors.	*Before:* Poor-risk customers were being approved for credit purchases because it was time-consuming to determine which customers had an overdue balance. *After:* Color was used as an attention-getter; now the name of every customer with an overdue balance is displayed in yellow.
Enhanced satisfaction: users feel comfortable with and supported by the system.	*Before:* Data entry screens were crowded and hard to read. *After:* Related fields were grouped into zones and each zone was separated by space.

For more information

Apple Computer. *Macintosh Human Interface Guidelines.* Reading, Mass.: Addison-Wesley, 1992.

General design principles for graphical user interfaces, targeted to Macintosh applications. Chapter Three provides detailed specification for parts of the presentation interface such as icons, windows, and scroll bars.

Galitz, W. O. *User-Interface Screen Design.* Boston: QED Publishing Group, 1993.

Chapter Five contains detailed guidelines and examples for the design of data entry screens. The chapter is divided into three parts:
• General design guidelines
• Data entry screens used with a dedicated source document
• Data entry screens used without a dedicated source document

IBM Corporation. *Common User Access: Advanced Interface Design Reference.* (Publication no. SC34-4290-00). 1991.

General design principles for graphical user interfaces, targeted to Windows-based applications. Chapter Two provides guidelines for designing parts of the presentation interface such as icons, windows, and scroll bars.

Marcus, A. *Graphic Design for Electronic Documents and User Interfaces.* New York: ACM Press, 1992.

Chapter Four contains guidelines for effective color use as well as an annotated bibliography of references for analysis, planning, design, and production of color displays. Chapter Seven compares six windowing (graphical user interface) systems: Apple Macintosh, NextStep, Open Look, Microsoft Windows, OS/2 Presentation Manager, and OSF/Motif.

Peddie, J. *Graphical User Interfaces and Graphic Standards.* New York: McGraw Hill, 1992.

Chapter Three discusses the history and elements of graphical user interfaces. The remainder of the book describes in detail and compares specific GUI operating systems (for example, XWindows, NeXT, Macintosh, NewWave).

Tufte, E. R. *Envisioning Information.* Cheshire, Conn.: Graphics Press, 1990.

In Chapter Five, "Color and Information," Tufte reflects on the care required to use color effectively: "Tying color to information is as elementary and straightforward as color technique in art. 'To paint well is simply this: to put the right color in the right place,' is Paul Klee's ironic prescription. The often scant benefits derived from coloring data indicate that even putting a good color in a good place is a complex matter. Indeed, [it is] so difficult and subtle that avoiding catastrophe becomes the first principle in bringing color to information: *Above all, do no harm*" (p. 81).

Evaluating Screen Displays

The purpose of this procedure

The way information is presented to users influences the way they perceive the system. Any interface review should include an overall review of the system's screen display even if no other presentation reviews are done. If this general review reveals extensive flaws, consider conducting additional presentation interface reviews—of menus, data entry screens, and any other presentation features that seem problematical.

When to use this procedure

It is especially important to evaluate and recommend redesign of screens when

- Items in Part 3 of the User Satisfaction Survey (see Chapter Two) are rated low

- During interviews or think-aloud observation (see Chapter Two), users have said things like "I find myself squinting at the monitor" or "I never display the graphs on the screen; I print them out so I can read them" or "When I get the information I need, I have to write it down so I can use it on the next screen" or "Everything on the screen runs together."

Terms you may not know

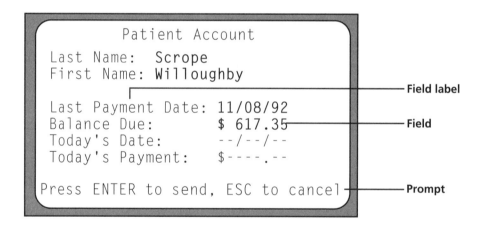

Field label Identifies the kind of information that goes into a field.
Prompt A system message that tells the user what to do next.

Before you start

Obtain some representative data for the system you are reviewing. From your set of evaluation tasks (see Chapter Two), select one or more to try out these interface activities:

- View several menus.
- Select an option from a menu.
- View several data entry screens.
- Enter data on a screen.
- Complete a multiscreen transaction.

Finding the problem

To discover the flaws in a system's screen display interface, work through your evaluation tasks using Presentation Interface Checklist #1: General Screen Design to evaluate the interface. (Resource C contains a reproducible copy of this checklist.) Every item that is checked "no" indicates an interface flaw. To correct these flaws, follow the instructions in the next section, "Solving the problem."

Many of the examples in the checklist refer to the sample screens that follow. Each screen element is labeled with the number on the checklist to which it refers.

Sample screen 1: Poor presentation

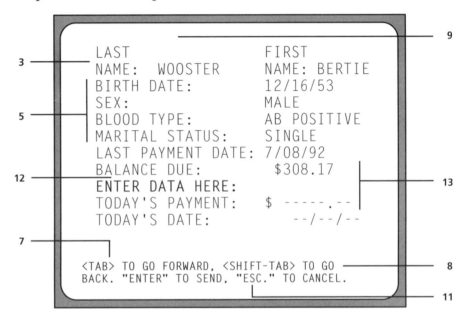

Sample Screen 2: Better presentation

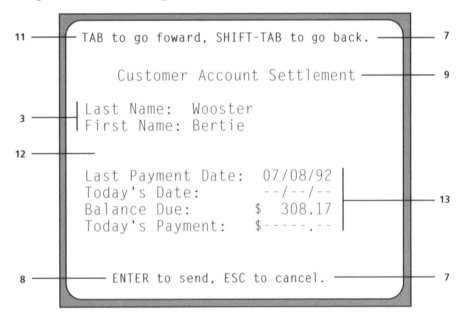

Presentation Interface Checklist #1: General Screen Design

#	Review Checklist	yes	no	n/a	Examples
1.	For question and answer interfaces, are visual cues and white space used to distinguish questions, prompts, instructions, and user input?	☐	☐	☐	Name? Glossop Please enter first and last name Name? Honoria Glossop Birthday? 5/20/63
2.	Does the data display start in the upper-left corner of the screen?	☐	☐	☐	
3.	Are multiword field labels placed horizontally (not stacked vertically)?	☐	☐	☐	When the two words in Last Name: are placed side-by-side, the eye can move naturally from left to right.
4.	Have industry or company formatting standards been followed consistently in all screens within a system?	☐	☐	☐	
5.	Is only (and all) information essential to decision making displayed on the screen?	☐	☐	☐	In sample screen 1, Birth Date, Sex, Blood Type, and Marital Status, while potentially important data, do not apply to this screen's purpose, which is to post payments to the customer's account.
✳ 6.	Are all data a user needs on display at each step in a transaction sequence?	☐	☐	☐	
7.	Are prompts, cues, and messages placed where the eye is likely to be looking on the screen?	☐	☐	☐	In sample screen 2, the instructions on how to fill out the screen are at the top, while the instructions on what to do once the screen is complete are on the bottom.
8.	Have prompts been formatted using white space, justification, and visual cues for easy scanning?	☐	☐	☐	In sample screen 1, the second sentence should begin on a new line. Also, the user is required to search for the ENTER DATA HERE prompt, which is buried in the middle of the screen.
✳ 9.	Does every display begin with a title or header that describes screen contents?	☐	☐	☐	The title Customer Account Settlement on sample screen 2 clearly identifies the purpose of the screen.

#	Review Checklist	yes	no	n/a	Examples
10.	Has a heavy use of all uppercase letters on a screen been avoided?	☐	☐	☐	The use of all capital letters in sample screen 1 makes it not only difficult to read but also nearly impossible to distinguish between field labels, prompts, and data entry fields.
11.	Do abbreviations not include punctuation?	☐	☐	☐	On sample screen 1, ESC would be easier to read than "ESC."; the punctuation is a redundant visual cue.
12.	Do text areas have "breathing space" around them?	☐	☐	☐	On sample screen 2, blank lines have been added to divide the screen into natural "chunks" of information.
13.	Are integers right-justified and real numbers decimal-aligned?	☐	☐	☐	On sample screen 1, the decimal points in the Balance Due and Enter Payment fields should be lined up.

Solving the problem

Every "no" on the checklist indicates an interface flaw that can interfere with performance.

- Ideally, you will be in a position to recommend an interface redesign to correct each flaw. Use checklist examples, where provided, as design guidelines. The answer to the item will then become either "yes" (because the feature was enhanced) or "n/a" (because the structure of the interface was changed to eliminate the feature).

- However, interface redesign is not always an option. In this case, you may be able to improve performance with an alternative strategy, such as a job aid. Any checklist item marked with an asterisk (*) is a candidate for one of these alternative strategies.

Interface Redesign Recommendations. If your analysis has uncovered flaws in the general screen presentation interface, use the design principles presented in checklist items 1 to 13 to guide you toward specific design revisions. For example:

- If screen displays include irrelevant information, this information should be removed.
- If information is presented in all capital letters, it should be changed to a combination of upper and lowercase.
- If information is crowded, elements should be rearranged into zones with adequate space between each zone (see Procedure 3.4, Evaluating Data Entry Screen Displays).

Alternative solutions (for items marked with *). Consider these alternatives if interface redesign is not possible.

#	IF the interface flaw is . . .	THEN recommend . . .
6	Not all the data a user needs are available at each step in a transaction sequence.	Providing a system function that will let users print full or partial screen images to capture data that are required for a future procedure
9	Screens are not titled.	A printed reference of screen images describing the purpose of each screen

<table>
<tr><td>

Procedure 3.2

</td><td>

Evaluating GUI Screen Displays

</td></tr>
</table>

The purpose of this procedure

Graphical User Interface (GUI) screens present a special set of interface problems. Such interfaces are touted as being not only easy to use but "intuitively" appealing. If your system is a GUI you may think that an interface review is unnecessary, but specific GUI systems vary widely in the quality of their presentation interface. As a result, it is important to do an overall review of the system's graphical display, even if you do no additional presentation interface reviews.

When to use this procedure

It is especially important to evaluate and recommend redesign of graphical displays when

- Items in Parts 3 and 7 of the User Satisfaction Survey are rated low

- During interviews or think-aloud observation, users have said things like "All those pictures look pretty much the same to me" or "I spend all my time looking for the icon I need" or "Clicking on icons was fun when I was first learning the system, but by now it's a little old" or "My screen gets all cluttered up with windows" or "I spend more time fiddling with windows than doing my work."

Terms you may not know

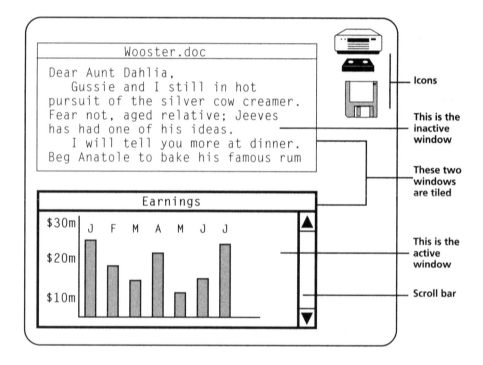

Active window The window that is available for manipulation. Several windows may be on the screen simultaneously, but the user can only manipulate the data in one at a time.

Icon A picture that represents an object (for example, annual report) or a process (for example, setting up a printer).

Scrolling Used to bring a different part of a document into view when a window offers a view of only a portion of the document. GUI interfaces often have *scroll bars,* which can be manipulated on screen to scroll horizontally or vertically.

Tiled windows A method of displaying several windows at once. Each window occupies its own portion of the screen, and there are no overlaps. Tiled windows are easy to find but displays may be too small if a number of windows are open.

Window A view into part of a document. GUI interfaces can often display several windows on the screen at once, each containing a different type of data (for example, a letter, a spreadsheet, and a graph).

Before you start

From your set of evaluation tasks, select one or more to try out these interface activities:

- View all the icons used in the system.
- Select an icon.
- Switch from icon to text display.
- Display multiple windows on the screen.
- Make a window active; make a different window active.
- Scroll in a window.
- Change the size and position of a window.

Finding the problem

To discover flaws in a system's GUI screen display interface, work through your evaluation tasks using Presentation Interface Checklist #2: GUI Screens to evaluate the interface. (See Resource C for a reproducible copy of the checklist.) Every item that is checked ''no'' indicates an interface flaw. To correct these flaws, follow the instructions in the next section, ''Solving the problem.''

Presentation Interface Checklist #2: GUI Screens

#	Review Checklist	yes	no	n/a	Examples
1.	Is there a consistent icon design scheme and stylistic treatment across the system?	☐	☐	☐	
2.	Is each individual icon a harmonious member of a family of icons?	☐	☐	☐	All files, regardless of content, are represented by a rectangular icon.
3.	Are icons concrete and familiar?	☐	☐	☐	All directory and subdirectory icons are shaped like file folders, visually reinforcing the concept that "files" (documents) reside in "folders" (directories).
4.	Are all icons in a set visually and conceptually distinct?	☐	☐	☐	The icon for the "printer setup" process resembles a laser printer. The icon for the "telecommunications setup" process resembles a telephone.
5.	Has excessive detail in icon design been avoided?	☐	☐	☐	
6.	Have large objects, bold lines, and simple areas been used to distinguish icons?	☐	☐	☐	
7.	Has color been used with discretion?	☐	☐	☐	All application icons are red, to set them apart from data files.
8.	Is a single, selected icon clearly visible when surrounded by unselected icons?	☐	☐	☐	When you click on an icon, it turns dark. The other (unselected) icons on the screen remain light.
9.	Does each icon stand out from its background?	☐	☐	☐	A black-and-white icon is easy to see against a pale gray background screen.
10.	Are icons labeled?	☐	☐	☐	

Set up printer   Select monitor

Presentation Interface Checklist #2 (Continued)

#	Review Checklist	yes	no	n/a	Examples
11.	Are there no more than twelve to twenty icon types?	☐	☐	☐	
12.	Can users choose between iconic and text display of information?	☐	☐	☐	The Show Icons command displays each file as an icon. The Show Names command removes the icons, and lists file names alphabetically.
13.	Are window operations easy to learn and use?	☐	☐	☐	
14.	Has the amount of required window housekeeping been kept to a minimum?	☐	☐	☐	The system automatically "tiles" all open windows. When you click in a window, it automatically "grows" to fill the entire screen.
15.	Are there salient visual cues to identify the active window?	☐	☐	☐	Active window Inactive window
16.	Does each window have a title?	☐	☐	☐	
17.	Are vertical and horizontal scrolling possible in each window?	☐	☐	☐	
✳ 18.	If setting up windows is a low-frequency task, is it easy to remember?	☐	☐	☐	

#	Review Checklist	yes	no	n/a	Examples
19.	In systems that use overlapping windows, is it easy for users to rearrange windows on the screen?	☐	☐	☐	To move a window, click to select it and, while holding down the mouse button, drag the window to its new location.
20.	In systems that use overlapping windows, is it easy for users to switch between windows?	☐	☐	☐	You can press (ESC) to "flip" from the front window to the one behind it. Continue pressing (ESC) to move through the entire stack of windows.

Solving the problem

Every "no" on the checklist indicates an interface flaw that can interfere with performance.

- Ideally, you will be in a position to recommend an interface redesign to correct each flaw. Use checklist examples, where provided, as design guidelines. The answer to the item will then become either "yes" (because the feature was enhanced) or "n/a" (because the structure of the interface was changed to eliminate the feature).

- However, interface redesign is not always an option. In this case, you may be able to improve performance with an alternative strategy such as a job aid. Any checklist item marked with an asterisk (*) is a candidate for one of these alternative strategies.

Interface redesign recommendations. If your analysis has uncovered flaws in the GUI presentation interface, use the design principles presented in checklist items 1 to 20 to guide you toward specific design revisions. For example, if the function of a particular icon is not readily apparent, two design principles that emerge are the following:

- Label each icon with a distinctive title that indicates its function.
- Redesign the icons to make each one visually distinctive.

If the active window cannot be distinguished from inactive windows, consider giving the active window a darker border to make it stand out.

Note: IBM and Apple, among others, have developed comprehensive standards for graphical user interfaces. Incorporating these standards into the design of interfaces will do much to resolve problems of this type, since a key feature of the GUI interface is consistency of presentation among all applications.

Alternative solutions (for items marked with *). Consider these alternatives if interface redesign is not possible.

#	IF the interface flaw is . . .	THEN recommend . . .
3	Icons are not concrete and familiar.	A printed "key" to icons, showing a reproduction of each icon and its function

#	IF the interface flaw is . . .	THEN recommend . . .
18	Setting up windows is a complex, infrequent task.	A set of instructions that describes and illustrates all the steps necessary to set up windows

Procedure 3.3   *Evaluating Menu Displays*

The purpose of this procedure

A menu is a list of options from which the user selects one. Chapters Four and Five, respectively, describe procedures for evaluating the menu conversation (see page 108) and navigation attributes (see page 134). However, menu presentation is also worth examining, since in many systems user tasks are performed by selecting options from menus. This procedure also includes the evaluation of soft function keys, if any, because they function as local menus to let users select function key commands.

When to use

It is especially important to evaluate and recommend redesign of menu displays when

- Items in Parts 3 and 7 of the User Satisfaction Survey are rated low.

- During interviews or think-aloud observation, users have said things like "These lists are too hard to read" or "Why did they put that option way up there? On the last menu, it was down on the bottom."

Terms you may not know

Menu choices The list of options available on a menu. Each menu offers multiple choices.

Menu title The name of the menu. Each menu has a single title.

Pull-down menu Many GUI systems display a permanent menu bar at the top of the screen. To select options, users click on one of the menu titles in the menu bar, causing all available choices in that menu to appear. Thus, with GUI systems, all options are visible at all times.

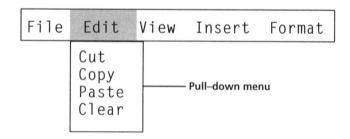

Soft function keys An on-screen display of the commands that correspond to function keys on the keyboard.

Before you start

From your set of evaluation tasks, select one or more to try out these interface activities:

- View all the high-use menus in the system.

- If the system uses soft function keys, view all displays that show them.

- If the system uses pull-down menus (typical in GUI systems), examine the contents of each menu.

Finding the problem   To discover flaws in a system's menu display interface, work through your evaluation tasks using Presentation Interface Checklist #3: Menus to evaluate the interface. (Resource C contains a reproducible copy of the checklist.) Every item that is checked "no" indicates an interface flaw. To correct these flaws, follow the instructions in the section after the checklist, "Solving the problem."

Presentation Interface Checklist #3: Menus

#	Review Checklist	yes	no	n/a	Examples
✻ 1.	Does the menu structure match the task structure?	☐	☐	☐	Personal Assistant A…Appointments E…Expense Tracking P…Phone Numbers T…To Do List
2.	Have industry or company standards been established for menu design, and are they applied consistently on all menu screens in the system?	☐	☐	☐	All menu titles are centered, all prompts appear on the bottom of the screen, and each menu choice is identified by a unique mnemonic code.
3.	Are menu choice lists presented vertically?	☐	☐	☐	
4.	Are menu choices ordered in the most logical way, given the user, the item names, and the task variables?	☐	☐	☐	Order Maintenance P…Place an Order C…Change an Order D…Delete an Order
5.	If there is a natural sequence to menu choices, has it been used?	☐	☐	☐	Schedule patient on: ___ Monday ___ Tuesday ___ Wednesday ___ Thursday ___ Friday
6.	If "exit" is a menu choice, does it always appear on the bottom of the list?	☐	☐	☐	Customer Accounts O…Open an account M…Modify an account C…Close an account E…Exit

Presentation Interface Checklist #3 (Continued)

#	Review Checklist	yes	no	n/a	Examples
7.	If the system uses a standard GUI interface where menu sequence has already been specified, do menus adhere to the specification whenever possible?	☐	☐	☐	In many GUI systems, the first item on the menu bar is the File menu, which handles file management functions (open, close, save, print, and so on). In addition, Exit is the last choice on the File menu.
8.	Are menu titles either centered or left-justified?	☐	☐	☐	Accounts O...Open an account M...Modify an account C...Close an account E...Exit
9.	Are menu items left-justified, with the item number or mnemonic preceding the name?	☐	☐	☐	Open a new account: 1...Checking 2...Savings 3...Money Market 4...SEP/Keogh
10.	Are meaningful groups of items separated by white space?	☐	☐	☐	File Edit Text N...New O...Open C...Close R...Rename ——— White space S...Save U...Preview P...Print

#	Review Checklist	yes	no	n/a	Examples
11.	Do menu instructions, prompts, and error messages appear in the same place(s) on each menu?	☐	☐	☐	Broker System __ Stock quotes __ Corporate bonds _X_ T-bills View today's T-bill rates
12.	Is there an obvious visual distinction made between "choose one" menus and "choose many" menus?	☐	☐	☐	Choose one → Select printer: ○ Imagewriter ● Laserwriter Choose many → Print options: ☐ Double sided ☒ Download fonts ☒ Manual feed
✱ 13.	Have spatial relationships between soft function keys (on-screen cues) and keyboard function keys been preserved?	☐	☐	☐	Help Save Copy Move [F1] [F2] [F3] [F4]
14.	Does the system gray out or delete labels of currently inactive soft function keys?	☐	☐	☐	The Print function does not apply unless the user has created a report, so this label only appears on report screens.

Solving the problem

Every "no" on the checklist indicates an interface flaw that can interfere with performance.

- Ideally, you will be in a position to recommend an interface redesign to correct each flaw. Use checklist examples, where provided, as design guidelines. The answer to the item will then become either "yes" (because the feature was enhanced) or "n/a" (because the structure of the interface was changed to eliminate the feature).

- However, interface redesign is not always an option. In this case, you may be able to improve performance with an alternative strategy such as a job aid. Any checklist item marked with an asterisk (*) is a candidate for one of these alternative strategies.

Interface redesign recommendations. If your analysis has uncovered flaws in the menu presentation interface, use design principles 1 to 14 to guide you toward specific design revisions. For example, it is often a simple matter to rearrange the sequence of menu choices on individual menus. Or, if the soft function key labeled EXIT on the screen is assigned to (F1) but appears in the lower right corner of the screen above (F15), here are two possible solutions:

- Rearrange the soft function key labels so that EXIT is moved to the lower left corner of the screen, above (F1).

- Reassign the function to the (F15) function key.

Alternative solutions (for items marked with *). Consider these alternatives if interface redesign is not possible.

#	IF the interface flaw is . . .	THEN recommend . . .
1	Menu structure does not match the task structure.	A printed list that matches frequent or complex user tasks to the menu(s) required to accomplish each task

IF you want to...	THEN go to...
Check a customer's credit information	Menus 1, 2, and 5
See if the product is in stock	Menu 7
Find out how long it will take to ship an order	Menus 3, 4, 6, and 8

#	IF the interface flaw is . . .	THEN recommend . . .
13	A mismatch between the placement of on-screen soft function keys and keyboard function keys.	Eliminate the soft function key display; replace with a keyboard template labeling each function key

Procedure 3.4 — Evaluating Data Entry Screen Displays

The purpose of this procedure

Think of a data entry screen as a fill-in form that structures the way in which users enter information into the system. Chapter Five (see page 142) describes procedures for evaluating the data entry screen navigation interface. But data entry screen presentation is also worth examining, since in database systems the greatest amount of user time will be spent viewing these screens.

When to use this procedure

These procedures apply only if you are evaluating a database system. Stand-alone applications—such as word processors or spreadsheets—do not have data entry screens. The other procedures in this chapter will help you evaluate the presentation interface of stand-alone applications.

Reviewing the presentation of data entry screens can have a high payoff because redesigning a data entry screen layout is usually one of the easiest system changes to make. It is especially important to evaluate and recommend redesign of data entry screen displays when

- Items in Part 3 of the User Satisfaction Survey are rated low.

- During interviews or think-aloud observation, users have said things like "These screens are too hard to read" or "On the application form the policy date is on the top, but on this screen it's down on the bottom" or "Why don't they put the claim number and the policy number in the same place?"

Terms you may not know

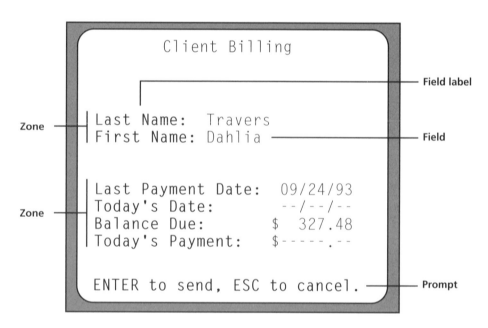

Database A data storage and retrieval system designed to capture data (*input*), manipulate it (*process*), and report on it (*output*).

Field The part of the data entry screen where the user enters information.

Field label Identifies the kind of information that goes into a field.

Prompt A system message that tells the user what to do next.

Zone An identifiable region of the data entry screen. Good screen design organizes related fields into zones in order to make them easier to find.

Before you start Obtain some representative data for the system you are reviewing. Identify the data entry screens that are used most frequently. From your set of evaluation tasks, select one or more to try out these interface activities:

- View a sample of the high-usage screens in the system.

- Conduct an Error Condition Test: Enter erroneous data to check the placement of error messages and prompts.

Finding the problem To discover flaws in a system's data entry screen display interface, work through your evaluation tasks using Presentation Interface Checklist #4: Data Entry Screens to evaluate the interface. (See Section Four for a reproducible copy of this checklist.) Every item that is checked "no" is an interface flaw. To correct these flaws, follow the instructions in the next section, "Solving the problem."

Presentation Interface Checklist #4: Data Entry Screens

#	Review Checklist	yes	no	n/a	Examples
1.	If users are working from hard copy, are the parts of the hard copy that go on-line marked?	☐	☐	☐	On an insurance claim, the applicant's name, address, and social security number are shaded.
✳ 2.	If users are working from hard copy, does the screen layout match the paper form?	☐	☐	☐	If the first line on the paper form shows the claim number, this should also be the first field on the screen.
3.	Does each data entry screen have a short, simple, clear, distinctive title?	☐	☐	☐	Claim Adjustment Claim #: ---- ----- -- Date: --/--/---- Status: -- Change: $-----.--
4.	In multipage data entry screens, is each page labeled to show its relation to others?	☐	☐	☐	Claim Adjustment Claim #: ---- ----- -- Date: --/--/---- Status: -- Change: $-----.-- 1 of 3
5.	Is white space used to create symmetry and lead the eye in the appropriate direction?	☐	☐	☐	
6.	Have items been grouped into logical zones, and have headings been used to distinguish among zones?	☐	☐	☐	Personal Name: ------------- Street: ------------- City: ------------ State: -- Zip: ----- Insurance Insurer: ------------ Copay: $---.--

Presentation Interface Checklist #4 (Continued)

#	Review Checklist	yes	no	n/a	Examples
7.	Are zones no more than twelve to fourteen characters wide and six to seven lines high?	☐	☐	☐	
8.	Have zones been separated by spaces, lines, color, letters, bold titles, ruled lines, or shaded areas?	☐	☐	☐	Order Placement Product: Item code: ---- Quantity: -- Color: -- Ship to: Name: ------------ Street: ------------ City: ------------ State: -- Zip: -----
9.	If the database includes groups of data, can users enter more than one group on a single screen?	☐	☐	☐	Order Entry Item# Qty Color Size G4-72 132 blue S G8-18 12 red M ----- --- ----- - ----- --- ----- - ----- --- ----- -
10.	If users are *experts*, usage is *frequent*, or the system has a *slow response time*, are there fewer screens (more information per screen)?	☐	☐	☐	
11.	If users are *novices*, usage is *infrequent*, or the system has a *fast response time*, are there more screens (less information per screen)?	☐	☐	☐	
12.	Are on-line instructions visually distinct?	☐	☐	☐	Prompts appear on the bottom of the screen and are displayed in yellow to make them stand out.
13.	Do embedded field-level prompts appear to the right of the field label?	☐	☐	☐	Status (A, P, C): ____

#	Review Checklist	yes	no	n/a
14.	Do on-line instructions appear in a consistent location across screens?	☐	☐	☐
15.	Are field labels and fields distinguished typographically?	☐	☐	☐
16.	Are field labels brief, familiar, and descriptive?	☐	☐	☐
17.	Are field labels close to fields, but separated by at least one space?	☐	☐	☐
18.	Are field labels consistent from one data entry screen to another?	☐	☐	☐
19.	Are fields and labels left-justified for alpha lists, and right-justified for numeric lists?	☐	☐	☐
20.	Are long columnar fields broken up into groups of five separated by a blank line?	☐	☐	☐

Examples

```
  Claim Adjustment
Claim #: ---- ----- --
Date:    --/--/----
Status:  --
Change:  $-----.--
F1 to send, ESC to cancel
```

Claim #: **124748MZ**
Date: **04/03/93**

Poor: Residence
Better: Address

Item #: 34-56G
Quantity: 7

If one screen uses the term "client," another screen should not refer to "customer."

```
Item      Lbs    Price
cheddar    2   $ 6.23
parmesan  13   $18.27
brie       5   $27.22
stilton   17   $54.49
```

```
     Order Entry
Item#  Qty  Color Size
G4-72   2   blue   S
G8-18   1   red    M
S5-33  10   grn    12
G2-77   5   brwn   44
G8-26  11   blue   XL

T5-42  10   grn    S
G8-18   3   red    M
```

Presentation Interface Checklist #4 (Continued)

#	Review Checklist	yes	no	n/a	Examples
✳ 21.	Are optional data entry fields clearly marked?	☐	☐	☐	Name: ------------------ *Salary*: $----------.--
22.	Are symbols used to break long input strings into "chunks"?	☐	☐	☐	Phone #: 801 - 581 - 4572
23.	Do field labels appear to the left of single fields and above list fields?	☐	☐	☐	See examples 20 and 21, above.
24.	Do related and interdependent fields appear on the same screen?	☐	☐	☐	
25.	Have dots or underscores been used to indicate field length?	☐	☐	☐	State: -- Phone: --- --- ----
26.	If overtype and insert mode are both available, is there a visible indication of which one the user is in?	☐	☐	☐	When the user is in "insert" mode, an I is displayed in the lower right corner of the screen. When the user is in "overtype" mode, this changes to an O.
27.	If pop-up windows are used to display error messages, do they allow the user to see the field in error?	☐	☐	☐	Claim Adjustment Claim #: 0520 1978 NE Date: 09/01/1993 Status: V Status code must be A, Change: $- P, or R

Solving the problem

Every "no" on the checklist indicates an interface flaw that can interfere with performance.

- Ideally, you will be in a position to recommend an interface redesign to correct each flaw. Use checklist examples, where provided, as design guidelines. The answer to the item will then become either "yes" (because the feature was enhanced) or "n/a" (because the structure of the interface was changed to eliminate the feature).

- However, interface redesign is not always an option. In that case, you may be able to improve performance with an alternative strategy such as a job aid. Any checklist item marked with an asterisk (*) is a candidate for one of these alternative strategies.

Interface redesign recommendations. If your analysis has uncovered flaws in the data entry presentation interface, use design principles 1 to 27 to guide you toward specific design revisions. Revising the layout of a data entry screen is often easier to accomplish than other kinds of system changes, and you are likely to find that a single data entry screen contains multiple design flaws. For example, if field labels are being revised to move embedded field-level prompts to the right of the label, other design flaws that can be fixed might be the following:

- Make the field labels bold so they stand apart from field entries.
- Edit field labels to make them brief, descriptive, and consistent across the system.
- Insert a single space between each field label and its field entry.

Alternative solutions (for items marked with ∗). Consider these alternatives if interface redesign is not possible.

#	IF the interface flaw is . . .	THEN recommend . . .
2	Users are working from hard copy, and the screen layout does not match the layout of the printed form.	A redesigned printed form that matches the layout of the screen
18	Field labels are inconsistent across the system.	A printed list of all synonymous terms

Synonyms:

Customer = client, payee

Policy# = i.d.#, policy, policy code

#	IF the interface flaw is . . .	THEN recommend . . .
21	Optional data entry fields are not marked.	A printed reference page for each screen indicating which fields are required and which are optional

Account Maintenance Screen

In this field...	Data entry is...
Last Name. . . .	*Required*
Middle.	*Optional*
First Name. . . .	*Required*
Title.	*Optional*
Client ID.	*Required*

Procedure 3.5 — *Evaluating Attention-Getting Techniques*

The purpose of this procedure

Many systems use one or more methods to get the user's attention. In some systems, these techniques are only used when the user makes an error. For example, selecting an inactive menu item might cause the system to "beep." Other systems use such techniques as multiple typefaces, color, and intensity of color or shade to draw the user's attention to various parts of the screen display. While these techniques can be effective when used in moderation, they can be distracting if overused.

When to use this procedure

It is especially important to evaluate and recommend redesign of attention-getting techniques when

- Items in Parts 3 and 7 of the User Satisfaction Survey are rated low.

- During interviews or think-aloud observation, users have said things like "The ##%$& system is always beeping at me" or "I think I just selected something but I can't tell."

Terms you may not know

Intensity   The color level or shade of an object (for example, the selected menu choice might appear in a bold typeface, while the unselected menu choices are in plain text).

Reverse video   A method of highlighting text information by placing a background behind the text and changing the text color; thus, while most on-screen text may be yellow on a black background, the reverse video would show black text on a yellow background.

Before you start

Obtain some representative data for the system you are reviewing. Identify which data entry screens are used most frequently. From your set of evaluation tasks, select one or more to try out these interface activities:

- View several data entry screens (if available).

- View several menus (if available).

- View several dialog boxes (if GUI interface).

- Conduct Error Condition Tests to elicit attention-getting techniques: enter erroneous data; select invalid menu options; attempt to bypass a system prompt; enter an invalid command.

Finding the problem

To discover flaws in a system's attention-getting interface, work through your evaluation tasks using Presentation Interface Checklist #5: Attention-Getting Techniques to evaluate the interface. (Resource C contains a reproducible copy of this checklist.) Every item that is checked "no" indicates an interface flaw. To correct these flaws, follow the instructions in the next section, "Solving the problem."

Presentation Interface Checklist #5: Attention-Getting Techniques

#	Review Checklist	yes	no	n/a	Examples
1.	Is reverse video or color highlighting used to get the user's attention?	☐	☐	☐	In a computer-based training (CBT) program, users must correctly answer a series of test questions before they can proceed to the next lesson. The program displays all incorrect answers and skipped items in red so that users can easily find and correct them.
2.	Is reverse video used to indicate that an item has been selected?	☐	☐	☐	In a GUI interface, an icon turns dark when you click on it.
3.	Are size, boldface, underlining, color, shading, or typography used to show relative quantity or importance of different screen items?	☐	☐	☐	Patient Information Name: - - - - - - - - - - - - - - - - - Street: - - - - - - - - - - - - - - - - - City: - - - - - - - - - - - - - - - - - State: - - Zip: - - - - - Insurer: - - - - - - - - - - - Copay: $ - - - . - -
4.	If shape is used as a visual cue, does it match cultural conventions?	☐	☐	☐	In a GUI interface, a dialog box encloses the command STOP in a red octagon.
5.	Are borders used to identify meaningful groups?	☐	☐	☐	Patient Information Name: - - - - - - - - - - - - - Street: - - - - - - - - - - - - - City: - - - - - - - - - - - - - State: - - Zip: - - - - - Sex: - DOB: - - / - - / - - Insurer: - - - - - - - - - - Copay: $ - - - . - -

Presentation Interface Checklist #5 (Continued)

#	Review Checklist	yes	no	n/a	Examples
6.	Is sound used to signal an error?	☐	☐	☐	When the system is displaying an error message, any action you take *other than* a response to the error message causes the system to "beep."
7.	Are attention-getting techniques used with care? • Intensity: two levels • Size: up to four sizes • Font: up to three fonts • Blink: two to four hertz • Color: up to four colors (additional colors for occasional use only) • Sound: soft tones for regular positive feedback, harsh for rare emergency conditions	☐	☐	☐	A CBT plane geometry program only uses these four colors: (1) The screen background is light blue. (2) Geometric objects are white. (3) Borders around and annotations to the geometric objects are black. (4) Explanatory information, prompts, and warnings are yellow.
8.	Are attention-getting techniques used only for exceptional conditions or for time-dependent information?	☐	☐	☐	A red message flashes on the screen every thirty minutes to remind you to save your data.

Solving the problem   Every "no" on the checklist indicates an interface flaw that can interfere with performance. Ideally, you will be in a position to recommend an interface redesign to correct each flaw. Use checklist examples, where provided, as design guidelines. The answer to the item will then become either "yes" (because the feature was enhanced) or "n/a" (because the structure of the interface was changed to eliminate the feature).

Interface redesign recommendations. If your analysis has uncovered flaws in the attention-getting presentation interface, use design principles 1 to 8 to guide you toward specific design revisions. For example, if it is difficult to locate information on a screen, consider the use of one or more of these attention-getting techniques:

- Use color or bold type to highlight the most important information.

- Shade screen elements that all perform the same function.

- Place borders or extra white space around clusters of information.

Alternative solutions (for items marked with *). Unfortunately, there are few solutions, other than training, to solve performance problems that result from poorly designed attention-getting devices. Such performance problems are usually caused by either underuse or overuse of attention-getting techniques.

IF the flaw is . . .	THEN performance may suffer because . . .
Too few attention-getting techniques	Users will not be alerted to error states, exceptional conditions, and time-dependent tasks. Training and documentation should caution users that they cannot rely on the system for these alerts.
Too many attention-getting techniques	Users may experience confusion, sensory overload, and fatigue. Training and documentation should recommend that users take scheduled breaks during the day.

Procedure 3.6	*Evaluating Color Displays*

The purpose of this procedure

More and more systems offer color display. In some systems, color is only used to draw the user's attention to various parts of the screen. Colors are assigned by the system and are outside the user's control. In other systems, virtually any part of the presentation interface can make use of color. While color is essential for some systems and can be effective in others when used in moderation, it can be distracting if overused.

When to use this procedure

It is especially important to evaluate and recommend redesign of color presentation when

- Items in Part 3 of the User Satisfaction Survey are rated low.

- During interviews or think-aloud observation, users have said things like "My eyes hurt after staring at this screen for too long" or "Someone told me that overdue accounts are displayed in red, but I'm color deficient so that doesn't do me any good."

Terms you may not know

Color coding Assigning colors to system states or conditions (for example, the system clock is displayed in green when running in real time and in yellow when running batch processes).

High chroma Bright saturated colors such as vivid reds, yellows, or oranges.

High contrast A maximum difference in brightness between the light and dark areas of a high-contrast image.

Low contrast A minimal difference in brightness between the light and dark areas of a low-contrast image.

Saturation The purity of the color in a scale from gray (low saturation) to the most vivid shade of the color (high saturation).

Spectrum The range of available colors.

Before you start

From your set of evaluation tasks, select one or more to try out these interface activities:

- View several data entry screens and menus (if available).

- Select several screen objects (if direct manipulation interface).

- View several dialog boxes (if GUI interface).

- Conduct Error Condition Tests to elicit color display: enter erroneous data, select invalid menu options, attempt to bypass a system prompt, and enter an invalid command.

Finding the problem

To discover flaws in a system's color interface, work through your evaluation tasks using Presentation Interface Checklist #6: Color to evaluate the interface. (See Resource C for a reproducible copy of the checklist.) Every item that is checked "no" is an interface flaw. To correct these flaws, follow the instructions in the next section, "Solving the problem."

Presentation Interface Checklist #6: Color

#	Review Checklist	yes	no	n/a	Examples
1.	Are there no more than four to seven colors, and are they far apart along the visible spectrum?	☐	☐	☐	*Poor*: Red, yellow, orange. *Better*: Red, white, green.
2.	Has color been used specifically to draw attention, communicate organization, indicate status changes, and establish relationships?	☐	☐	☐	While most patient accounts are displayed in white, past-due accounts are displayed in red.
3.	Has the same color been used to group related elements?	☐	☐	☐	**Green**
✳ 4.	Is color coding consistent throughout the system?	☐	☐	☐	Red always signals a system alert. On-line help messages are always displayed in green.
✳ 5.	Do the selected colors correspond to common expectations about color codes?	☐	☐	☐	From our experience with automobiles, red signals "stop" or "danger." If the system displays a red symbol to indicate that the printer is warmed up, users may misinterpret this as a printer problem.
✳ 6.	Does the system automatically color-code items, with little or no user effort?	☐	☐	☐	The system automatically changes the claim number to red if the claim is being audited.
7.	Can users turn off automatic color coding if necessary?	☐	☐	☐	
8.	Is color used in conjunction with some other redundant cue?	☐	☐	☐	Overdue accounts are displayed in red and the customer code is italicized.

(In the Examples column, for item 3:)

Green

```
    Patient Information
  Name:    ------------
  Street:  ------------
  City:    ------------
  State:   -- Zip: -----

  Insurer: ----------
  Copay:   $---.--
```

Blue

Presentation Interface Checklist #6 (Continued)

#	Review Checklist	yes	no	n/a	Examples
9.	Is a legend provided if color codes are numerous or not obvious in meaning?	☐	☐	☐	Customer Account Codes: Blue: New account. 　　　ASK FOR PICTURE ID. Green: Cancelled account. 　　　DO NOT CASH CHECKS. Black: Balance overdue. 　　　DO NOT ISSUE CREDIT.
10.	Are high-value, high-chroma colors used to attract attention?	☐	☐	☐	Critical system messages are displayed in high-chroma red.
11.	Have pairings of high-chroma, spectrally extreme colors been avoided?	☐	☐	☐	*Poor*: Saturated red letters on a blue background; purple bars on a yellow graph; magenta figures in a green spreadsheet. In each case, the information will appear to "vibrate" on the screen. *Better*: Black letters on a white background, white bars on a blue graph, navy figures in a light blue spreadsheet.
12.	Are saturated blues avoided for text or other small, thin line symbols?	☐	☐	☐	
13.	Is there good color and brightness contrast between image and background colors?	☐	☐	☐	Application icons are displayed in dark blue on a white background.
14.	Have light, bright, saturated colors been used to emphasize data and have darker, duller, desaturated colors been used to de-emphasize data?	☐	☐	☐	**Red** Patient Accounts Name　　　　Balance Alcester　　$132.27 Aldershot　$456.23 Appleby　　$000.00 Ashcroft　　$000.00 **Light blue**

❋

Solving the problem

Interface redesign recommendations. If your analysis has uncovered flaws in the color presentation interface, use design principles 1 to 14 above to guide you towards specific design revisions. For example, revise color assignments if

- Color codes do not conform to common cultural expectations of this user group
- Color coding is not consistent throughout the system
- The colors used for coding are too close on the color spectrum
- Error messages and warnings use a color that is *not* high chroma

Alternative solutions (for items marked with *). Consider these alternatives if interface redesign is not possible.

#	IF the interface flaw is . . .	THEN recommend . . .
4,5	Color codes are confusing or inconsistent.	A printed reference of colors and their associated meanings; if the codes are inconsistent, multiple references may be necessary

Color	Meaning
Blue	This question is optional
Yellow	Your answer is wrong
Orange	Your answer is right
Purple	You finished this lesson
White	You still have work to do

#	IF the interface flaw is . . .	THEN recommend . . .
6	Users must color-code items manually.	A macro to partially automate this procedure, or a printed set of instructions
9	The system uses numerous color codes, but there is no on-line explanation of their meanings.	A keyboard template (in color) that indicates the meaning of each color code

The Conversation Interface: Facilitating Communication Between User and Computer

---

Introduction

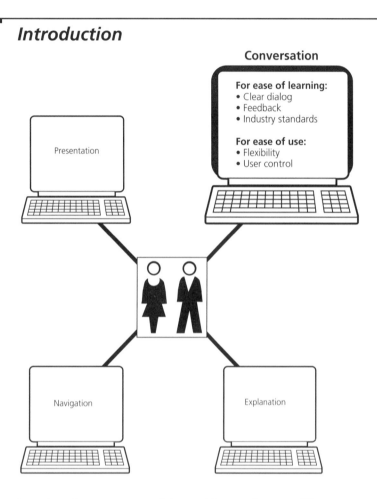

Conversation

For ease of learning:
• Clear dialog
• Feedback
• Industry standards

For ease of use:
• Flexibility
• User control

Presentation

Navigation

Explanation

What is conversation? Imagine that you are talking with a colleague. The conversation might go something like this:

> **You:** Chris, did you get the draft of the annual report I sent you?
>
> **Chris:** No, I haven't seen it.
>
> **You:** That's funny, I put it in E-mail at 1:00.
>
> **Chris:** Oh, I thought you meant you sent me a hard copy. Sorry about that . . . let me check my E-mail. Yup, there it is.
>
> **You:** When do you think we can meet to review it?
>
> **Chris:** How about tomorrow at 3:00 or Friday at 10:00?
>
> **You:** Friday is better for me.
>
> **Chris:** Great . . . I'll see you then.

There are two participants in this example, as there are in any dialogue: the sender and the receiver. And as in all conversations, the roles alternate. When you are sending, Chris is receiving, and vice versa.

The same is true when people and computers have a conversation. The system sends information to the user in the form of *prompts, feedback,* and *menus.* The user sends information to the system in the form of *commands* and *data input.* However, there is one key difference between person-to-person and person-to-computer conversations: while in person-to-person conversations the *locus of control* (who initiates, who responds) alternates, in person-to-computer interactions, the locus of control should rest with the person.

What is the purpose of this chapter?

This chapter shows you how to review and recommend redesign of a system's conversation interface. Optimally, of course, you want to evaluate all four components of a system's interface: presentation, conversation, navigation, and explanation. If you have only one shot at interface redesign, however, work on the system's conversation interface because

- A system's conversation interface makes a big difference in how that system is perceived by users; it is the system's "personality."

- Conversation interfaces are usually easier and cheaper to redesign than other interfaces because such redesigns do not require adding or revising functions. Often, significant improvements can be accomplished with a simple rewrite of existing messages.

- Performance problems caused by a flawed conversation interface are harder to solve with alternative solutions such as performance aids.

How is this chapter organized?

This chapter contains six procedures to help you review and redesign the conversation interface. The procedures have been organized by the *direction of the conversation;* that is, beginning with the sender and proceeding to the receiver.

System sends, user receives:

IF you want to evaluate . . .	THEN see page . . .	Related procedures elsewhere in this book . . .
Prompts	96	How to evaluate error-handling (p. 168)
Feedback	101	How to evaluate error-handling (p. 168)
Menus	108	How to evaluate menu displays (p. 69)
		How to evaluate menu navigation (p. 134)

User sends, system receives:

IF you want to evaluate . . .	THEN see page . . .	Related procedures elsewhere in this book . . .
Locus of control	114	How to evaluate performance support (p. 172)
Commands	119	How to evaluate performance support (p. 172)
Data input	124	How to evaluate data entry screen displays (p. 75)
		How to evaluate navigation with a single screen (p. 142)
		How to evaluate navigation among screens (p. 147)

Most systems contain literally hundreds of system messages. To help make the message review process easier, I have classified these messages into two types: *prompts* and *feedback*. However, sometimes, the distinction between a prompt (see page 96) and feedback (see page 101) is blurred. For example, when the user selects the Empty Trash command (this command, common in GUI interfaces, deletes all files that are currently in an electronic "holding bin"), the system response may be "The trash contains one item, using 126K of disk space. Are you sure you want to permanently remove it?" The first sentence is feedback, because it informs the user about the current state of the trash. The second sentence is a prompt. This is why, if you are reviewing the *prompts* interface, you will probably want to evaluate the *feedback* interface as well.

What are the results of following the procedures in this chapter?

Using the procedures in this chapter to discover and correct flaws in the conversation interface can improve user performance in these ways:

Potential result . . .	For example . . .
Decreased learning time: more users can acquire more skills in less time.	*Before:* Field-level prompts provided little useful information; for example, the prompt for the Item Code field read Enter the code for the item.
	After: Field-level prompts were rewritten to make them more informative. The Item Code prompt was changed to a pop-up list of all available item codes.
Increased proficiency: more users can use more system functions.	*Before:* A complex command language made it difficult for users to master all but the most basic system functions.
	After: Macros were designed to let users bypass complex commands.
Increased productivity: users can accomplish a task in less time, and with less effort.	*Before:* Data entry screens required users to enter commas, decimals, and dollar signs in numeric fields.
	After: The system now automatically enters this information for users, thus saving time and reducing the amount of typing required.
Improved quality: users can produce more accurate work, with less time spent correcting errors.	*Before:* Users were constantly correcting data entry errors in the Customer ID field, a fifteen-character numeric string.
	After: The string was broken up into three five-character chunks, with a space between each chunk, resulting in fewer data entry errors.

Potential result . . .	For example . . .
Greater satisfaction: users feel comfortable with and supported by the system.	*Before:* Medical students using a computer-based training (CBT) program on pulmonary immunology found the tone of system feedback patronizing. For example, the system responded "Good job!" to every correct answer.
	After: Feedback was rewritten to make it more appropriate to a medical school setting.

For more information

Bailey, R. W. *Human Error in Computer Systems.* Englewood Cliffs, N.J.: Prentice-Hall, 1983.
Chapter Eight describes how poorly designed messages can cause an increase in the number and severity of user errors.

Galitz, W. O. *User-Interface Screen Design.* Boston: QED Publishing Group, 1993.
Section Five provides guidelines for the structure and content of input data.

Mayhew, D. J. *Principles and Guidelines in Software User Interface Design.* Englewood Cliffs, N.J.: Prentice-Hall, 1992.
Chapter Seven presents research findings and design guidelines for command language interfaces. Chapter Fifteen discusses experimental results of system response time on cognitive processing.

Powell, J. E. *Designing User Interfaces.* San Marcos, Calif.: Microtrend Books, 1990.
Chapter Six presents guidelines for the design of menus and commands. The case study at the end of the chapter describes a menu design task and alternative interface design solutions.

Rubenstein, R., and Hersh, H. M. *The Human Factor: Designing Computer Systems for People.* Bedford, Mass.: Digital Press, 1984.
Chapters Five (Language) and Nine (Responding to Users) are thoughtful looks at the issue of conversations between people and computers.

Shneiderman, B. *Designing the User Interface: Strategies for Effective Human-Computer Interaction.* Reading, Mass.: Addison-Wesley, 1992.
Chapter Eight presents guidelines for designing effective system messages.

Smith, B. R. *Soft Words for a Hard Technology: Humane Computerization.* Englewood Cliffs, N.J.: Prentice-Hall, 1984.
Chapter Two discusses the impact of "hostile" prompts on user perceptions of a system.

Procedure 4.1 — *Evaluating Prompts*

Direction of the conversation	Conversation interface
System sends, user receives	**Prompts**
	Feedback
	Menus
User sends, system receives	Locus of control
	Commands
	Data input

The purpose of this procedure

Prompts set the tone of the interaction between people and computers. Menus, data entry screens, reports, and other screen displays are fixed sources of information; the information is present on the screen at all time, regardless of what the user does. Prompts, on the other hand, are driven by user actions; they inform users about what action they should take next. Such information can be a powerful aid to performance because it is directly linked to user behavior. This is only true, however, if the information sent via prompts is both useful and understandable to the receiver. Prompts that are confusing or incomplete will either have no impact on performance (because users will simply learn to ignore the prompts), or they will cause errors and lead to user frustration.

When to use this procedure

It is especially important to evaluate and recommend redesign of prompts when

- Items in Part 4 of the User Satisfaction Survey (see Chapter Two) are rated low.

- During interviews or think-aloud observation (see Chapter Two), users have said things like "I don't bother looking at the message line at the bottom of the screen—I never know what it's telling me" or "All those messages were helpful when I was just learning the system, but now they just clutter up the screen" or "I don't like this computer's personality—it makes me feel stupid."

Terms you may not know

Feedback Describes the result of a user's action and informs the user of the system's current state. See p. 102 for examples of system feedback.

Prompt A system message that tells the user what to do next, after the user takes an action. For example:

After the user takes this action . . .	The system responds with this prompt . . .
Moves the cursor to a data entry field	Enter status code (A, P, or R)
Completes the last field on a data entry screen	Press ENTER to save data, ESC to cancel
Displays a menu	Enter choice # and press RETURN

Before you start

Obtain some representative data for the system you are reviewing. From your set of evaluation tasks (see Chapter Two), select one or more to try out these interface activities:

- Select options from several menus.
- Issue different commands that cause the system to display a prompt.
- Enter information on several data entry screens.
- Perform several tasks from beginning to end.
- Leave some tasks without finishing.

Finding the problem

To discover flaws in a system's prompt interface, work through your evaluation tasks using Conversation Interface Checklist #1: Prompts to evaluate the interface. (See Resource D for a reproducible copy of the checklist.) Every item that is checked "no" is an interface flaw. To correct these flaws, follow the instructions in the next section, "Solving the problem."

Conversation Interface Checklist #1: Prompts

#	Review Checklist	yes	no	n/a	Examples
1.	Is the most important information placed at the beginning of the prompt?	☐	☐	☐	*Poor:* Do not leave this screen before you press SEND. *Better:* Press SEND to leave this screen.
2.	Do the instructions follow the sequence of user actions?	☐	☐	☐	*Poor:* Press RETURN after you enter status code. *Better:* Type status code and press RETURN.
3.	When prompts imply a necessary action, are the words in the message consistent with that action?	☐	☐	☐	*Poor:* Field is empty. *Better:* Type dealership code in field.
4.	Are user actions named consistently across all prompts in the system?	☐	☐	☐	If some prompts tell users to "delete" information, other prompts should not refer to "removing" information.
5.	Are system objects named consistently across all prompts in the system?	☐	☐	☐	If some menu prompts refer to their choices as "items," other menus should not refer to them as "options."
✱ 6.	Do keystroke references in prompts match actual key names?	☐	☐	☐	If the key is labeled (CTL) on the keyboard: *Poor:* Press CONTROL to stop. (users will look for a key labeled (CONTROL), or may even type c-o-n-t-r-o-l) *Better:* Press CTL to stop.
7.	On data entry screens, are tasks described in terminology familiar to users?	☐	☐	☐	*Poor:* Domicile: - - - - - - - - *Better:* Home Address: - - - - -
✱ 8.	Are field-level prompts provided for data entry screens?	☐	☐	☐	*Field:* Region: ____ *Field-level prompt:* Type dealership region: N(orth), S(outh), E(ast), W(est)
9.	Do field-level prompts provide more information than a restatement of the field name?	☐	☐	☐	*Field:* Date: - - - - - - - - *Poor:* Type date. *Better:* Type date when the claim was submitted (mm/dd/yyyy).

#	Review Checklist	yes	no	n/a	Examples
10.	For question and answer interfaces, are the valid inputs for a question listed?	☐	☐	☐	What is your marital status? (s= single, m=married, w=widowed, d=divorced): m When did you file the claim? (mm/dd/yy): 12/06/93
11.	For question and answer interfaces, are questions stated in clear, simple language?	☐	☐	☐	*Poor:* Enter the name of the person with whom you are filing jointly. *Better:* What is your spouse's name?
12.	Are prompts expressed in the affirmative and do they use the active voice?	☐	☐	☐	*Poor:* Cannot quit until file is backed up. *Better:* Back up file before quitting.
13.	Are prompts stated constructively, without overt or implied criticism of the user?	☐	☐	☐	*Poor:* Illegal entry. Cannot compute. *Better:* Type date as mm/dd/yy.
14.	Do prompts imply that the user is in control?	☐	☐	☐	*Poor:* Type menu selection. *Better:* Ready for menu selection.
15.	Are prompts brief and unambiguous?	☐	☐	☐	*Poor:* If you want to cancel printing, press the ESC key now. *Better:* Printing . . . press ESC to cancel.
16.	If the system supports both novice and expert users, are multiple levels of detail available?	☐	☐	☐	The system automatically displays detailed prompts. However, experienced users can reconfigure the system to display brief prompts. *Detailed prompt:* Account status codes are A (active), P (pending approval), D (credit denied), and C (closed). *Brief prompt:* A, P, D, C.

Solving the problem

Every "no" on the checklist indicates an interface flaw that can interfere with performance.

- Ideally, you will be in a position to recommend an interface redesign to correct each flaw. Use checklist examples, where provided, as design guidelines. The answer to the item will then become either "yes" (because the feature was enhanced) or "n/a" (because the structure of the interface was changed to eliminate the feature).

- However, interface redesign is not always an option. In this case, you may be able to improve performance with an alternative strategy such as a job aid. Any checklist item marked with an asterisk (*) is a candidate for one of these alternative strategies.

Interface redesign recommendations. If your analysis has uncovered flaws in the prompt interface, use design principles 1 to 16 to guide you toward specific design revisions. Generally, if system prompts are problematical you will find that multiple design principles have been violated; within a single prompt you may find errors of consistency, clarity, grammar, and accuracy! However, one rewrite session can solve a plethora of problems.

*Alternative solutions (for items marked with *).* Consider these alternatives if interface redesign is not possible.

#	IF the interface flaw is . . .	THEN recommend . . .
6	Keystroke messages in prompts do not match actual key names.	A keyboard template that translates key names in prompts to actual key names
		Applying labels over the keys to match the names in the prompts (for example, relabel the CTL key CONTROL, to match the system prompts)
8	Field-level prompts are not provided.	*Syntactic support:* a printed list of systemwide data entry rules (for example, always enter the date as dd/mm/yyyy)
		Semantic support: a printed list of the data entry codes, organized by screen name

Direction of the conversation	Conversation interface
System sends, user receives	Prompts
	Feedback
	Menus
User sends, system receives	Locus of control
	Commands
	Data input

The purpose of this procedure

Menus, data entry screens, reports, and other screen displays are fixed sources of information. In other words, this kind of information is always present on the screen, no matter what the user does. System prompts (for example, Enter today's date) are driven by user actions and give information about what to do next. In addition to prompts, systems use *feedback* to inform users of the success or failure of actions (for example, File copied successfully) and to tell users what state the system is in (for example, Printing in progress). Such information can be a powerful aid to performance if it is presented in a useful and understandable way. But feedback that is confusing or incomplete will either have no impact on performance—a shame, since this is a lost opportunity—or will cause users to become frustrated with the system.

When to use this procedure

It is especially important to evaluate and recommend redesign of feedback when

- Items in Part 4 of the User Satisfaction Survey are rated low.

- During interviews or think-aloud observation, users have said things like "I'm never sure if the system did what I just told it to do" or "Huh? What does FATAL ERROR 1257Q mean?" or "Is the computer processing or is it waiting for me to do something?" or "I hate it when the computer patronizes me . . . it talks to me like I'm a three year old."

Terms you may not know

Feedback Describes the result of a user's action and informs the user of the system's current state. For example:

When the user takes this action (or the system is in this state) . . .	The system responds with this feedback . . .
User issues a command to save a file to a disk.	Unable to save file. Disk full.
In a word processor, user pulls down the Edit menu with no text selected.	The system grays out the Cut, Copy, and Clear commands on the Edit menu.
A system action is taking a long time to complete.	Printing in progress . . . 10% complete.

Prompt Explains what to do next, after the user takes an action. See p. 97 for examples of system prompts.

Before you start

Obtain some representative data for the system you are reviewing. Obtain a list of typical (made frequently) and serious (high-risk) errors. From your set of evaluation tasks, select one or more to try out these interface activities:

- Select options from several menus.
- Select objects on the screen (direct manipulation interface only).
- Enter information on several data entry screens.
- Perform several tasks from beginning to end.
- Conduct Error Condition Tests: enter invalid data in fields; select invalid menu options; fail to respond correctly to a system prompt; leave a task unfinished; enter illegal commands; press an incorrect key.

Finding the problem

To discover flaws in a system's feedback interface, work through your evaluation tasks using Conversation Interface Checklist #2: Feedback to evaluate the interface. (See Resource D for a reproducible copy of the checklist.) Every item that is checked "no" indicates an interface flaw. To correct these flaws, follow the instructions in the next section, "Solving the problem."

Conversation Interface Checklist #2: Feedback

#	Review Checklist	yes	no	n/a	Examples
1.	Is there some form of system feedback for every operator action?	☐	☐	☐	In a computer-based training (CBT) program for third-graders, a chime sounds after every correct answer. Every incorrect answer results in an "uh-oh" noise.
2.	After the user completes an action (or group of actions), does the feedback indicate that the next group of actions can be started?	☐	☐	☐	While the system is recalculating a spreadsheet, an icon in the shape of an hourglass appears on screen and the user cannot enter data. After the recalculation is complete, the hourglass disappears and the cursor returns to the first cell.
3.	Is there visual feedback in menus or dialog boxes about which choices are selectable?	☐	☐	☐	Unless the first column in the spreadsheet is selected, the Sort command does not appear on the menu.
4.	Is there visual feedback in menus or dialog boxes about which choice the cursor is on now?	☐	☐	☐	cursor is here To Printer: "Glory" Copies: [1] Pages: ◉ All ○ From: [ ] To: [ ] Paper Source: ○ Paper Tray ◉ Manual Feed Print: ◉ Black & White ○ Gray Scale ○ Color [OK] [Cancel] [Help]
5.	If multiple options can be selected in a menu or dialog box, is there visual feedback about which options are already selected?	☐	☐	☐	These two options are selected Type Style: ☐ Plain [X] Bold [X] Italic ☐ Outline
6.	Is there visual feedback when objects are selected or moved?	☐	☐	☐	When the cursor is on a menu choice, the choice is highlighted in reverse video.
7.	Is the current status of an icon clearly indicated?	☐	☐	☐	Icons of files that have been changed, but not backed up, are displayed in red. Their file names are also italicized.

Conversation Interface Checklist #2 (Continued)

#	Review Checklist	yes	no	n/a	Examples
8.	Is there feedback when function keys are pressed?	☐	☐	☐	(F6) changes the data entry mode from *overtype* to *insert*. When you press this key, you will see an I in the lower right corner of the screen.
9.	Are error messages worded so the system, not the user, takes the blame?	☐	☐	☐	*Poor:* Bad file name. *Better:* File names must be eight characters or less.
10.	If humorous error messages are used, are they appropriate and inoffensive to the user population?	☐	☐	☐	If the users are computer-savvy engineers, the system response to a particularly egregious error might be "You've gotta be kidding!" However, even with this population such messages can quickly become irritating.
11.	Are error messages grammatically correct?	☐	☐	☐	*Poor:* Unable to print file its too big. *Better:* Field is too large to print. Print fewer pages or increase printer memory allocation.
12.	Do error messages avoid the use of exclamation points?	☐	☐	☐	*Poor:* Field out of range!!!! *Better:* February days range from 1 to 29.
13.	Do error messages avoid the use of violent or hostile words?	☐	☐	☐	*Poor:* DISASTROUS OVERFLOW: RUN TERMINATED *Better:* An error caused the print job to stop. Try again? (Y,N)
14.	Do error messages avoid an anthropomorphic tone?	☐	☐	☐	*Poor:* I'm sorry, Dave . . . I'm afraid I can't do that. *Better:* File name cannot contain punctuation.
15.	Do all error messages in the system use consistent grammatical style, form, terminology, and abbreviations?	☐	☐	☐	

#	Review Checklist	yes	no	n/a	Examples
16.	If the system supports both novice and expert users, are multiple levels of error message detail available?	☐	☐	☐	The system automatically displays detailed feedback. However, experienced users can reconfigure the system to display brief feedback. *Detailed feedback:* Cannot copy file: disk is full. Insert another disk. *Brief feedback:* Disk full.
❃ 17.	If there are observable delays (greater than fifteen seconds) in the system response time, is the user kept informed of the system's progress?	☐	☐	☐	Saving file . . .
❃ 18.	Are response times appropriate to the task? • *Typing, cursor motion, mouse selection:* 50–150 milliseconds • *Simple, frequent tasks:* less than 1 second • *Common tasks:* 2–4 seconds • *Complex tasks:* 8–12 seconds	☐	☐	☐	• *Common task:* sending a file to the printer • *Complex task:* copying and pasting a complicated drawing
❃ 19.	Are response times appropriate to the user's cognitive processing? • *Continuity of thinking is required and information must be remembered throughout several responses:* less than two seconds • *High levels of concentration aren't necessary or remembering information is not required:* two to fifteen seconds	☐	☐	☐	• *Continuity of thinking required:* a word processing program should never lag behind the typing speed of a user because her thinking processes will be slowed if she must wait for the system to catch up. • *Remembering information is not required:* after the user has finished typing a report and sends the document to the printer, the original cognitive task (writing the report) is completed; a slow printer response time will not jeopardize his performance.

Solving the problem

Every "no" on the checklist indicates an interface flaw that can interfere with performance.

- Ideally, you will be in a position to recommend an interface redesign to correct each flaw. Use checklist examples, where provided, as design guidelines. The answer to the item will then become either "yes" (because the feature was enhanced) or "n/a" (because the structure of the interface was changed to eliminate the feature).

- However, interface redesign is not always an option. In this case, you may be able to improve performance with an alternative strategy such as a job aid. Any checklist item marked with an asterisk (*) is a candidate for one of these alternative strategies.

Interface redesign recommendations. If your analysis has uncovered flaws in the feedback interface, use design principles 1 to 19 to guide you toward specific design revisions. For example, if users do not receive feedback about the success (or failure) of their actions, such feedback can be provided in the following forms:

- System messages (for example, "Report saved")
- Visual cues (for example, screen display is dimmed while spreadsheet is recalculating; it brightens when user entry is possible)

Error messages are an important component of feedback. Generally, if these messages are problematical you will find that multiple design principles have been violated; within a single error message you may find errors of consistency, clarity, grammar, and accuracy! However, one rewrite session can solve a plethora of problems.

Alternative solutions (for items marked with *). Consider these alternatives
if interface redesign is not possible.

#	IF the interface flaw is ...	THEN recommend ...
8	No feedback when function keys are pressed	A keyboard template indicating the consequences of pressing each function key
9–15	Poorly worded or vague error messages	A printed reference (alphabetized) of all error messages with a comprehensive explanation of • the probable cause of the error • the seriousness of the error • ways to fix the problem
17–19	Response-time delays	A printed job aid alerting users to the kinds of tasks that may result in processing delays; without this information, users may think the system is either broken or waiting for them to take an action

Procedure 4.3   *Evaluating Menu Language*

Direction of the conversation	Conversation interface
System sends, user receives	Prompts
	Feedback
	Menus
User sends, system receives	Locus of control
	Commands
	Data input

The purpose of this procedure

Menus are a standard approach used by many systems to let users move from one screen to another. Each option on a menu is really a system command, but rather than having to remember these commands, users simply select the one they want from an on-screen display of those available.

Although not having to remember complex command strings can be a performance advantage, the advantage is lost if the language menus use is obscure, confusing, or inconsistent. Users should always have a clear idea of what will happen when they select an option from a menu. They lose time when they have to interpret what the language means, and errors occur when they select the wrong options.

When to use this procedure

It is especially important to evaluate and recommend redesign of menu language when

- Items in Parts 4 and 7 of the User Satisfaction Survey are rated low.

- During interviews or think-aloud observation, users say things like "What's the difference between DELETE ENTRY and CLEAR ENTRY?" or "Where did this list come from? I never saw it before!" or "This menu isn't telling me what I want to know. How do I make a new spreadsheet column?"

Terms you may not know

Menu choices The list of options available on a menu. Each menu offers multiple choices.

Menu level A hierarchical structure frequently used by non-GUI systems to organize menus. Selecting an option from a high-level menu displays a lower-level menu and this progression continues until an option on the lowest-level menu is selected, allowing the user to accomplish a task. For example:

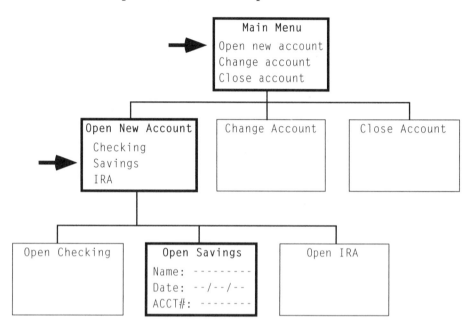

Menu title The name of the menu. Each menu has a single title.

Pull-down menu A permanent menu bar displayed at the top of many GUI system screens. To select options, users click on a menu name, which causes the options for that menu to appear. With this method, all system options are visible at all times. For example:

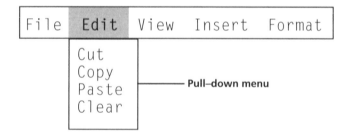

Before you start

From your set of evaluation tasks, select one or more to try out these interface activities:

- View the main menu.

- For non-GUI systems, select options from the main menu to display a representative sample of lower-level menus.

- For GUI systems, pull down each menu on the menu bar.

Finding the problem

To discover flaws in a system's menu language interface, work through the evaluation tasks using Conversation Interface Checklist #3: Menus to evaluate the interface. (See Resource D for a reproducible copy of the checklist.) Every item that is checked "no" is an interface flaw. To correct these flaws, follow the instructions in the next section, "Solving the problem."

Conversation Interface Checklist #3: Menus

#	Review Checklist	yes	no	n/a	Examples
1.	Do menu choices fit logically into categories that have readily understood meanings?	☐	☐	☐	Sales Regions ___ North ___ South ___ East ___ West
2.	Is each lower-level menu choice associated with only one higher-level menu?	☐	☐	☐	**Level 1 menu:** Sales Regions _X_ North ___ South ___ East ___ West **Level 2 menu:** North Region ___ Division A _X_ Division B ___ Division C **Level 3 menu:** Division B ___ Sales ___ Marketing ___ R & D
3.	Is the menu choice name on a higher-level menu used as the menu title of the lower-level menu?	☐	☐	☐	City Transport _X_ Bus schedules ___ Subway routes ___ Taxi rates Bus Schedules ___ Boston _X_ North Shore ___ Cape Cod

Conversation Interface Checklist #3 (Continued)

#	Review Checklist	yes	no	n/a	Examples
4.	Are menu titles parallel grammatically?	☐	☐	☐	If one menu title is View Heading, another menu title should *not* be Viewing the Footnotes.
5.	Are menu titles brief, yet long enough to communicate?	☐	☐	☐	*Poor:* Tools *Poor:* Setting up your page print options *Better:* Page Setup
6.	Are menu choices logical, distinctive, and mutually exclusive?	☐	☐	☐	*Non-example:* The difference between Transportation and Bus schedules is unclear. Exploring the City ____ Bus schedules ____ Museum tours ____ Transportation
7.	Is the first word of each menu choice the most important?	☐	☐	☐	Exploring the City ____ Bus schedules ____ Museum tours ____ Restaurant reviews
8.	Are menu choice names consistent, both within each menu and across the system, in grammatical style and terminology?	☐	☐	☐	If most menu options are one or two words (Transfer Funds, Change Beneficiary), an option should *not* be named Assigning a New Executor.
9.	Does the structure of menu choice names match their corresponding menu titles?	☐	☐	☐	Menu title ——— Insert __ Insert File __ Insert Column Menu choices __ Insert Row
10.	Is the menu-naming terminology consistent with the user's task domain?	☐	☐	☐	If the medical school divides the academic year into quarters, menu names should *not* refer to semesters.

✱

#	Review Checklist	yes	no	n/a	Examples
✳ 11.	If menu choices are ambiguous, does the system provide additional explanatory information when a choice is selected?	☐	☐	☐	As each menu choice is highlighted, a prompt on the bottom of the screen explains the function of the highlighted choice.

Solving the problem

Every "no" on the checklist indicates an interface flaw that can interfere with performance.

- Ideally, you will be in a position to recommend an interface redesign to correct each flaw. Use checklist examples, where provided, as design guidelines. The answer to the item will then become either "yes" (because the feature was enhanced) or "n/a" (because the structure of the interface was changed to eliminate the feature).

- However, interface redesign is not always an option. In this case, you may be able to improve performance with an alternative strategy such as a job aid. Any checklist item marked with an asterisk (*) is a candidate for one of these alternative strategies.

Interface redesign recommendations. If your analysis has uncovered flaws, use design principles 1 to 11 to guide you toward specific revisions. For example, if the names on menus are not part of the user's terminology, meet with users to identify appropriate names and revise the menu accordingly.

Alternative solutions (for items marked with *). Consider these alternatives if interface redesign is not possible.

#	IF the interface flaw is . . .	THEN recommend . . .
8	Menu names are ambiguous, and no on-line prompts are available.	A printed "dictionary" of menu names, translated into user terms
11	Terms on menus are not used consistently throughout the system.	A printed list of all synonymous terms

Term	Synonym(s)
Student. . . .	Learner, Registree
Semester. . .	Session
Course i.d. . .	Course #, Course code

Procedure 4.4   *Evaluating Locus of Control*

Direction of the conversation	Conversation interface
System sends, user receives	Prompts
	Feedback
	Menus
User sends, system receives	**Locus of control**
	Commands
	Data input

The purpose of this procedure

In any interaction, there is an initiator and a responder. The locus of control rests with the initiator. In person-to-person conversations, the locus of control is usually shared. However, person-to-computer conversations are most satisfying (and less frustrating) if the person maintains the locus of control. People need to feel that they are in charge of the system and that the system responds to their actions.

Locus of control is a subtle feature of the conversation interface. For example, the prompt "Enter command" places the locus of control with the system, because it is phrased as an instruction. The same prompt restated as "Ready for command" puts the user in charge of the interaction.

When to use this procedure

It is especially important to evaluate and recommend redesign of locus of control when

- Items in Part 4 of the User Satisfaction Survey are rated low.

- During interviews or think-aloud observation, users say things like "Oops! I didn't mean to hit that key. Now I have to do it all over again" or "It takes me five minutes just to get past all those menus to the screen I need. Why can't I just type the name of the screen I want?"

Terms you may not know

Mapping The relationship between a system control and a user's actions. For example, clicking on a menu name in a GUI interface (user action) pulls down the menu (system control).

Typing ahead A method of bypassing multiple menu levels. Each menu option is assigned a code; users enter a string of codes to jump directly to the lowest level in the hierarchy.

Undo An error-handling feature that allows users to "take back" their last action or set of actions. For example, after a column of figures has been moved to another position in a spreadsheet, the undo function will move the column back to its original location.

Visibility The user's ability to determine what actions are possible simply by looking at the system. For example, reverse video in a data entry field indicates that data can be typed into that field.

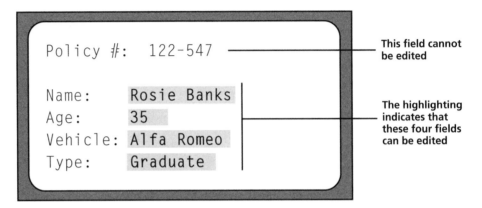

Policy #:   122-547 ———————— **This field cannot be edited**

Name: Rosie Banks
Age: 35   **The highlighting indicates that these four fields can be edited**
Vehicle: Alfa Romeo
Type: Graduate

Before you start

Obtain a representative sample of data for the system you are reviewing. From your set of evaluation tasks, select one or more to try out these interface activities:

- Navigate down a menu hierarchy.

- Enter data on a data entry screen.

- Execute time-consuming operations, such as printing a lengthy document.

- Execute high-risk functions, such as data deletion.

Finding the problem

To discover flaws in a system's locus of control interface, work through your evaluation tasks using Conversation Interface Checklist #4: Locus of Control to evaluate the interface. (See Resource D for a reproducible copy of the checklist.) Every item that is checked "no" is an interface flaw. To correct these flaws, follow the instructions in the next section, "Solving the problem."

Conversation Interface Checklist #4: Locus of Control

#	Review Checklist	yes	no	n/a	Examples
1.	Are users the initiators of actions rather than the responders?	☐	☐	☐	You can select commands from a pull-down menu or you can assign your own keystroke shortcuts to bypass menus.
2.	Do messages place users in control of the system?	☐	☐	☐	*Poor:* Disk full error. *Better:* Cannot save. C(ancel) or R(etry)?
3.	Does the system provide *visibility:* that is, by looking, can the user tell the state of the system and the alternatives for action?	☐	☐	☐	*Poor:* C) *Better:* Main Menu ___ Registration ___ Dorm assignment ___ Loan processing
✳ 4.	Does the system provide *mapping:* that is, are the relationships between controls and actions apparent to the user?	☐	☐	☐	In a system with multiple windows, clicking on a window causes the window to become darker.
5.	When a user's task is complete, does the system wait for a signal from the user before processing?	☐	☐	☐	After the dialog box entry is complete, the system does not take action until you press (ENTER) or click on the (OK) icon.
6.	Can users type-ahead in a system with many nested menus?	☐	☐	☐	To register a student for three credits of English 101 in the the Liberal Arts school, type R L 3 E101.
✳ 7.	Are users prompted to confirm commands that have drastic, destructive consequences?	☐	☐	☐	Enter command: **format** Are you sure? This will erase all data on your hard drive. Y to format, N to cancel. **N**

#	Review Checklist	yes	no	n/a	Examples
8.	Is there an "undo" function at the level of a single action, a data entry, or a complete group of actions?	☐	☐	☐	You select a text block, and select clear instead of copy. Oops! The text disappears. You select undo to restore the text.
✳ 9.	Can users cancel out of operations in progress?	☐	☐	☐	You begin printing a 100-page document and then discover that you have run out of company letterhead. You press (HOLD) to pause printing while you find more paper.

Solving the problem

Every "no" on the checklist indicates an interface flaw that can interfere with performance.

- Ideally, you will be in a position to recommend an interface redesign to correct each flaw. Use checklist examples, where provided, as design guidelines. The answer to the item will then become either "yes" (because the feature was enhanced) or "n/a" (because the structure of the interface was changed to eliminate the feature).

- However, interface redesign is not always an option. In this case, you may be able to improve performance with an alternative strategy such as a job aid. Any checklist item marked with an asterisk (*) is a candidate for one of these alternative strategies.

Interface redesign recommendations. If your analysis has uncovered flaws in the menu interface, use design principles 1 to 9 to guide you toward specific design revisions. For example:

- Prompts can be added to inform users if they are about to take a potentially destructive action.

- Shortcuts can be provided to give expert users the option of bypassing such prompts.

Alternative solutions (for items marked with *). Consider these alternatives if interface redesign is not possible.

#	IF the interface flaw is . . .	THEN recommend . . .
4	Relationship between key assignments and user actions not clearly mapped	A keyboard template that indicates which keys perform which actions
7	No confirmation of potentially destructive user actions	Posting a list of "high-risk" commands in clear view
9	Inability to cancel out of time-consuming operations	A printed list of operations that are likely to take a significant amount of system processing time

Procedure 4.5	*Evaluating Commands*

Direction of the conversation	*Conversation interface*
System sends, user receives	Prompts
	Feedback
	Menus
User sends, system receives	Locus of control
	Commands
	Data input

The purpose of this procedure

Commands are the original, traditional method of user-initiated conversation. The user types a command (for example, copy a:*.* b:) and the system carries out the action specified (in this example, the system will copy all the files from the disk in drive A to the disk in drive B). Commands are an extremely powerful and efficient way for users to converse with systems, and are particularly suited to high-frequency, expert users. However, command languages that are inconsistent, complex, and unforgiving can increase the time it takes to master the system and lead both to errors and to user dissatisfaction.

When to use this procedure

Evaluating the command conversation interface obviously only applies in systems that use a command language. Many systems offer a combination of commands and menus; in such systems, consider how often users need to use the command interface. It is especially important to evaluate and recommend redesign of commands when

- Items in Part 4 of the User Satisfaction Survey are rated low.
- During interviews or think-aloud observation, users say things like "I only use these three commands, because I get the others confused" or "I'm too dumb to remember all those commands" or "When I first started learning the system I liked being able to talk to it in English, but now I wish I could use abbreviations."

Terms you may not know

Character edit Allows the user to revise a command simply by typing over the incorrect characters rather than retyping the entire command.

Command An instruction that can be interpreted and acted upon by the system.
Example: find region 1.

Lexicon The specific names used in a command language.
Example: copy, find, delete, rename.

Semantics The complete set of functions in a system and how those functions are driven by the command language.

Examples of functions	Examples of commands
Combine text and graphics	Insert picture
Add a column of numbers in a table	Calculate
Move a paragraph	• Cut • Paste

Syntax The structure of a command language. Syntax rules govern the order of words and the use of punctuation.
Example: The syntax for the instruction "Change the name of this file from 1992Report to 1993Report" might be "rename 1992report 1993report" in one command language and "fnr 1992report : 1993report" in another.

Before you start

Obtain a list of all system commands, as well as a set of syntax rules. From your set of evaluation tasks, select one or more that let you try out these parts of the interface:

- Enter individual commands.

- Conduct Error Condition Tests: enter invalid commands, and make typographical errors during command entry.

Finding the problem

To discover flaws in a system's command interface, work through your evaluation tasks using Conversation Interface Checklist #5: Commands to evaluate the interface. (See Resource D for a reproducible copy of the checklist.) Every item that is checked "no" is an interface flaw. To correct these flaws, follow the instructions in the next section, "Solving the problem."

Conversation Interface Checklist #5: Commands

#	Review Checklist	yes	no	n/a	Examples
✳ 1.	Are the commands used the same way, and do they mean the same thing, in all parts of the system?	☐	☐	☐	An asterisk always means a "wildcard." Therefore, the command copy *.* means "copy everything," and the command search Sm* means "search for any name that starts with the letters Sm."
2.	Does the command language have a consistent, natural, and mnemonic syntax?	☐	☐	☐	Command to copy all files from drive A to drive B *Poor:* pip b: a: *Better:* copy a: to b:
3.	Does the command language use normal action-object syntax?	☐	☐	☐	*Poor:* myfile send *Better:* send myfile
4.	Does the command language avoid arbitrary, non-English use of punctuation, except for symbols that users already know?	☐	☐	☐	*Poor:* RS:/EW/, /EAW/;* *Better:* change all EW to EAW
5.	Does the system allow novices to use a keyword grammar and experts to use a positional grammar?	☐	☐	☐	*Novice user:* copy all a: to b: *Experienced user:* copy a:*.* b:
✳ 6.	Does the command language employ user jargon and avoid computer jargon?	☐	☐	☐	*Poor:* transmit myfile *Better:* send myfile
7.	Are command names specific rather than general?	☐	☐	☐	*Poor:* change *Better:* move
8.	Does the command language allow both full names and abbreviations?	☐	☐	☐	To exit from an application, you can type either q or quit.
9.	Do abbreviations follow a simple primary rule and, if necessary, a simple secondary rule for abbreviations that otherwise would be duplicates?	☐	☐	☐	*Primary:* Truncate to the first three letters (for example, delete = del, insert = ins) *Secondary:* Drop vowels (for example, delay) = dly)
10.	Is the secondary rule used only when necessary?	☐	☐	☐	
11.	Are abbreviated words all the same length?	☐	☐	☐	del, ins, hlp, esc, end, opt, ctl

Conversation Interface Checklist #5 (Continued)

#	Review Checklist	yes	no	n/a	Examples
12.	Can users define their own synonyms for commands?	☐	☐	☐	Instead of typing twelve lines of computer instructions every time you start the system, you can enter these commands once, define them as a batch file, and just type start at the beginning of a session.
13.	Are character edits allowed in commands?	☐	☐	☐	You type rename nowrpt.doc oldrpt.doc. Oops! Then you discover a typo: you meant to type newrpt.doc. You move your cursor to the left, and change "o" to an "e."
14.	Does the system allow novice users to enter the simplest, most common form of each command and allow expert users to add parameters?	☐	☐	☐	*Novice:* format b: *Expert:* format b:/v\s/720/ archive
15.	Do expert users have the option of entering multiple commands in a single string?	☐	☐	☐	Entering p myreport 3 will print three copies of the file myreport. These commands can also be entered one line at a time: command: print file name: myreport # of copies: 3
16.	Does the system provide function keys for high-frequency commands?	☐	☐	☐	You can either type the command pause, or you can press the (Break) key.

Solving the problem

Every "no" on the checklist indicates an interface flaw that can interfere with performance.

- Ideally, you will be in a position to recommend an interface redesign to correct each flaw. Use checklist examples, where provided, as design guidelines. The answer to the item will then become either "yes" (because the feature was enhanced) or "n/a" (because the structure of the interface was changed to eliminate the feature).

- However, interface redesign is not always an option. In this case, you may be able to improve performance with an alternative strategy such as a job aid. Any checklist item marked with an asterisk (*) is a candidate for one of these alternative strategies.

Interface redesign recommendations. If your analysis has uncovered flaws in the command interface, use design principles 1 to 16 to guide you toward specific design revisions. For example:

- Macros and function key shortcuts can be predefined for users to bypass complex command sequences.
- Abbreviations can be revised to follow a primary rule for most commands, and a simple, secondary rule for exceptions.

*Alternative solutions (for items marked with *).* Consider these alternatives if interface redesign is not possible.

#	IF the interface flaw is . . .	THEN recommend . . .
1	The command language is not consistent throughout the system.	A printed decision table listing all user tasks and the different commands that accomplish the task:

IF you want to...	AND you are in a...	THEN type...
Save a file	Menu	save
	Data entry screen	transfer

#	IF the interface flaw is	THEN recommend
6	Commands use computer terms rather than user terms.	A printed usage primer of all system commands, organized by user task, that includes the following: • The command name • The purpose of the command, in user terms • Command syntax, if any • One or more task-specific examples

Procedure 4.6   *Evaluating Data Input*

Direction of the conversation	Conversation interface
System sends, user receives	Prompts
	Feedback
	Menus
User sends, system receives	Locus of control
	Commands
	Data input

The purpose of this procedure

Many corporate systems, and virtually all database systems, are data-intensive. In other words, users spend most of their time entering data. For such systems, any interface redesign that expedites the data entry process will have performance benefits in terms of time and error reduction.

In the initial design of an interface, attention is frequently paid to the layout of data entry screens while the data that go into these screens are ignored. Sometimes, the data are not under the control of interface designers; if the organization requires the storage and retrieval of sixteen highly confusing status codes, nothing more can be said. In other cases, however, the input data can be redesigned—especially when such revisions can be shown to reduce errors and rework time.

When to use this procedure

Good-bet systems to review are large databases that have many users. It is especially important to evaluate and recommend redesign of input data when

- Items in Part 4 of the User Satisfaction Survey are rated low.

- During interviews or think-aloud observation, users have said things like "Is that a B or an 8? I can't tell" or "The computer makes me enter all measurements in centimeters, but I think in inches" or "It's such a waste of time to type a dollar sign on every line."

Terms you may not know	***Alpha data*** Input data that consist only of letters. Example: Month: January.

Terms you may not know

Alpha data Input data that consist only of letters.
    Example: Month: January.

Alphanumeric data Input data that consist of both letters and numbers.
    Example: Address: 33 Southern Road.

Data code A short string of numbers or letters that represents a longer entry.
    Example: The data entry code P may represent the status Pending.

Leading zero Used to fill in the blank spaces in fields that can accept numbers of different lengths (different number of digits).
    Example: Quantity: 0037.

Numeric data Input data that consist only of numbers.
    Example: Issue Date: 03/27/93.

Before you start

Obtain a representative sample of data for the system you are reviewing; focus particularly on data that are entered frequently. Obtain a list of special data entry codes. From your set of evaluation tasks, select one or more to try out these interface activities:

- Enter alpha data.

- Enter numeric data.

- Enter alphanumeric data.

- Enter data codes, if any.

- Conduct an Error Condition Test: Make typographical errors in data entry fields.

Finding the problem

To discover flaws in a system's data input interface, work through your evaluation tasks using Conversation Interface Checklist #6: Data Input to evaluate the interface. (See Resource D for a reproducible copy of the checklist.) Every item that is checked ''no'' is an interface flaw. To correct these flaws, follow the instructions in the next section, ''Solving the problem.''

Conversation Interface Checklist #6: Data Input

#	Review Checklist	yes	no	n/a	Examples
1.	For data entry screens with many fields or in which source documents may be incomplete, can users save a partially filled screen?	☐	☐	☐	Issuing a new insurance policy requires twelve data entry screens, each containing up to fifteen fields. You can stop whenever you like, and any information in the completed screens will be saved automatically.
2.	Can users reduce data entry time by copying and modifying existing data?	☐	☐	☐	To create a new contract, you can find a similar contract, issue the Save As... command to copy it under a new name, and then make any changes.
✳ 3.	Does the system perform data translations for users?	☐	☐	☐	Time: - - : - - *You type:* 1:30 *System displays:* 13:30
✳ 4.	Are input data codes meaningful?	☐	☐	☐	Marital Status: —— *Codes:* m, s, w, d
5.	Are input data codes distinctive?	☐	☐	☐	*Poor:* INC and JNC *Better:* INC and JTN
6.	Have frequently confused data pairs been eliminated whenever possible?	☐	☐	☐	The uppercase letter I is not used as a data entry code in this system, because it is easily confused with the number 1.
7.	Have large strings of numbers or letters been broken up into chunks?	☐	☐	☐	Social Sec #: 010-38-6270
8.	Are data inputs case-blind whenever possible?	☐	☐	☐	Month: - - - - - - - *You type:* January, january, or JANUARY
9.	Do field values avoid mixing alpha and numeric characters whenever possible?	☐	☐	☐	*Poor:* B7J78 *Better:* 37978
10.	Have uncommon letter sequences been avoided whenever possible?	☐	☐	☐	*Poor:* xz *Better:* an
11.	Does the system automatically enter leading zeros?	☐	☐	☐	Date: - - - - - - *You type:* 4 3 89 *System displays:* 04 03 89

#	Review Checklist	yes	no	n/a	Examples
12.	Does the system automatically enter leading or trailing spaces to align decimal points?	☐	☐	☐	*You type:* 35.27 1872.66 *System displays:* 35.27 1872.66
13.	Does the system automatically enter a dollar sign and decimal for monetary entries?	☐	☐	☐	*You type:* 93325 *System displays:* $933.25
14.	Does the system automatically enter commas in numeric values greater than 9999?	☐	☐	☐	*You type:* 10234 *System displays:* 10,234
15.	Are character edits allowed in data entry fields?	☐	☐	☐	*Poor:* You make an error in a 32-character address field. The system deletes the address, and you retype it. *Better:* You make a typographical error in the address field. You position your cursor over the incorrect letter, and change it.
✳ 16.	Is the structure of a data entry value consistent from screen to screen?	☐	☐	☐	If most screens use the date structure mm/dd/yy, others should *not* use mm/dd/yyyy.
17.	Are typing requirements minimal for question and answer interfaces?	☐	☐	☐	*Poor:* What is your status? pending *Better:* What is your status (A, P, R)? P

Solving the problem Every "no" on the checklist indicates an interface flaw that can interfere with performance.

- Ideally, you will be in a position to recommend an interface redesign to correct each flaw. Use checklist examples, where provided, as design guidelines. The answer to the item will then become either "yes" (because the feature was enhanced) or "n/a" (because the structure of the interface was changed to eliminate the feature).

- However, interface redesign is not always an option. In this case, you may be able to improve performance with an alternative strategy such as a job aid. Any checklist item marked with an asterisk (*) is a candidate for one of these alternative strategies.

Interface redesign recommendations. If your analysis has uncovered flaws in the data input interface, use design principles 1 to 17 to guide you toward specific design revisions. For example:

- Prompts can be added to explain data codes that are not meaningful.

- A dollar sign can be prepended to monetary fields.

- Data values can be changed to ensure consistency throughout the system.

Alternative solutions (for items marked with *). Consider these alternatives if interface redesign is not possible.

#	IF the interface flaw is . . .	THEN recommend . . .
3	The system does not provide data translation for users.	A translation table that calculates all conversions (for example, 12-hour to 24-hour clock, inches to centimeters)
4	Data input codes are not meaningful.	For each screen in the system, an on-screen list (preferable) or printed list of field names and their associated data input codes

Field	Codes
Status	1 (active) 2 (pending) 3 (cancelled)
Vehicle	1 (car) 2 (motorcycle) 3 (van) 4 (truck)

#	IF the interface flaw is . . .	THEN recommend . . .
16	Structure of data entry values is not consistent throughout the system.	A printed list of all synonymous data entry values, indicating which screen requires which synonym

## CHAPTER 5

The Navigation Interface: Making It Easy for Users to Get Around in the System

Introduction

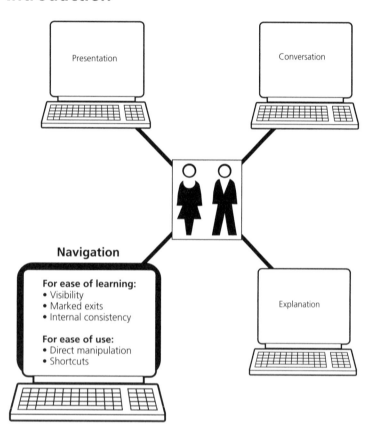

What is navigation?

Imagine taking a business trip to an unfamiliar city.

1. You land at the airport.

2. You pick up your rental car.

3. You drive to your hotel.

What's wrong with this picture? You won't get very far without either a good set of directions or a road map. Sometimes even these won't help. In Boston, a city known for its twisty little streets that disappear suddenly, only to reemerge as other twisty little streets with new names, the common response to a lost traveler is, ''You can't get there from here.''

This example raises two navigation issues. To make your way around a city, you need to have a picture in your mind of its general layout, and you need to be able to get to where you want to go without getting lost. The same is true when users make their way around a computer system. For example, in a word processing system, users need to know what editing options are available, and how to select the one they want. In a data entry system, users need to advance easily from one screen to another. They also must be able to move around efficiently within a data entry screen. Users of a direct manipulation interface need to know which objects on a screen can be selected, and the consequence of selecting an object.

What is the purpose of this chapter?

This chapter explains how to review and recommend redesign of a system's *navigation* interface. The navigation interface is the method or methods by which users move around the system. Navigating a computer system requires the knowledge of what options are available and how to get the correct option with a minimum of time and effort. A clumsy or inefficient navigation interface increases the time it takes both to learn and to use a system. If users continually get lost and "can't get there from here," they will be frustrated and dissatisfied with the system as a whole. If the procedure for getting from one part of the system to another requires multiple steps, then the time it takes to perform any system task will be increased, leading to a resulting decrease in productivity.

How is this chapter organized?

This chapter contains five evaluative procedures, which are organized around the five navigation categories.

IF you want to evaluate . . .	THEN see page . . .	Related procedures elsewhere in this book . . .
The system's use of menus to move from one task to another	134	How to evaluate menu displays (p. 69) How to evaluate menu language (p. 108)
Methods for moving around within a single screen or dialog box	142	How to evaluate data entry screen displays (p. 75) How to evaluate data input (p. 124)
Methods for moving between screens	147	None
Ease of navigation in a direct-manipulation interface	151	How to evaluate GUI screen displays (p. 63)
How well the system's hardware supports navigation	156	None

What are the results of following the procedures in this chapter?

Using the procedures in this chapter to discover and correct flaws in the navigation interface can improve user performance in these ways:

Potential result . . .	For example . . .
Decreased learning time: more users can acquire more skills in less time.	*Before:* Users had to remember a complex set of commands to move from one screen to another. *After:* The commands were replaced with labeled function keys; instead of learning commands, users simply press a single key to move to another screen.
Increased proficiency: more users can use more system functions.	*Before:* In a computer-based training (CBT) remedial reading program for adults, learners had difficulty deciphering on-screen instructions. *After:* The program was redesigned to be a direct-manipulation interface. Icons were designed to replace written instructions, allowing learners to simply click on the program option they want.
Increased productivity: users can accomplish a task in less time and with less effort.	*Before:* A "deep" menu structure required users to pass through at least five menus before arriving at the screen they needed. *After:* A type-ahead function was added to let experienced users bypass menus and go directly to the appropriate screen.

Potential result . . .	For example . . .
Improved quality: users can produce work that is more accurate, with less time spent correcting errors.	*Before:* In a payroll system with multiple data entry screens, users could not return to a previous screen to correct their work. Because errors had to be remembered and corrected after an entire transaction was complete, users frequently missed these errors.

After: The system was redesigned to let users move easily among multipage transactions, thus allowing error correction to take place as soon as an error is discovered. |
| Greater satisfaction: users feel comfortable with and supported by the system. | *Before:* In a direct manipulation system, users were only able to navigate by using a mouse to select objects on the screen. While novice users liked this design, experienced users found it time-consuming.

After: The direct manipulation interface was enhanced with the addition of keystroke shortcuts to give users the option of either selecting with a mouse or typing on the keyboard. |

For more information

Apple Computer. *Macintosh Human Interface Guidelines.* Reading, Mass.: Addison-Wesley, 1992.
General design principles for graphical user interfaces targeted to Macintosh applications. Chapter Three provides detailed specification for parts of the navigation interface such as menus, dialog boxes, windows, and object selection.

IBM Corporation. *Common User Access: Advanced Interface Design Reference.* (Publication no. SC34-4290-00). 1991.
General design principles for graphical user interfaces, targeted to Windows-based applications. Chapter Two presents design guidelines for parts of the navigation interface such as menus, dialog boxes, and object selection.

Mayhew, D. J. *Principles and Guidelines in Software User Interface Design.* Englewood Cliffs, N.J.: Prentice-Hall, 1992.

Chapter Four describes research and design principles for menu selection mechanisms. Chapter Nine describes navigation in direct-manipulation interfaces.

Powell, J. E. *Designing User Interfaces.* San Marcos, Calif.: Microtrend Books, 1990.

Chapter Six describes guidelines for effective menu design.

Rubenstein, R., and Hersh, H. M. *The Human Factor: Designing Computer Systems for People.* Bedford, Mass.: Digital Press, 1984.

Chapter Eight describes menu and direct manipulation interface styles.

Shneiderman, B. *Designing the User Interface.* Reading, Mass.: Addison-Wesley, 1992.

Chapter Three describes alternative menu designs, methods for moving through menus quickly, and selection mechanisms. Chapter Five describes navigation in direct-manipulation interfaces.

Tognazzini, B. *TOG on Interface.* Reading, Mass.: Addison-Wesley, 1992.

Appendix B (index of principles and guidelines) contains general guidelines for reducing or eliminating navigation and improving the effectiveness of menus. The index serves as a guide to text passages in the book that further explain the guidelines and provide examples of applications that implement them.

Procedure 5.1 *Evaluating Menu Navigation*

The purpose of this procedure

All system navigation was originally accomplished through the use of commands. In an attempt to bypass complex command languages, many systems evolved to menu navigation. In these systems, users move from one screen or function to another by selecting choices from an on-screen list of options. Menu navigation can reduce training time and errors, because users don't need to memorize command sequences. However, in a poorly designed menu navigation system, users can get lost in low-level menus, navigation is cumbersome for expert users, and users either select incorrect choices or can't find the function they need.

When to use this procedure

It is especially important to evaluate and recommend redesign of menu navigation when

- Items in Parts 5 and 7 of the User Satisfaction Survey (see Chapter Two) are rated low.

- During interviews or think-aloud observation (see Chapter Two), users say things like "It takes too long to bring up the screen I need" or "I never know where I am in this system" or "I wanted to do [some system function], but I forgot what menu it was on."

Terms you may not know

Broad menus A menu containing many choices (in contrast with *deep menus*, following). Users are frequently able to move directly from a single menu to the screen they need.

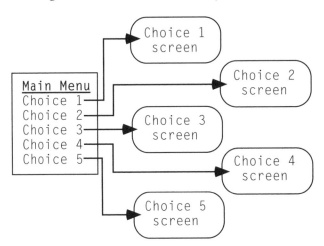

Deep menus A menu containing only a few choices. When users select a choice, they are brought down to a lower menu level, and the process continues until the required screen is reached. Deep menus are also called nested menus.

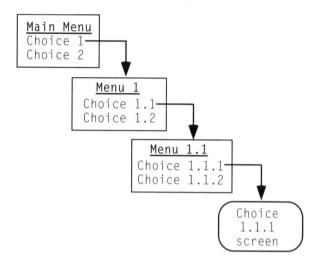

Inactive item A choice not currently available to the user, usually because of the system state. For example, in a word processor, if a document is not open, the "Save" choice is inactive because there is nothing for the system to save. Once a document is opened, the "Save" choice becomes active.

Menu map A graphic illustration of the menu hierarchy, often in the form of an organization chart. Users can display the menu map on the screen to determine where they are and where they can go next.

Typing ahead A method of bypassing nested menus. Each menu is assigned a code (generally a number or a letter); users enter a string of codes to jump directly to the desired menu level.

Before you start

From your set of evaluation tasks (see Chapter Two), select one or more to try out these interface activities:

- View the main menu.

- Conduct an Error Condition Test: Enter an invalid menu option.

- Navigate forward ("down" menu levels).

- Navigate backward ("up" menu levels) by stepping back one level at a time, and by jumping from the lowest level directly to the main menu.

Finding the problem

To discover flaws in a system's menu navigation interface, work through your evaluation tasks using Navigation Interface Checklist #1: By Menus to evaluate the interface. (See Resource E for a reproducible copy of the checklist.) Every item that is checked "no" indicates an interface flaw. To correct these flaws, follow the instructions in the next section, "Solving the problem."

Navigation Interface Checklist #1: Via Menus

#	Review Checklist	yes	no	n/a	Examples
1.	If menu lists are *short* (seven items or fewer), can users select an item by moving the cursor?	☐	☐	☐	On the main menu for a computer-based training program with five lessons, Lesson One is highlighted. Pressing the **down** arrow on the keyboard moves you to Lesson Two.
2.	If menu lists are *long* (more than seven items), can users select an item either by moving the cursor or by typing a mnemonic code?	☐	☐	☐	NYC Transportation A...Airline schedules B...Bus map C...Cab rates F...Ferry schedules L...Limo services R...Road map S...Subway map T...Train schedules
3.	If the system uses a pointing device, do users have the option of either clicking on menu items or using a keyboard shortcut?	☐	☐	☐	To print the ferry schedule, you can pull down the File menu and click on Print. Or you can simultaneously press (ALT) (P).
4.	Are inactive menu items grayed out or omitted?	☐	☐	☐	Ferry schedules does not appear as an option on the Chicago Transportation menu because Chicago does not have a ferry system.
5.	Are there menu selection defaults?	☐	☐	☐	The NYC Transportation menu comes up with Bus schedules already selected because analysis revealed that users selected this choice most frequently. NYC Transportation A...Airline schedules B...Bus schedules F...Ferry schedules T...Train schedules

Navigation Interface Checklist #1 (Continued)

#	Review Checklist	yes	no	n/a	Examples
6.	Are menus broad (many items on a menu) rather than deep (many menu levels)?	☐	☐	☐	This is a *deep* menu structure. If possible avoid this design since it takes users longer to reach the screen they need.
7.	If the system has deep (multilevel) menus, do users have the option of typing ahead?	☐	☐	☐	Typing T B M B will bypass the Transportation, Bus, and Metro menus to display today's Bay Area bus schedule.
✲ 8.	If the system uses a type-ahead strategy, do the menu items have mnemonic codes?	☐	☐	☐	*Poor:* Type 1 5 3 to bypass the Transportation, Bus, and Metro menus. *Better:* Type T B M to bypass the Transportation, Bus, and Metro menus.
✲ 9.	If the system has many menu levels or complex menu levels, do users have access to an on-line spatial menu map?	☐	☐	☐	

#	Review Checklist	yes	no	n/a	Examples
10.	If the system has multiple menu levels, is there a mechanism that allows users to go back to previous menus?	☐	☐	☐	From the Metro submenu, you can press (PgUp) to move back to the Bus menu. You can press (Shift) (PgUp) to jump directly to the main menu.
11.	If users can back up to a previous menu, can they change their earlier menu choice?	☐	☐	☐	If you back up from the Bus menu to the Transportation menu, you can then select Train to go down to the Train menu.
12.	Do GUI (Graphical User Interface) menus offer *affordance*, that is, make obvious where selection is possible?	☐	☐	☐	On the pull-down Edit menu, the Copy choice appears in a lighter color because no text has been selected. Once you select a block of text to copy, the Copy command reappears in black.

Edit

```
Cut
Copy  ◄───      This option is
Paste           not available
Clear
Select All
```

#	Review Checklist	yes	no	n/a	Examples
13.	Do GUI menus make obvious the item that has been selected?	☐	☐	☐	Each choice on the pull-down menu is highlighted in turn as you slide your pointer down the list.
14.	Do GUI menus make obvious whether deselection is possible?	☐	☐	☐	Items that can be turned on or off via a pull-down menu have a check mark beside them if they are on. Selecting these items causes the check mark to disappear.

View

```
Normal
✓Outline  ◄───   These options
                 are turned on
Show Ribbon
✓Show Ruler  ◄──
Show Tools
```

Navigation Interface Checklist #1 (Continued)

#	Review Checklist	yes	no	n/a	Examples
15.	Do GUI menus offer *activation:* that is, make obvious how to say "Now do it"?	☐	☐	☐	The Print dialog box contains a (PRINT) button which, when clicked, prints the document.

```
To Printer: "Memories"

Copies: [1]    Pages: ○All ●From:[12] To:[25]

Paper Source: ●Paper Tray ○Manual Feed

Print: ●Black & White ○Gray Scale ○Color
        [Print]      [Cancel]      [Help]
```
↑————Click here to print

Note: Because dialog boxes frequently present options, they serve as menus in GUI interfaces.

Solving the problem

Every "no" on the checklist indicates an interface flaw that can interfere with performance.

- Ideally, you will be in a position to recommend an interface redesign to correct each flaw. Use checklist examples, where provided, as design guidelines. The answer to the item will then become either "yes" (because the feature was enhanced) or "n/a" (because the structure of the interface was changed to eliminate the feature).

- However, interface redesign is not always an option. In this case, you may be able to improve performance with an alternative strategy such as a job aid. Any checklist item marked with an asterisk (*) is a candidate for one of these alternative strategies.

Interface redesign recommendations. If your analysis has uncovered flaws in the menu navigation interface, use design principles 1 to 15 to guide you toward specific design revisions. For example, if the system contains a deep menu structure, two design alternatives that emerge from the checklist principles are the following:

- Revise the menu structure to create fewer menus that each offer more choices.

- Assign a mnemonic code to each menu choice and create a type-ahead function to allow expert users to bypass deep menus.

Alternative solutions (for items marked with ∗). Consider these alternatives if interface redesign is not possible.

#	IF the interface flaw is . . .	THEN recommend . . .
8	The system provides type-ahead, but menu choices are numbered (not mnemonic), so users must remember multiple numeric strings.	A printed list of the type-ahead numeric strings for the most common user tasks

<table>
<tr><td>IF you want to...</td><td>THEN type...</td></tr>
<tr><td colspan="2">Send out a bill. . . . . .1 5 5 3</td></tr>
<tr><td colspan="2">Change an account. .1 3 5 2 2</td></tr>
<tr><td colspan="2">Place an order. . . . . .2 2 4</td></tr>
</table>

#	IF the interface flaw is . . .	THEN recommend . . .
9	There is a deep menu structure and no on-line spatial map.	A printed system-organization chart that shows the complete menu hierarchy

Evaluating Navigation in a Single Screen or Dialog Box

The purpose of this procedure

Data entry screens. Many of the systems installed in organizations are database systems. The primary functions of a database system are to capture data (*input*), manipulate it (*process*), and report on it (*output*). For example, a company payroll system, through which data flows in this manner, is a database. Its word processor is not a database.

The primary interface to a database system is the *data entry screen.* When people pay attention to the data entry screen interface, it is usually from the standpoint of layout: the amount of information that appears on each screen and the way this information is arranged. These considerations certainly have an impact on performance, and are discussed in Chapter Three, "The Presentation Interface." But equally important—and frequently overlooked—is the interface for navigating within a screen. An awkward or inconsistent navigation interface, especially when high-use screens are involved, can cost users time and cause frustration with the system.

Dialog boxes. In direct manipulation interfaces, the dialog box is a data entry screen with the same functions of input, process, and output.

1. Input: The user enters instructions in the dialog box ("Print three copies of this report").

2. Process: The system processes those instructions ("Someone just told me to print three copies of the report").

3. Output: The system then returns a result ("Here you go . . . three copies of the report, hot off the printer").

When to use this procedure

It is especially important to evaluate and recommend redesign of navigation within a single screen or dialog box when:

• Items in Parts 5 and 7 of the User Satisfaction Survey are rated low.

• During interviews or think-aloud observation, users say things like "There's one screen I really hate. I have to waste time moving the cursor all the way down to *here,* when all I really need to do is enter one code way up *here*" or "They keep changing the keys I'm supposed to use."

Terms you may not know

Auto-tabbing Automatic movement of the cursor by the system after the user enters a character in the last position of a field (instead of the user pressing a key to move to the next data entry field). The purpose of auto-tab is to save keystrokes; however, some studies have shown that while auto-tab may be appropriate for frequent users, it can actually slow performance for others.

Dialog box A pop-up display that elicits one or more responses from a user. A sample dialog box is shown on the next page.

Before you start

Obtain some representative data for the system you are reviewing. From your set of evaluation tasks, select one or more to try out these interface activities:

- Bring up a high-frequency data entry screen.

- Complete all fields on the screen.

- Conduct Error Condition Tests: correct a data entry error while you are still in the field; correct a data entry error after you have left a field; attempt to enter data in a protected field.

- Repeat all of these tasks for at least three other data entry screens.

Finding the problem

To discover flaws in a system's screen or dialog box navigation interface, work through your evaluation tasks using Navigation Interface Checklist #2: In a Single Screen or Dialog Box to evaluate the interface. (See Resource E for a reproducible copy of the checklist.) Every item that is checked "no" indicates an interface flaw. To correct these flaws, follow the instructions in the next section, "Solving the problem."

Sample screen:

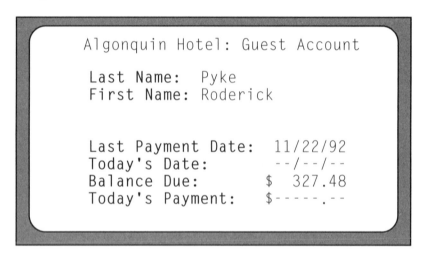

Sample dialog box:

Navigation Interface Checklist #2: In a Single Screen or Dialog Box

#	Review Checklist	yes	no	n/a	Examples
1.	When the user enters a screen or dialog box, is the cursor already positioned in the field users are most likely to need?	☐	☐	☐	*Screen:* The cursor starts out in the Today's Date field, since the first four fields on the screen display information already in the database (that is, they display information that cannot be changed). *Dialog Box:* The cursor starts out in the Copies field.
2.	Can users move forward and backward within a field?	☐	☐	☐	*Screen:* if you type 132092, when you meant to type 032092, you can back up and type over the 1. *Dialog Box:* If you type From: 6, when you meant to type From: 16, you can back up and type a 1 in front of the 6.
3.	Can users move forward and backward between fields or dialog box options?	☐	☐	☐	*Screen:* If you enter today's payment, and then realize that you entered an incorrect date, you can go back to the Today's Date field. *Dialog Box:* If you leave the Copies field and then realize that you meant to print five copies, you can go back to the Copies field.
✻ 4.	Is the method for moving the cursor to the next or the previous field both simple and visible?	☐	☐	☐	*Screen:* The system uses (TAB) to move forward, and (SHIFT) (TAB) to move backward. Although this method is simple, it is *not* visible. *Dialog Box:* Because this is a direct-manipulation interface, you make selections by pointing and clicking on each dialog box option.

#	Review Checklist	yes	no	n/a	Examples
✳ 5.	Is the method for moving the cursor to the next or previous field consistent throughout the system?	☐	☐	☐	*Screen:* Because (TAB) moves you to the next field on the Patient Account screen, it also moves you to the next field on all the other screens in the Patient Billing system. *Dialog Box:* One feature of direct-manipulation interfaces is their consistency; you use the point-and-click method for navigating all dialog boxes in the system.
6.	If the system uses a pointing device, do users have the option of either clicking on fields or using a keyboard shortcut?	☐	☐	☐	*Dialog Box:* You can press (TAB) to move from the Copies field to the From field; you can press (RETURN) instead of clicking on (OK) to print the document.
7.	Has auto-tabbing been avoided *except* when fields have fixed lengths or users are experienced?	☐	☐	☐	*Screen:* In this system, all dates are six characters long (for example, 032793). When you enter today's date, the cursor immediately moves to today's payment.
8.	Are protected areas completely inaccessible?	☐	☐	☐	*Screen:* The cursor never even goes to Last Name, First Name, Last Payment Date, and Balance Due because the information in these fields cannot be changed.

Solving the problem

Every "no" on the checklist indicates an interface flaw that can interfere with performance.

- Ideally, you will be in a position to recommend an interface redesign to correct each flaw. Use checklist examples, where provided, as design guidelines. The answer to the item will then become either "yes" (because the feature was enhanced) or "n/a" (because the structure of the interface was changed to eliminate the feature).

- However, interface redesign is not always an option. In this case, you may be able to improve performance by using an alternative strategy such as a job aid. Any checklist item marked by an asterisk is a candidate for one of these alternative strategies.

Interface redesign recommendations. If your analysis has uncovered flaws in the within-screen navigation interface, use design principles 1 to 8 to guide you toward specific design revisions. For example, if the screen comes up with the cursor in the first data entry field but most users want to enter data on the sixth field, the following are three design alternatives:

- Display the cursor in the sixth field.

- Change the position of the sixth field so that it becomes the first field.

- Create a Function Key shortcut that "jumps" the cursor to the sixth field.

Alternative solutions (for items marked with *). Consider these alternatives if interface redesign is not possible.

#	IF the interface flaw is . . .	THEN recommend . . .
4	The method for moving the cursor is not visible.	A keyboard template indicating which keys move the cursor
5	The method for moving the cursor is inconsistent from one part of the system to another.	For each data entry screen in the system, on-screen (preferable) or printed instructions explaining which keys move the cursor

Procedure 5.3	*Evaluating Navigation Between Screens*

The purpose of this procedure

Navigation between screens is similar to navigation within menus (see Procedure 5.1 on page 134). In both cases, users will have a tendency to "get lost" if the navigation interface is not highly visible. People are most likely to use interscreen navigation as follows:

- In complex database systems with "multipage" data entry screens

- During database queries, when they are searching through the database for one or more records

When to use this procedure

It is especially important to evaluate and recommend redesign of interscreen navigation when

- Items in Part 5 of the User Satisfaction Survey are rated low.

- During interviews or think-aloud observation, users say things like "It takes too long to find the information I need" or "I never know how to make this screen go away so I just keep hitting keys until it vanishes" or "Am I through entering this claim? I can't remember which screens I finished."

Terms you may not know

Field The part of the data entry screen into which the user enters information.

Multipage Information that is too extensive to fit onto a single screen and spills over onto additional screens; because each screen is usually called a "page," these entry screens are "multipage."

Query Search of the database to find a particular record or set of records. For example, a query might ask the system to display all customers with accounts that are more than three months overdue.

Record A single instance of a collection of data in a database. For example, in a payroll database, an employee record contains the name, home address, and hourly wage for a particular employee.

Before you start　　　　Obtain some representative data for the system you are reviewing. From your set of evaluation tasks, select one or more to try out these interface activities:

- Bring up a multipage data entry screen.
- Complete all fields on the first screen.
- Go to the next screen and complete all fields. Repeat for all pages.
- Switch from one type of data entry screen to another.
- Switch from a data entry screen back to the main menu.
- Search for a particular record or set of records.
- Switch from a query screen back to the main menu.
- Conduct Error Condition Tests: correct a data entry error while you are still on a screen; correct a data entry error after you have left a screen.

Finding the problem　　　To discover flaws in a system's interscreen navigation interface, work through your evaluation tasks using Navigation Interface Checklist #3: Between Screens to evaluate the interface. (See Resource E for a reproducible copy of the checklist.) Every item that is checked "no" indicates an interface flaw. To correct these flaws, follow the instructions in the next section, "Solving the problem."

Navigation Interface Checklist #3: Between Screens

#	Review Checklist	yes	no	n/a	Examples
✸ 1.	If users must navigate between multiple screens, does the system use context labels, menu maps, and place markers as navigational aids?	☐	☐	☐	In a computer-based training program with multiple learning paths, pressing the (HELP) key will display this graphic. Your current location in the training program will be shaded. You are here
2.	If the system has multipage data entry screens, do all pages have the same title?	☐	☐	☐	In a life insurance company's system there are seven screens for the system function that adds a new policy holder to the database. Each screen has the title Add Client.
✸ 3.	If the system has multipage data entry screens, does each page have a sequential page number?	☐	☐	☐	Each Add Client screen has a page number in the upper-right corner. The first reads 1 of 7, the second 2 of 7, the third 3 of 7, and so on.
4.	If the system has multipage data entry screens, can users move backward and forward among all the pages in the set?	☐	☐	☐	From the sixth Add Client screen, users can tab to the upper-right corner, type 1, and jump back to the first screen.
5.	If the system uses a question and answer interface, can users go back to previous questions or skip forward to later questions?	☐	☐	☐	What is your name? Ginger Winship What is your age? 40 What is your claim #? back What is your age? 39
6.	Does the system offer "find next" and "find previous" shortcuts for database searches?	☐	☐	☐	When you query the database for Jones, you are shown the information for Albert Jones. Pressing the (PgDown) key displays information for Alice Jones.

Solving the problem

Every "no" on the checklist indicates an interface flaw that can interfere with performance.

- Ideally, you will be in a position to recommend an interface redesign to correct each flaw. Use checklist examples, where provided, as design guidelines. The answer to the item will then become either "yes" (because the feature was enhanced) or "n/a" (because the structure of the interface was changed to eliminate the feature).

- However, interface redesign is not always an option. In this case, you may be able to improve performance with an alternative strategy such as a job aid. Any checklist item marked with an asterisk (*) is a candidate for one of these alternative strategies.

Interface redesign recommendations. If your analysis has uncovered flaws in the interscreen navigation interface, use design principles 1 to 6 to guide you toward specific design revisions. For example, if the screens in a multipage procedure are not titled, it is often a simple matter to add a title to each page.

Alternative solutions (for items marked with *). Consider these alternatives if interface redesign is not possible.

#	IF the interface flaw is . . .	THEN recommend . . .
1	The relationship between screens is not clear or visible.	A printed system-organization chart that shows the complete screen hierarchy

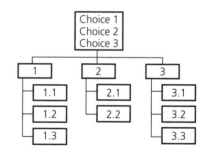

#	IF the interface flaw is . . .	THEN recommend . . .
3	Multipage data entry screens are not sequentially numbered.	A printed list of the most frequent (or most complex) user tasks, with a checklist of the screens that must be used to complete each task

| **Procedure 5.4** | *Evaluating Navigation by Direct Manipulation* |

The purpose of this procedure

A direct manipulation interface allows users to perform actions directly on objects they see on the screen. This book uses the term "direct manipulation" to describe systems in which

- An on-screen *pointer* indicates the user's position on the screen.
- A *pointing device* (generally a mouse or trackball) is used to move the pointer around the screen.
- Objects on the screen are selected by *clicking* the mouse or trackball.

A special kind of direct manipulation interface is the graphical user interface (GUI). Such interfaces use graphic symbols (called *icons*) to represent objects and actions. Many GUI systems use *windows* to present several kinds of information on the screen at the same time. GUI navigation uses the same point-and-click method that other, nongraphic direct manipulation interfaces do. Direct manipulation interfaces are becoming increasingly popular because people often find them easier to use than other types. However, direct manipulation in and of itself is no guarantee of simplicity or ease of use. If the navigation interface is awkward, such interfaces can actually be more complicated and confusing than others.

When to use this procedure

It is especially important to evaluate and recommend redesign of direct manipulation navigation when

- Items in Parts 5 and 7 of the User Satisfaction Survey are rated low.
- During interviews or think-aloud observation, users say things like "Help! I just lost my spreadsheet" or "Sometimes it's a real pain to take my hand off the keyboard just to click on the mouse."

Terms you may not know

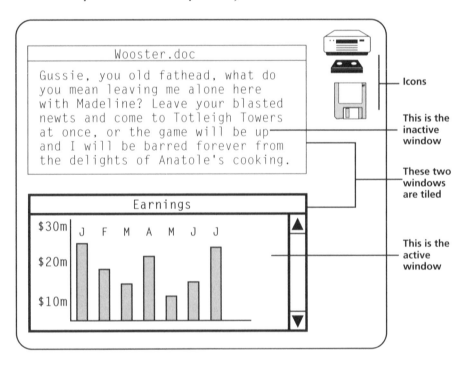

Active window The window that is available for user manipulation. Although several windows may be on the screen simultaneously, the user can only manipulate one window at a time.

Dialog box A pop-up display that elicits one or more responses from a user.

GUI The acronym for graphical user interface. GUIs use icons to create the illusion that the system is composed of objects, which users can manipulate.

Icon A picture that represents an object (for example, an annual report) or process (for example, setting up a printer).

Window A view into a document. GUI interfaces are often characterized by the ability to display several windows on the screen at once, each containing a different type of data (for example, a letter, a spreadsheet, and a graph).

Before you start

From your set of evaluation tasks, select one or more to try out these interface activities:

- Select an option from a menu.
- Conduct an Error Condition Test: select an invalid menu option.
- Open multiple windows and switch between them.
- Request a system action via a dialog box.
- Enter information on a data entry screen.

Finding the problem

To discover flaws in a system's direct manipulation navigation interface, work through your evaluation tasks using Navigation Interface Checklist #4: Direct Manipulation to evaluate the interface. (See Resource E for a reproducible copy of the checklist.) Every item that is checked ''no'' indicates an interface flaw. To correct these flaws, follow the instructions in the next section, ''Solving the problem.''

Navigation Interface Checklist #4: Direct Manipulation

#	Review Checklist	yes	no	n/a	Examples
1.	**Windows:** If the screen displays multiple windows, is navigation between windows simple and visible?	☐	☐	☐	Although stacked windows save space, it may be easier to navigate between tiled windows because stacked windows can become "buried."
2.	**Windows:** Are there salient visual cues to identify the active window?	☐	☐	☐	The active window is highlighted. Information in the inactive window is grayed-out.
3.	**Data Entry Screens:** Do users have the option of either clicking directly on a field or using a keyboard shortcut?	☐	☐	☐	You can either click on (DONE) when you have finished entering data or you can press the (Send) key on the keyboard.

Tiled windows   Stacked windows

Active window   Inactive window

```
       Payment Posting
Name: Stilton Cheesewright

Balance Due:        $1,225.47
Today's Date:      --/--/--
Today's Payment: $-----.--
 (PREV)    (NEXT)    (DONE)
```

Navigation Interface Checklist #5 (Continued)

#	Review Checklist	yes	no	n/a	Examples
4.	**Menus:** Do the users have the option of either clicking directly on a menu item or using a keyboard shortcut?	☐	☐	☐	To copy an object, first click on the object to select it. Then, either select Copy from the Edit menu, or type (Alt) (C).
5.	**Dialog Boxes:** Do users have the option of either clicking directly on a dialog box option or using a keyboard shortcut?	☐	☐	☐	You can either click on the word Color, or you can type (Ctrl) (C).
6.	**Dialog Boxes:** Can expert users bypass nested dialog boxes with either type-ahead, user-defined macros, or keyboard shortcuts?	☐	☐	☐	Selecting Manual Feed in the Print dialog box displays another dialog box of paper size options. After selecting a paper size, you can either • Click (OK) to redisplay the first dialog box and then click (OK) again to print your document, or • Just type (Alt) (Enter) to print immediately

For item 5, the example includes the dialog box illustration:

```
To Printer: "Bunker"

Copies: [1]    Pages: ◉All ○From:[  ] To:[  ]

Paper Source: ○Paper Tray ◉Manual Feed

Print: ◉Black & White ○Gray Scale ○Color
```
Click here ⬏

Solving the problem

Every "no" on the checklist indicates an interface flaw that can interfere with performance. Ideally, you will be in a position to recommend an interface redesign to correct each flaw. Use checklist examples, where provided, as design guidelines. The answer to the item will then become either "yes" (because the feature was enhanced) or "n/a" (because the structure of the interface was changed to eliminate the feature).

Interface redesign recommendations. If your analysis uncovers flaws in the direct manipulation navigation interface, use design principles 1 to 6 to guide you toward specific design revisions. For example:

- If a mouse must be used to select from a menu, the most frequently used options can be identified and assigned to function keys.

- If a frequent system task requires users to access many nested dialog boxes, a macro can be created to automate the process.

Alternative solutions (for items marked with *).* Unfortunately, there are few alternative solutions, other than training, to solve performance problems cause by awkward or complex navigation methods in direct manipulation interfaces. If the navigation interface does not provide both mouse and keyboard navigation, selection and data entry may be slowed. If navigation among multiple windows is either not readily apparent or overly complex, users may lose time as they search for their data.

The development of standards for graphical user interfaces will do much to resolve these performance problems because a key feature of the GUI interface is consistency among all applications.

Procedure 5.5 | *Evaluating Hardware-Based Navigation*

The purpose of this procedure

Although the primary focus of the procedures in this book is on software, a critical component of the navigation interface is the input device or devices with which the user directs the system. Most systems use a keyboard for input; others also have pointing devices such as a mouse or a trackball. Still others use pressure-sensitive screens, which users touch to point directly to an object.

The selection and redesign of input devices is generally not open to negotiation. However, a poorly designed hardware-based navigation interface can seriously impede performance. Therefore, it is important to review this aspect of navigation and recommend alternative solutions where appropriate.

When to use this procedure

It is especially important to evaluate and recommend redesign of hardware-based navigation tools when

- Items in Part 5 of the User Satisfaction Survey are rated low.

- During interviews or think-aloud observation, users say things like "I'm always hitting the wrong key" or "Where's that (DELETE) key?" or "I can never remember whether I'm supposed to press (SHIFT) (G) or (ALT) (G)."

Terms you may not know

Function key "Shortcut" keys that allow users to perform actions by pressing a key rather than by either entering a command or selecting an option from a menu. Function key labels on the keyboard can be *generic* ((F1), (F2), (F3)), *dedicated* ((ESC), (HOME), (DEL)), or a combination of the two.

Qualifier key A key that is pressed in combination with another key. Qualifier keys increase the number of available keyboard shortcuts (for example, (F1), (ALT) (F1), and (SHIFT) (F1) can each perform a different function), but their overuse can make the interface confusing.

Soft function keys An on-screen display of the commands that correspond to function keys on the keyboard. They help users to remember the actions of generic function keys.

Before you start

Obtain some representative data for the system you are reviewing. Obtain a list of all keyboard shortcuts. From your set of evaluation tasks, select one or more to try out these interface activities:

- Select options from several menus.
- Enter information on several data entry screens.
- Try out each keyboard shortcut.
- Conduct Error Condition Tests: press invalid function keys; identify and press keys with similar-sounding names.

Finding the problem

To discover flaws in a system's hardware interface, work through your evaluation tasks using Navigation Interface Checklist #5: Input Devices to evaluate the interface. (See Resource E for a reproducible copy of the checklist.) Every item that is checked "no" is an interface flaw. To correct these flaws, follow the instructions in the next section, "Solving the problem."

Navigation Interface Checklist #5: Input Devices

#	Review Checklist	yes	no	n/a	Examples
✻ 1.	Do the selected input device(s) match user capabilities?	☐	☐	☐	Users with special needs may not be able to press multiple keys and would do better with an interface that can be manipulated with one hand.
2.	Do the selected input device(s) match environmental constraints?	☐	☐	☐	A mouse may not be appropriate at a teller window, where counter space is at a premium.
3.	If the system uses multiple input devices, has hand and eye movement between input devices been minimized?	☐	☐	☐	The trackball is placed right beside the keyboard, so users don't have to take their eyes off the keyboard to look for it.
4.	If the system supports graphical tasks, has an alternative pointing device been provided?	☐	☐	☐	In a graphics package, a drawing can be resized either by dragging its boundaries or by entering exact measurements in a dialog box.
5.	Are cursor keys arranged in either an inverted T or a cross configuration?	☐	☐	☐	Cross Inverted T
6.	Is the numeric keypad located to the right of the alpha key area?	☐	☐	☐	Alpha keys Numeric keys
✻ 7.	Are important keys (for example, (ENTER), (TAB)) larger than other keys?	☐	☐	☐	
8.	Has the system been designed so that keys with similar names do not perform opposite (and potentially dangerous) actions?	☐	☐	☐	If the (ENTER) key saves data, the (RETURN) key should not exit from the system. Users could conceivably press (RETURN) and assume they have saved a file, only to discover the next day that their file is nowhere to be found!

#	Review Checklist	yes	no	n/a	Examples
9.	Are there enough function keys to support functionality, but not so many that scanning and finding are difficult?	☐	☐	☐	
10.	Are function keys reserved for generic, high-frequency, important functions?	☐	☐	☐	Typical function key assignments are Save, Exit, Insert, Delete, Home, Next, Previous, and Help.
11.	Does the system follow industry or company standards for function key assignments?	☐	☐	☐	Many systems have standardized on (F1) to bring up the on-line help system.
12.	Are function keys arranged in logical groups?	☐	☐	☐	On a word processing system, all function keys that support editing (move, copy, insert, delete) are grouped in one cluster, while all keys that support file management (open file, save, print) are in another.
13.	Are the most frequently used function keys in the most accessible positions?	☐	☐	☐	The (PgUp) and (PgDn) keys are immediately to the right of the alpha keys on the keyboard.
14.	Are the function keys that can cause the most serious consequences in hard-to-reach positions?	☐	☐	☐	The (BREAK) key, which causes the system to reset, is in the upper right corner of the keyboard, away from all the other keys.
15.	Are the function keys that can cause the most serious consequences located far away from low-consequence and high-use keys?	☐	☐	☐	The (Delete) key is on the opposite end of the keyboard from the (Enter) key.
16.	Do function keys that can cause serious consequences have an undo feature?	☐	☐	☐	When you press (Delete), the system displays the message "Do you really want to delete this file?"

Navigation Interface Checklist #5 (Continued)

#	Review Checklist	yes	no	n/a	Examples
✳ 17.	Has the use of qualifier keys been minimized?	☐	☐	☐	The system only uses the function keys (F1) through (F10). Additional key combinations (for example, (SHIFT) (F1), (ALT) (F1)) are available for experienced users, but are not required to operate the system.
18.	If the system uses qualifier keys, are they used consistently throughout the system?	☐	☐	☐	(F2) = select paragraph (SHIFT) (F2) = select page (F3) = copy paragraph (SHIFT) (F3) = copy page
✳ 19.	Are function keys labeled clearly and distinctly, even if this means breaking consistency rules?	☐	☐	☐	The "escape" key is labeled (ESC) (name is truncated), while the "help" key is labeled (HLP) (vowel is dropped).
20.	Are function key assignments consistent across screens, subsystems, and related products?	☐	☐	☐	You indicate the end of all actions by pressing (ENTER), whether you are in a menu, a dialog box, or a data entry screen.

Solving the problem

Every "no" on the checklist indicates an interface flaw that can interfere with performance.

- Ideally, you will be in a position to recommend an interface redesign to correct each flaw. Use checklist examples, where provided, as design guidelines. The answer to the item will then become either "yes" (because the feature was enhanced) or "n/a" (because the structure of the interface was changed to eliminate the feature).

- However, interface redesign is not always an option. In this case, you may be able to improve performance with an alternative strategy such as a job aid. Any checklist item that is marked with an asterisk (*) is a candidate for one of these alternative strategies.

Interface redesign recommendations. It is unlikely that you will be able to redesign the hardware-based interface, even if your analysis has uncovered flaws in it. Most organizations have corporate standards for hardware selection, and these cannot readily be bypassed. In addition, buying new hardware is expensive, especially if the organization has invested heavily in the hardware it already has.

However, two hardware-based navigation flaws can be fixed by modifying the software:

- Design principle 16: Provide an undo capability for any "dangerous" function keys.

- Design principle 20: Identify and revise inconsistent function-key assignments.

Alternative solutions (for items marked with ∗). Because interface redesign is not generally an option, consider these alternatives.

#	IF the interface flaw is . . .	THEN recommend . . .
1	Inappropriate input device.	Evaluating the cost of providing a secondary input device, especially for users with special needs.
7	Key labels of important keys are difficult to read.	Buying a set of replacement keycaps that fit over existing keys; these are less expensive than replacing the entire keyboard. In some environments, color-coding keys may be appropriate; however, remember that 8 percent of the men and 1 percent of the women in European and North American communities have some degree of color deficiency (Bailey, 1982; Shneiderman, 1992).
17	Overuse of qualifier keys.	A printed list of all qualifier-key shortcuts, sorted by user task.

IF you want to...	THEN press...
Open a file.	CTL SHIFT O
Save a file.	OPT S
Print a file.	SHIFT ALT P

Note: Although many systems print lists of shortcuts, these are generally sorted in order of keystroke rather than task. As a result, users have to know which keystroke they need before they can find it!

#	IF the interface flaw is . . .	THEN recommend . . .
19	Unlabeled function keys.	Either soft function keys or a paper template that fits over the keyboard. Some manufacturers sell "generic" templates, with a laminated surface, which let you create a personalized template. For a high volume of users, however, it may be more cost-effective to purchase professionally printed templates.

The Explanation Interface: Incorporating Features That Help Users Learn About the System

---

Introduction

What is explanation?

A novice user sits at a computer console, staring at the message "Task not applicable at this time." She asks herself: What is a task? Does "Not Applicable" mean I don't need to do this, or that I have to do it but not this way? If I sit here and wait for some time to pass, will it work then? (Carroll, 1982, p. 49).

This anecdote illustrates an all-too-common user interface flaw. The system is attempting to explain itself; whoever wrote "Task not applicable at this time" thought that the message was sufficient explanation and that users would be able to read the message, understand what it was telling them, and solve the problem. Nevertheless, this explanation is phrased in a way that leaves the user scratching her head.

What is the purpose of this chapter?

This chapter shows you how to review and recommend redesign of a system's *explanation* interface. A well-designed user interface teaches you about itself as you use it. This is accomplished with the explanation interface through

- Error-handling: protect users from making errors, forgive them when they do, explain the reason for the error, and provide solutions.
- Performance support: interpret variations in user actions, provide memory aids for complex tasks, and allow users to customize the interface to meet their own performance requirements.
- On-line help: provide visible, understandable on-screen references that follow all user interface design guidelines for navigation, presentation, and conversation.

How is this chapter organized?

This chapter contains three procedures organized around the three categories of explanation.

IF you want to evaluate . . .	THEN see page . . .	Related procedures elsewhere in this book . . .
The system's ability to handle user errors	168	How to evaluate prompts (p. 96) How to evaluate feedback (p. 101)
The degree of performance support provided by the system	172	How to evaluate data input (p. 124)
The availability and adequacy of on-line help	178	None

What are the results of following the procedures in this chapter?

Using the procedures in this chapter to discover and correct flaws in the explanation interface can improve user performance in these ways:

Potential result . . .	For example . . .
Decreased learning time: more users can acquire more skills in less time.	*Before:* Users had to memorize complex data entry codes. *After:* When the user moves the cursor to a data entry field, the system displays a list of all valid data entry codes for that field. The user simply selects the code from this list.

Potential result . . .	For example . . .

Increased proficiency: more users can use more system functions.

Before: In a sophisticated graphics application, users usually employed only the most basic system functions.

After: When users click on any drawing tool, they receive on-line help about the uses of the tool.

Increased productivity: users can accomplish a task in less time and with less effort.

Before: The art department's new page layout program was powerful . . . but setting up new publications was time-consuming.

After: Templates were set up for typical page layout tasks. Now users can simply modify an existing template rather than create a publication from scratch each time.

Improved quality: users can produce work that is more accurate, with less time spent correcting errors.

Before: If users accidentally closed a file without saving their work, any changes they had made to the file were lost.

After: The system was redesigned with an "oops" capability that allows users to reverse their last action. Now if users attempt to close a file without saving first, a warning message asks if they want to save the file.

Greater satisfaction: users feel comfortable with and supported by the system.

Before: Error messages were written in a language that only remotely resembled English.

After: Error messages were rewritten and supplemented with an on-line help function. Each message now fully describes the error. If the user presses the (HELP) key, the system explains the cause of the error and offers suggestions about how to correct it.

For more information

Barrett, E. (ed.). *The Society of Text: Hypertext, Hypermedia, and the Social Construction of Information.* Cambridge, Mass.: MIT Press, 1991.

This collection of readings covers topics such as designing systems for the on-line user, multimedia design, and working in an on-line environment.

Carr, C. "Performance Support Systems—The Next Step?" *Performance & Instruction,* 1992, *31*(2), 23–26.

Proposes that any performance effort is actually composed of four different performance types: wasted efforts, distracting duties, ancillary duties, and value-added duties. Describes the design challenges implicit in designing electronic performance support systems to meet the requirements of each performance type.

Carroll, J. M. *The Nurnberg Funnel: Designing Minimalist Instruction for Practical Computer Skill.* Cambridge, Mass.: MIT Press, 1990.

Chapter Two, "Getting to Know a Computer," discusses the difficulty of error recovery when users fail to recognize that they have made an error. It also describes the phenomenon of errors leading to other errors, causing "side effects and tangles."

Gery, G. *Electronic Performance Support Systems.* Boston: Weingarten Publications, 1991.

Presents the theory of electronic support systems. Describes, through the use of detailed case studies, the application of electronic support systems to solve human performance problems.

Harmon, P., Maus, R., and Morrissey, W. *Expert Systems: Tools and Applications.* New York: Wiley, 1988.

Section Three covers the methodology of expert systems development, including procedures for front-end analysis, task analysis, prototype development, system development, testing, implementation, and maintenance. Section Four presents a catalog of over 100 commercial expert system applications including applications in the fields of finance, training, and manufacturing.

Horn, R. E. *Mapping Hypertext.* Lexington, Mass.: The Lexington Institute, 1989.

This book actually employs the principles of hypertext, using a graphical layout and embedded "links" to describe the history, cognitive principles, and design guidelines for hypertext systems.

Horton, W. *Designing and Writing Online Documentation: Help Files to Hypertext.* New York: Wiley, 1990.

Chapter Ten describes guidelines for designing and presenting five kinds of on-line help: reference summary, reference topic, context-sensitive help, diagnostic help, and active help.

Puterbaugh, G., Rosenberg, M., and Sofman, R. "Performance Support Tools: A Step Beyond Training." *Performance & Instruction,* 1989, *28*(10), 1–5.

Moving from theory to application, the authors describe the development of an electronic performance support system designed to improve the performance of training test developers.

Ridgway, L. "Read My Mind: What Users Want from Online Information." *IEEE Transactions On Professional Communication,* June 1987, *PC-30*(2), 87–90.

The author offers three explanations for why people do not use on-line help, including the following: it may break the user's train of thought; it is disorienting because navigation changes are required to access it; it often does not provide the answer the user needs.

Sellen, A., and Nicol, A. "Building User-Centered On-Line Help." In B. Laurel (ed.), *The Art of Human-Computer Interface Design.* Reading, Mass.: Addison-Wesley, 1990.

The authors describe five design flaws of on-line help systems: they make it difficult to find information; they fail to deliver relevant information; it is difficult to switch between on-line help and the working context; they are complex; their quality and layout are poor.

Yang, Y. "Undo Support Models." *International Journal of Man-Machine Studies,* 1988, *28,* 457–481.

The author proposes three types of support features to help users recover from errors and unwanted situations: escapes (for example, press the (CANCEL) button in a dialog box to leave without taking action); stops (for example, press (ESC) to pause printing partway through the print job); undos (for example, press the (DELETE) key and text vanishes; press the (UNDO) key and it reappears).

| **Procedure 6.1** | ***Evaluating Error-Handling*** |

The purpose of this procedure

My object all sublime, I shall achieve in time. To let the punishment fit the crime ... the punishment fit the crime (*The Mikado,* Gilbert and Sullivan, 1898).

A well-designed user interface is forgiving; it protects users from making errors wherever possible, provides understandable feedback regarding the nature of the errors, and provides error recovery, allowing users to bail out of error states gracefully.

When to use this procedure

It is especially important to evaluate and recommend redesign of error-handling when

- Items in Part 6 of the User Satisfaction Survey (see Chapter Two) are rated low.

- During interviews or think-aloud observation (see Chapter Two), users say things like "Oops! I didn't mean to do that. Now I have to start all over again" or "I don't bother looking at the message line at the bottom of the screen—I never know what it's telling me" or "It says I made an error, but it doesn't tell me what to do about it."

Terms you may not know

Semantics The complete set of functions in a system and how they are driven by the command language. For example, the four valid data entry codes for the Region: field are N, S, E, W.

Syntactic The structure of information. For example, when you assign a name to a file, the name must be no more than eight characters and cannot contain any special characters.

Undo Feature that lets users "take back" their last action. For example, select a block of text in a document. Select the Delete command by mistake. Oops! The text vanishes. Select the Undo command and it reappears.

Before you start

Obtain some representative data for the system you are reviewing. Interview or observe users to obtain a set of typical errors. From your set of evaluation tasks (see Chapter Two), select one or more that let you replicate

- Common (frequent) user errors. For example, type a date in the format mm/dd/yy instead of mm/dd/yyyy.

- Serious (potentially destructive) user errors. For example, issue the Quit command without first saving your work.

Finding the problem

To find flaws in a system's error-handling interface, work through your evaluation tasks using Explanation Interface Checklist #1: Error-Handling. (See Resource F for a reproducible copy of the checklist.) Every item checked "no" indicates an interface flaw. To correct these flaws, follow the instructions in the next section, "Solving the problem."

Explanation Interface Checklist #1: Error-Handling

#	Review Checklist	yes	no	n/a	Examples
1.	Does the system prevent users from making errors whenever possible?	☐	☐	☐	If you attempt to close a file without saving your work, the system prompts "Do you want to save this document?"
2.	Does the system warn users if they are about to make a potentially serious error?	☐	☐	☐	Initializing the disk will destroy all data on your hard drive. Do you really want to do this? (Y,N)
3.	Can users easily reverse their actions?	☐	☐	☐	After accidentally deleting a paragraph you meant to copy, you can type undo and the paragraph will reappear.
4.	If the system allows users to reverse their actions, is there a retracing mechanism to allow for multiple undos?	☐	☐	☐	Typing undo reverses your last command. Typing undo again reverses the command you placed before that.
5.	If an error is detected in a data entry field, does the system place the cursor in that field or highlight the error?	☐	☐	☐	
6.	Do error messages inform the user of the error's severity?	☐	☐	☐	*Poor:* Bad boot block. *Better:* WARNING: Bad boot block found. Back up all important files to prevent data from being lost.
✳ 7.	Do error messages suggest the cause of the problem?	☐	☐	☐	*Poor:* Unable to recalculate worksheet. *Better:* Unable to recalculate worksheet: there is an invalid formula in cell C3.
8.	Do error messages provide appropriate semantic information?	☐	☐	☐	*Poor:* Invalid entry. *Better:* Day-of-week codes are 1 (Monday) through 7 (Sunday).
✳ 9.	Do error messages provide appropriate syntactic information?	☐	☐	☐	*Poor:* Illegal command. *Better:* File names cannot contain punctuation (% ! *).

#	Review Checklist	yes	no	n/a	Examples
❋ 10.	Do error messages indicate what action the user needs to take to correct the error?	☐	☐	☐	*Poor:* Memory management error. *Better:* Out of memory. Exit from all open applications and restart your computer.
11.	If the system supports both novice and expert users, are multiple levels of error-message detail available?	☐	☐	☐	*Novice message:* Cannot delete a locked file. Type "unlock ⟨filename⟩" and try again. *Expert message:* File locked.

Solving the problem

Every "no" on the checklist indicates an interface flaw that can interfere with performance.

- Ideally, you will be in a position to recommend an interface redesign to correct each flaw. Use checklist examples, where provided, as design guidelines. The answer to the item will then become either "yes" (because the feature was enhanced) or "n/a" (because the structure of the interface was changed to eliminate the feature).

- However, interface redesign is not always an option. In this case, you may be able to improve performance with an alternative strategy such as a job aid. Any checklist item marked with an asterisk (*) is a candidate for one of these alternative strategies.

Interface redesign recommendations. If your analysis has uncovered flaws in the error-handling interface, use design principles 1 to 11 to guide you toward specific design revisions. For example:

- Rewrite error messages that do not provide the appropriate semantic (content) information.

- Rewrite error messages that do not provide the appropriate syntactic (structure) information.

- Expand error messages to include information on the severity of the error or to offer possible solutions to the problem.

Alternative solutions (for items marked with *). Consider these alternatives if interface redesign is not possible.

#	IF the interface flaw is . . .	THEN recommend . . .
7, 10	Error messages do not suggest the cause of the error or what action the user needs to take to recover from the error.	A printed troubleshooting reference in the form of an alphabetized table of each error message, describing • Why the message may have appeared • How serious the error is • How to correct the error
9	Error messages do not provide appropriate syntactic information.	A printed set of syntax rules. For example:

Data Entry Rules
Date format is always mm/dd/yyyy. **Type this:**   03/27/1994 **Not this:**   3/27/1994
File names must be 8 characters or less. **Type this:**   94budget **Not this:**   1994annualbudget
Titles are not punctuated. **Type this:**   Dr **Not this:**   Dr.

Evaluating Performance Support

The purpose of this procedure

Performance support is a relatively new concept defined and described by Gery in *Electronic Performance Support Systems* (1991). The goal of an electronic performance support system (EPSS) is to provide the information necessary to generate performance and learning at the time this information is needed by performers. For example:

IF the question or need is . . .	THEN the response of an EPSS is . . .
Why do this?	Explanation
	Example and consequences
What is it?	Definitions
	Illustrations
	Descriptions
How do I do it?	Procedure
	Interactive advisors
	Structured paths
	Demonstration
How or why did this happen?	Explanation
	Example or demonstration
Where am I?	Monitoring systems
	Navigation systems
	Views of context ("You are here . . .")
What next?	Directions, prompts, coaching
	Lists of options or paths

Applying this concept to user interface design, the explanation interface supplies performance support to users when

- Users can initiate requests for additional information as they perform a task.
- Users are not required to memorize lengthy or complex commands.
- Users are protected from extensive typing or retyping.
- Users can customize the system to meet their individual or organizational needs.

When to use

It is especially important to evaluate and recommend redesign of performance support when

- Items in Part 6 of the User Satisfaction Surveys are rated low.

- During interviews or think-aloud observation, users say things like "I sure get tired of typing today's date three hundred times a day" or "Okay, I finished entering data—where do I go from here?" or "Do I have to enter the customer's home phone number?"

Terms you may not know

Default A value that is assigned automatically by the system and that remains in effect unless the user deliberately changes it.

Dependent field A field in which information must be entered (for example, Spouse Name) after a particular value is entered in another field (for example, Marital Status = married).

Dialog box A pop-up display that elicits one or more responses from a user.

```
┌─────────────────────────────────────────────────────┐
│  To Printer: "Crispin"                               │
│ ┌───────────────────────────────────────────────────┐
│ │ Copies: ☐    Pages:  ◉All  ○From:☐ To:☐          │
│ │                                                    │
│ │ Paper Source:   ◉Paper Tray    ○Manual Feed       │
│ │                                                    │
│ │ Print: ○Black & White  ○Gray Scale  ◉Color       │
│ │         ╭──────╮      ╭──────╮      ╭──────╮       │
│ │         │  OK  │      │Cancel│      │ Help │       │
│ │         ╰──────╯      ╰──────╯      ╰──────╯       │
│ └───────────────────────────────────────────────────┘
└─────────────────────────────────────────────────────┘
```

Optional field A data entry field that the user may leave blank. Many database systems require entry of some information (for example, social security number) and allow users the option of entering other information (for example, middle name).

Partial input An incomplete value that is entered by the user and completed by the system. For example, users can type jan and the system will record the entry as January.

Before you start
Obtain some representative data for the system you are reviewing. From your set of evaluation tasks, select one or more to try out these interface activities:

- Customize the system (if that option is available).
- Issue several commands that cause the system to display a prompt.
- Enter information on high-use data entry screens or dialog boxes. Select at least one screen or dialog box with optional fields and one with dependent fields.
- Perform several tasks from beginning to end.
- Leave some tasks without finishing.
- Select tasks from several menus.

Finding the Problem
To discover flaws in a system's performance support interface, work through your evaluation tasks using Explanation Interface Checklist #2: Performance Support to evaluate the interface. (See Resource F for a reproducible copy of the checklist.) Every item that is checked "no" indicates an interface flaw. To correct these flaws, follow the instructions in the next section, "Solving the problem."

Explanation Interface Checklist #2: Performance Support

#	Review Checklist	yes	no	n/a	Examples
1.	Does the system intelligently interpret variations in user commands?	☐	☐	☐	You enter exut. System replies "No such command exists. Do you mean exit? (Y,N)"
2.	Do data entry screens and dialog boxes indicate the number of character spaces available in a field?	☐	☐	☐	Last Name: _ _ _ _ Date: _ _ / _ _ / _ _
❋ 3.	Do data entry screens and dialog boxes indicate when fields are optional?	☐	☐	☐	Salary (opt.): _ _ _ _
4.	Does the system complete unambiguous partial input on a data entry field?	☐	☐	☐	*You enter:* Month: A *System supplies:* Month: APRIL
❋ 5.	Are there pop-up or pull-down menus within data entry fields that have many, but well-defined, entry options?	☐	☐	☐	When you enter the Country field, the system displays a list of all country codes. You click on the country code you need.
6.	On data entry screens and dialog boxes, are dependent fields displayed only when necessary?	☐	☐	☐	The Medicare # field is only displayed if a number greater than or equal to 65 is entered in the Age field.
7.	Do fields in data entry screens and dialog boxes contain default values whenever appropriate?	☐	☐	☐	In the Print dialog box, the number of copies is preset to 1 and the page range is preset to All, since these are the most likely user choices. These defaults can be changed if necessary.
8.	Can users set their own system, session, file, and screen defaults?	☐	☐	☐	You can set up your system to automatically load your word processing and spreadsheet programs whenever you turn the system on.
9.	Are data entry screens and dialog boxes supported by navigation and completion instructions?	☐	☐	☐	Guest Account Last Name: Fink-Nottle First Name: Augustus Last Payment: $ 54.67 Balance Due: $125.47 Today's Date: --/--/-- Payment: $----.-- F1 to send, ESC to cancel

Explanation Interface Checklist #2 (Continued)

#	Review Checklist	yes	no	n/a	Examples
10.	If menu items are ambiguous, does the system provide additional explanatory information when an item is selected?	☐	☐	☐	FastWrite Tutorial 1...Lesson 1 2...Lesson 2 3...Lesson 3 Lesson 2 teaches you how to format the letter you wrote in Lesson 1
* 11.	Are there memory aids for commands, either through on-line quick reference or prompting?	☐	☐	☐	Enter new file name (nnnnnnnn.nnn):
12.	Does the system correctly anticipate and prompt for the user's probable next activity?	☐	☐	☐	After you open a checking account for a customer, the system asks "Do you want to place an order for checks? (Y,N)" Selecting "Y" automatically displays the Check Order screen.

Solving the problem

Every "no" on the checklist indicates an interface flaw that can interfere with performance.

- Ideally, you will be in a position to recommend an interface redesign to correct each flaw. Use checklist examples, where provided, as design guidelines. The answer to the item will then become either "yes" (because the feature was enhanced) or "n/a" (because the structure of the interface was changed to eliminate the feature).
- However, interface redesign is not always an option. In this case, you may be able to improve performance with an alternative strategy such as a job aid. Any checklist item marked with an asterisk (*) is a candidate for one of these alternative strategies.

Interface redesign recommendations. If your analysis has uncovered flaws in the performance support interface, use design principles 1 to 12 to guide you toward specific design revisions. For example, if the system does not currently supply memory aids for commands, the following are two design alternatives:

- Embed the memory aid in the prompt. For example, the dialog box field Year of birth could contain the characters YYYY in the field.
- Allow users to request further help. For example, typing ? in a data entry field will display a list of valid codes or syntactic rules.

Alternative solutions (for items marked with *). Consider these alternatives if interface redesign is not possible.

#	IF the interface flaw is . . .	THEN recommend . . .
3	No indication of optional data entry fields	For each screen in the system, a printed list of each field indicating if it is required or optional
5	No pop-up or pull-down menus within data entry fields that have many entry options	For each screen in the system, a printed list of field names and their associated data input codes, or an alphabetized list of high-use data entry fields and their valid data entry codes
11	No on-line memory aids for the syntax of commands	A printed list of systemwide syntax rules

Command Hints	
Hint	**Example**
* is a wildcard	`copy a:*.* b:`
File names are 8 characters or less	`myreport`
Leave one space between commands	`save myfile a:`

Procedure 6.3 — *Evaluating On-Line Help*

The purpose of this procedure

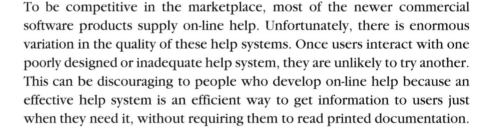

In the beginning, documentation was written by programmers, and it could only be understood by other programmers.

And lo, the software companies said, "We shall hire Technical Writers to create User Guides that can be understood by all users." And so they did. And it was good.

But behold, users did not open the documents because they weighed well–nigh unto 100 pounds. And the users did grumble, because they resisted the idea of reading a 700-page book just to learn how to recalculate a spreadsheet.

And lo, the software companies said, "We shall hire Instructional Designers to put our documentation on-line so users shalt not risk hernias." And so they did. And it was good.

But behold, the users did not use the on-line documents, because they resisted the idea of reading 700 help screens just to learn how to recalculate a spreadsheet.

And lo, the software companies said, "We shall hire Performance Technologists to build interactive on-line systems so the users can get the kind of help they need, just when they need it." And so they did. And it was good.

But behold, ugly rumors do abound that users are not using the on-line help. And the software companies doth scratch their heads. And darkness hath spread across the land…

To be competitive in the marketplace, most of the newer commercial software products supply on-line help. Unfortunately, there is enormous variation in the quality of these help systems. Once users interact with one poorly designed or inadequate help system, they are unlikely to try another. This can be discouraging to people who develop on-line help because an effective help system is an efficient way to get information to users just when they need it, without requiring them to read printed documentation.

When to use this procedure

It is especially important to evaluate and recommend redesign of on-line help when:

- Items in Part 6 of the User Satisfaction Survey are rated low.

- During interviews or think-aloud observation, users say things like "I only tried the help system once . . . never again!" or "I'm afraid that if I ask for help, I'll lose all my work" or "Help system? What help system?"

Terms you may not know

Context sensitivity The changeability of the content (and sometimes the structure) of the on-line help. Context sensitivity depends on what the user is doing when help is requested.

Example: If a user is in a data entry field, pressing the (HELP) key displays instructions on what to type in the field. If a user is viewing a menu, pressing the (HELP) key displays information on each menu choice.

Before you start

Talk to a knowledgeable user or programmer to discover the kinds of on-line references available on the system, if any. For each kind of on-line help, do the following:

- Display several help screens and evaluate the quality of their content and structure.

- Attempt to switch between several system tasks and on-line help.

- Try accessing on-line help while you are in the middle of a system task.

- Move from one part of the on-line help system to another.

Finding the problem

To discover flaws in a system's on-line help interface, work through your evaluation tasks using Explanation Interface Checklist #3: On-Line Help to evaluate the interface. (See Resource F for a reproducible copy of the checklist.) Every item that is checked "no" indicates an interface flaw. To correct these flaws, follow the instructions in the next section, "Solving the problem."

Explanation Interface Checklist #3: On-Line Help

#	Review Checklist	yes	no	n/a	Examples
1.	Is the help function visible; for example, a key labeled HELP or a special menu?	☐	☐	☐	Each dialog box contains a (HELP) button. The (F1) key on the keyboard is clearly labeled HELP.
2.	Is the help system interface (navigation, presentation, and conversation) consistent with the navigation, presentation, and conversation interfaces of the application it supports?	☐	☐	☐	If the application uses menus for navigation, the help system should use menus as well. If the (Enter) key is used to select a menu choice in the application, the help system should not use the (Return) key.
3.	Navigation: Is information easy to find?	☐	☐	☐	Pressing the (HELP) key on the keyboard displays an index of system commands, sorted alphabetically.
4.	Presentation: Is the visual layout well designed?	☐	☐	☐	Help screens use white space to break up large blocks of text and bold type to emphasize major topics.
5.	Conversation: Is the information accurate, complete, and understandable?	☐	☐	☐	Each error message box contains a (HELP) button. Clicking on this button displays a help screen that describes what caused the error and how to recover from it.
6.	Is the information relevant? • Goal-oriented (What can I do with this program?) • Descriptive (What is this thing for?) • Procedural (How do I do this task?) • Interpretive (Why did that happen?) • Navigational (Where am I?)	☐	☐	☐	*Poor:* The copy command is used to copy data. *Better:* Purpose: Use the copy command to copy the numbers in one set of cells to another set of cells. Syntax: copy ⟨range⟩ to ⟨range⟩ Example: copy A1C15 to C3F18

#	Review Checklist	yes	no	n/a	Examples
7.	Is there context-sensitive help?	☐	☐	☐	In a computer-based training (CBT) program, typing ? at any question displays a hint to guide the learner toward the correct answer.
8.	Can the user change the level of detail available?	☐	☐	☐	Highlighting a menu choice and pressing the (HELP) key displays a brief explanatory sentence. Pressing the (HELP) key again provides more detail about the menu choice.
✳ 9.	Can users easily switch between help and their work?	☐	☐	☐	The help screen is displayed in a pop-up window, allowing users to view their work at the same time.
✳ 10.	Is it easy to access and return from the help system?	☐	☐	☐	Pressing (F1) displays the help screen. On the bottom of this screen is the message "Press ESC to return to your work."
✳ 11.	Can users resume work where they left off after accessing help?	☐	☐	☐	

Solving the problem   Every "no" on the checklist indicates an interface flaw that can interfere with performance.

- Ideally, you will be in a position to recommend an interface redesign to correct each flaw. Use checklist examples, where provided, as design guidelines. The answer to the item will then become either "yes" (because the feature was enhanced) or "n/a" (because the structure of the interface was changed to eliminate the feature).

- However, interface redesign is not always an option. In this case, you may be able to improve performance with an alternative strategy such as a job aid. Any checklist item marked with an asterisk (*) is a candidate for one of these alternative strategies.

Interface redesign recommendations. If your analysis has uncovered flaws in the on-line help interface, use design principles 1 to 11 to guide you toward specific design revisions. For example:

- Rewrite on-line help messages that do not state information in user (task-oriented) terms.

- Modify the layout of help screens, using white space, bold type, and other attention-getting devices to make them more readable.

- Add messages to help screens that explain how to get back to the application.

Alternative solutions (for items marked with ∗). Consider these alternatives if interface redesign is not possible.

#	IF the interface flaw is . . .	THEN recommend . . .
1	The help function is available but not visible.	A keyboard template that indicates the key, or keystroke sequence, required to access the help function
9–11	Switching between on-line help and the application is a complex task.	Printed instructions on how to access on-line help and how to get back into one's work; if additional user actions are required (for example, saving work before accessing on-line help), these should be included

## CHAPTER 7

Ensuring Successful Implementation of Solutions

Introduction

What is the purpose of this chapter?

This chapter is about following up. It is about the work you need to do after you have discovered interface flaws and designed preliminary solutions to fix these flaws. Following up ensures that the solutions you design are communicated to the people who must implement them and that these solutions are effective in improving the performance problems of users.

How is this chapter organized?

This chapter addresses the two procedures necessary to follow up after a user interface review.

Procedure	Results	See page . . .
Document your interface design recommendations.	By performing this procedure, you will be able to communicate your findings to the person who has the authority to modify the user interface.	186
Evaluate the impact of interface redesign.	By performing this procedure, you will ensure that your interventions had a positive impact on user performance.	189

For more information

Brinkley, R. C. "Getting the Most from Client Interviews." *Performance & Instruction,* 1989, *28*(4), 5–8.
Describes types of interview questions, methods for posing questions, and techniques for framing questions.

Burley-Allen, M. *Listening: The Forgotten Skill.* New York: Wiley, 1982.
Chapter Six contains a list of problems that can occur during an interview accompanied by an excellent set of sample questions to solve each one.

Freedman, D. P., and Weisberg, G. M. *Handbook of Walkthroughs, Inspections, and Technical Reviews: Evaluating Programs, Projects, and Products.* New York: Dorset House, 1990.
Describes methods for evaluating the effectiveness of programs, projects, and products.

Gause, D. C., and Weinberg, G. M. *Exploring Requirements: Quality Before Design.* New York: Dorset House, 1989.
Part V, "Greatly Improving the Odds of Success," describes methods for measuring user satisfaction and developing test cases. Chapter Twenty-Four, "Making Agreements," discusses implementation strategies.

McConnell, V. C., and Koch, K. W. *Computerizing the Corporation: The Intimate Link Between People and Machines*. New York: Van Nostrand Reinhold, 1990.

Chapters Five and Six describe the technology implementation life cycle, an eight-phase planning method designed to maximize the effectiveness of system implementations.

Shneiderman, B. *Designing the User Interface: Strategies for Effective Human-Computer Interaction*. Reading, Mass.: Addison-Wesley, 1992.

The User Satisfaction Survey described in this book was adapted from Shneiderman's QUIS user-evaluation questionnaire (pp. 485–492). For information on the development and refinement of this instrument, see also Chin, J. P., Diehl, V. A., and Norman, K. L., "Development of an Instrument Measuring User Satisfaction of the Human-Computer Interface."

van Steenis, H. *How to Plan, Develop, and Use Information Systems: A Guide to Human Qualities and Productivity*. New York: Dorset House, 1990.

Part IV, "Organizing and Managing for Quality," discusses organizational characteristics that allow system implementations to be successful.

Weinberg, G. M. *Rethinking Systems Analysis & Design*. New York: Dorset House, 1988.

Although this book is targeted to programmers, it is also helpful for anyone involved in systems design. Part IV describes specific behaviors to avoid when interviewing users.

Procedure 7.1   How to Document Interface Design Recommendations

The purpose of this procedure

If you have employed the procedures in Chapters Three through Six, chances are you have discovered a number of flaws in the system's presentation, conversation, navigation, and explanation interfaces. If you are a programmer, your task at this point is clear: Start coding! However, you are probably not a programmer . . . and therefore you are not in a position to make changes to a system directly. To change the parts of the system that are causing problems for users, you must communicate your redesign recommendations to the people who are responsible for developing and maintaining the system.

When to use this procedure

While most of the procedures in this book are meant to be selected only as needed, documenting your interface design recommendations must be performed immediately after carrying out the procedures in Chapters Three to Six.

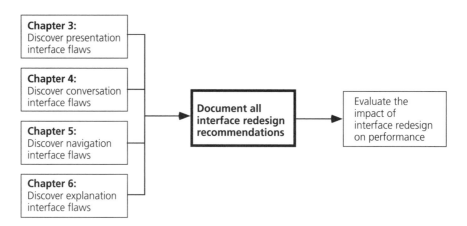

Terms you may not know

MIS Acronym for management information systems.

MIS group The organization that has primary responsibility for data processing within a company. In many companies, this group is responsible for developing and maintaining internal systems.

Before you start

Pull together all the checklists you filled out during your interface review. If you reviewed every aspect of the interface, you will have twenty checklists. However, you are more likely to have a smaller number, since your front-end data gathering probably pointed you to a subset of the interface that was causing most user problems.

**Documenting your
interface design
recommendations**

1. Read through each checklist and pull out each item that was
checked "no" during your interface review. For example:

Merged Checklist Items	y	n	n/a
1. Does the system perform data translations for users?	☐	☑	☐
2. Are input data codes meaningful?	☐	☑	☐
3. Are input data codes distinctive?	☐	☑	☐
4. In multipage data entry screens, is each page labeled to show its relation to others?	☐	☑	☐
5. Are menu titles parallel grammatically?	☐	☑	☐
6. Is the first word of each menu item the most important?	☐	☑	☐
7. Are menu items named consistently, within each menu and across the system?	☐	☑	☐
8. Are menu titles brief, yet long enough to communicate?	☐	☑	☐

2. For each item, describe the specific interface flaw that led to the
"no" rating. For example:

#	Flaw	Example
1	Does the system perform data translations for users?	On the "Accident Description" screen, users must enter the accident date in military time. For example, 1:30 P.M. is entered as 13:30. These users are unfamiliar with military time.
2	Are input data codes meaningful?	The "Policy Setup" screen uses many identical numeric codes. For example, in the "marital status" field, 0 = single and 1 = married. In the "policy status" field, 0 = new policy and 1 = policy renewal.

3. Read through your list from Step 2, and look for commonalities among the checklist items. Combine items that could potentially be solved together by a single interface redesign. For example:

   - Items 2 and 3 deal with data codes.
   - Items 5 and 8 deal with menu titles.
   - Items 6 and 7 deal with menu item names.

4. List your recommendations for improving each interface flaw. Include alternative recommendations where possible. For example:

#	Flaw	Alternatives
1	Does the system perform data translations for users?	*Alternative 1:* Allow users to enter time on a 12-hour clock and have the system translate their entry to a 24-hour clock.
		Alternative 2: Design on-line performance support for all "time" fields. When user presses a "help me" key, the system displays a translation table that looks something like this: 1 = 13 2 = 14 3 = 15, and so on.
		Alternative 3: Same as design alternative 2, but print the translation table on a small card that users can tape to their computers.

5. Summarize your findings and conclusions in a memo to the person responsible for approving system design changes. The way you frame this memo depends on who is receiving it. The case study in Chapter Eight shows a sample memo that could be sent to a manager in an internal management information systems (MIS) department.

The purpose of this procedure

The goal of this book is to make things better: to improve the performance of people who use computers by redesigning the user interface so that it is easy to learn and easy to use. Thus, if you have used the procedures in this book to find and fix flaws in the user interface, it is reasonable to expect that performance will improve, that people will have more effective interactions with computers. But how can you be sure? This procedure describes five strategies for evaluating the impact of your interface redesign on performance by examining the following:

- Learning time
- Proficiency
- Productivity
- Quality
- User satisfaction

When to use this procedure

These strategies are performed after interface redesigns and alternative strategies have been implemented. Realize, however, that picking an "ideal" time for evaluating the impact of these interventions is tricky because it is unlikely that everything will be implemented at the same time. Making the situation even more complicated, some of your recommendations may never be implemented because of time and cost constraints. Others may be implemented immediately but not evaluated until users are trained on the changes.

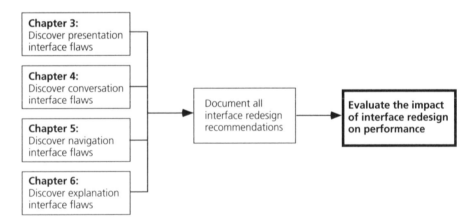

Terms you may not know

Productivity A measure of the amount of output that can be produced in a given period of time.

Proficiency A measure of the number of system functions being used by a representative sample of the user population.

Quality A measure of the degree to which output meets or exceeds an established standard.

Before you start

The following strategies are offered based on the assumption that, before the interface was redesigned, you had already gathered baseline data on proficiency, productivity, and quality, as well as on learning time and user satisfaction. If you were not able to gather these data, you can still use these strategies to describe "what is," but you will not be able to demonstrate that there has been an improvement.

Evaluating the impact of interface redesign

Evaluating the impact of any performance intervention can be a complex activity. The strategies that follow are offered as guidelines only; it is beyond the scope of this book to deal at a detailed level with implementation and evaluation methods. Such information can be found in any number of excellent books and articles. (See page 184 for a list of references.)

Strategy 1: Look at impact on learning time. Improving the user interface should decrease the amount of time it takes new users to learn a system. If there is an in-house course on the system, interview instructors to determine if training is taking less time, if instructors are able to cover more material in class, and if learners seem to be grasping the course material more quickly. If users are essentially self-taught or learn through on-the-job training, interview users or their managers to see if they perceive that the learning curve has been shortened.

For example, before interface redesign, the inventory management system course was five days long and covered only the basic system functions. Users were expected to learn advanced system features independently by reading the user guide. After interface redesign, course instructors reported that students were able to master the basic system functions in four days. They now give students a choice: leave after four days or remain in class one more day to learn advanced features.

Strategy 2: Look at impact on proficiency. Improving the user interface should allow more people to use more system functions. Some systems can automate the process of gathering these data by tracking the amount of time users spend on individual applications or how often users select specific functions from menus. You can also interview a representative sample of users to see if they perceive that the number of system functions they use has increased.

For example, before interface redesign, very few people used the mail-merge component of the company's in-house word processing system because it was too complicated to learn. Instead, they created each return address individually and used a typewriter to type addresses on envelopes. After the mail-merge interface was redesigned, the number of people who used this feature increased dramatically.

Strategy 3: Look at impact on productivity. Improving the user interface should allow users to accomplish their work more efficiently. Productivity can be measured in several ways, including the following:

- Rate *(for example, the number of customer orders processed per hour)*

- Timeliness *(for example, the percentage of orders that customers receive by the date promised)*

- Volume *(for example, the total number of proposals written)*

Such measurements require that either you or the users be willing to collect these data over a period of time. Productivity measurement is probably not useful unless baseline productivity data already exist. However, for a large system with many users, measuring improvements in rate, timeliness, and volume are excellent ways to cost-justify redesigning the user interface.

For example, before interface redesign, it took a data entry clerk three hours to enter a new loan application on the system. Applications were severely backlogged, and the manager frequently had to bring in temporary employees to help her group catch up. As part of the redesign of the interface, data entry screen layout was improved and input data codes were changed to make them easier to enter. When the processing rate was measured again, the time had been reduced by 50 percent to 1.5 hours.

Strategy 4: Look at impact on quality. Improving the user interface should decrease the number and severity of errors. Some systems can automate the process of error tracking by counting keystrokes, system edits, or error states. Another way to measure quality improvements is to track the amount of time spent on rework. Finally, users can simply be interviewed to see if they believe they are producing more accurate work.

For example, before interface redesign, data entry errors were a serious problem for the billing department. Many errors were not discovered until the day after they were made, when an overnight error report was generated. Error-correction procedures required clerks to search the system for each error on the report and to retype the correct information. The retyping process often introduced new errors. As part of the redesign of the interface, the system's error-handling function was completely revamped to include edits for all data entry fields so that clerks would be alerted to mistakes as they were doing the work. Although initially this was a costly investment, the costs were offset within six months by the total elimination of rework time.

Strategy 5: Look at impact on user satisfaction. Improving the user interface should make users feel comfortable with and supported by the system. The same User Satisfaction Survey that you use to gather initial data from users before reviewing the interface (see Chapter Two) can help you determine if your interface redesign makes a difference in the way users perceive the system. You can also interview again some of the users you spoke to before conducting the interface review.

For example, initial survey and interview data revealed that novice users were confused by the system's crowded data entry screens and that experienced users were frustrated by the system's inability to let them use shortcuts to bypass menus they did not need. When the User Satisfaction Survey was administered three months after interface redesign, users rated both these items as satisfactory.

SECTION THREE

TECHNIQUES IN ACTION

Overview

What is this section about?

In Section Two of this book you found twenty-six individual procedures to help you identify and design solutions to flaws in the user interface. The goal of Section Three is to synthesize these procedures, showing how they work together in a real-world setting. To accomplish this goal, this section presents a case study that shows a practitioner solving a performance problem that was caused by a flawed user interface. By improving the interactions between the users and the system, performance was measurably improved.

How should this section be read?

The performance problem and the system itself are fictitious; they are a conglomerate of many common situations. As a result, do not be surprised if the case study does not match your own business problem exactly. Instead, as you read through the case study ask yourself the following questions:

- Which aspects of this performance problem have I seen, or am I likely to see, in my work?

- How did the practitioner in this case apply the procedures? Can I use similar procedures in my setting?

- How did the practitioner in this case solve the performance problem? Would I have solved the problem in the same way? If not, what other designs can I see myself developing?

- What were the benefits achieved by the solution? Would my organization accept these as indicators of success? If not, what would I have to do to demonstrate measurable benefits?

How is this section organized?

## CHAPTER 8

When Training Stops Working: Case Study of First Atlantic Bank

The Performance Problem

The setting

First Atlantic Bank (FAB) is a medium-size financial institution with fifty branches located on the East coast. The company's headquarters are in Baltimore. Many of the branches service major cities (Boston, New York, Atlanta) and employ an average of fifteen to twenty tellers each.

The performers

Most of the tellers are young and have little prior work experience. The teller line is the entry-level position for most new bank hires, and turnover is high. Tellers have always been required to operate two automated systems.

- TTM (Teller Transaction Manager) manages all the basic teller transactions. TTM tasks include cashing checks, entering deposits, and issuing money orders. Tellers spend approximately 65 percent of their time using the TTM system.

- CAM (Client Account Manager) manages customer accounts. CAM tasks include opening a new account for an existing customer, setting up a joint trust, and selling certificates of deposit. Tellers spend approximately 35 percent of their time using the CAM system.

The system

In response to increased competition in the banking industry, the bank's management information systems department switched last year from CAM to a more powerful system: the Customer Account Sales Helper (CASH). CASH is designed to streamline the account management process, enabling tellers to sell more bank services. CASH was purchased from an outside vendor, but is being maintained in-house.

The practitioner

Mort Gage works in the bank's training department. He is based in the home office in Baltimore. One of the training department's responsibilities is to develop and deliver training for new-hire tellers. Tellers are required to attend this three-week course before they can start on the teller line. The course is delivered five times a year at regional sites in Boston, New York, Baltimore, and Atlanta. The course is divided into two sections:

- During weeks 1 and 2, new hires learn how to use TTM to manage basic teller transactions.

- During week 3, new hires learn how to use CASH to manage customer accounts and sell bank services.

Mort was the manager in charge of CAM training development and delivery for four years. When the bank switched over to the CASH system, he was responsible for managing the modification of CAM training materials. For example, he saw to it that overhead transparencies of CAM data entry screens were replaced with shots of CASH screens, that the user guide was revised to incorporate new CASH functions, and that hands-on practice sessions were modified to emphasize critical CASH procedures. However, he retained the basic design of the course.

The problem

Mort has been receiving a lot of complaints recently from FAB branch managers that the quality of the teller training program has deteriorated. Since Mort knows that neither the basic course design nor the instructors have changed, he interviews the branch managers and learns that tellers are coming back from their three-week training course with a limited understanding of how to use the CASH system. To compensate for this problem, managers say they must supplement the formal training with an extra week of on-the-job CASH training. This consumes branch resources because the head teller must spend additional time working with the new hires.

Every branch manager Mort interviews insists that the course be increased to four weeks, to give tellers more practice on CASH before they begin work at the branch. But Mort's boss says no way. The department is currently running five courses a year in each location; a total of 300 instructor-days a year. Adding an additional week to each course would increase this to 400 instructor-days. There is a hiring freeze in effect, and there simply aren't enough instructors available to cover the additional 100 days. Because this performance problem has only appeared since the CAM system was replaced by the CASH system, Mort decides he'd better find out more about CASH.

The Response

Step 1: Gather data from users

1. Mort explains to the branch managers that he is committed to solving this performance problem and would like an opportunity to learn more about the specific problems tellers are having with the CASH system. He gets their permission to administer the User Satisfaction Survey in all fifty branches. He receives a 75 percent response rate, and summarizes the survey data (see Exhibit 8.1).

2. Mort selects fifteen tellers in the Baltimore area to interview. Five have just been through CASH training, five have worked on the teller line for at least three months, and five are head tellers. He designs his interview questions to focus especially on parts of the CASH interface which, based on survey data, seem to be causing problems for users.

3. From the group of fifteen interviewees, Mort selects three tellers to observe using the system. He selects tellers who have just completed CASH training because these are the users that currently need additional on-the-job training.

Step 2: Select evaluation tasks

1. Mort arranges to meet with Blanche Carte, the management information systems manager in charge of the CASH system, to learn more about how CASH works. Blanche lends him copies of the functional requirements that the outside vendor developed; this document, although not designed to be an instruction guide for users, gives Mort a good picture of the major system functions. During this meeting, Mort also obtains Blanche's permission to gain access to a test version of the system so he can conduct the CASH interface review.

2. Mort uses what he has learned from his conversation with Blanche and the functional requirements to come up with a "first cut" set of CASH system tasks.

3. From the group of fifteen interviewees he met when he gathered user data, Mort selects three head tellers to help him identify which of these tasks are

   • Core (crucial to CASH operation)

   • Frequent (performed by most tellers, most of the time)

   • High risk (prone to serious consequences)

4. Mort documents these core, frequent, and high-risk tasks as the evaluation tasks he will use as he reviews the CASH interface.

Step 3: Conduct the interface review

Based on data gathered from users, Mort targets his interface review to the six areas that seem to be causing the most problems for users. These are the following:

Interface component	Specific problem area	For details, see page . . .
Presentation	1. Data entry screen display	75
Conversation	2. Menu language	108
	3. Data input	124
Navigation	4. Navigating via menus	134
	5. Navigating between screens	147
Explanation	6. Error-handling	168

To review each potential problem area, Mort obtains representative data for the CASH system and selects appropriate evaluation tasks. He works through each evaluation task, using the checklist to identify interface flaws.

To review this problem area . . .	Mort selects evaluation tasks that let him . . .	And uses this checklist . . .
1. Data entry screen display	• View a sample of the CASH screens that tellers use most frequently • Enter erroneous data	Presentation Checklist #4: Data Entry Screens (see Exhibit 8.2)
2. Menu language	• View the CASH main menu • Select options from the main menu to display a sample of lower-level menus	Conversation Checklist #3: Menus (see Exhibit 8.3)
3. Data input	• Enter alpha, numeric, and alphanumeric data • Enter data codes • Make typographical errors in data entry fields	Conversation Checklist #6: Data Input (see Exhibit 8.4)
4. Navigating via menus	• View the CASH main menu • Enter an invalid menu option • Navigate forward ("down") and backward ("up") menu levels	Navigation Checklist #1: Via Menus (see Exhibit 8.5)
5. Navigating between screens	• Display a multipage data entry screen. Complete all fields on the first screen. Go to the next screen. Repeat for all screens in the series. • Correct data entry errors while still on a screen. Correct data entry errors after leaving the screen. • Switch from one type of data entry screen to another. • Switch between data entry screens and menus.	Navigation Checklist #3: Between Screens (see Exhibit 8.6)

To review this problem area . . .	Mort selects evaluation tasks that let him . . .	And uses this checklist . . .
6. Error-handling	• Replicate common (frequent) teller errors • Replicate serious (potentially destructive) teller errors	Explanation Checklist #1: Error-Handling (see Exhibit 8.7)

The Solution

Putting it all together

Mort reads through his completed checklists and focuses on each item that has been checked "no." For each one, he makes notes to himself on the specific interface flaw that led to the "no" rating. He looks for commonalities to see if several flaws can be solved at the same time. For example, redesigning one CASH menu can solve flaws in both the conversation and the navigation interfaces.

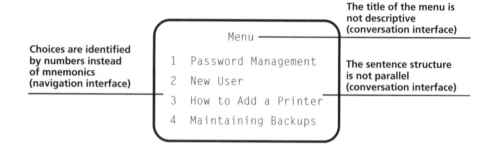

The title of the menu is not descriptive (conversation interface)

The sentence structure is not parallel (conversation interface)

Choices are identified by numbers instead of mnemonics (navigation interface)

```
              Menu

     1   Password Management

     2   New User

     3   How to Add a Printer

     4   Maintaining Backups
```

Mort's interface redesign recommendations

Mort summarizes his findings in a memo to Blanche Carte. A copy of the memo follows:

Background. At the request of the FAB branch managers, and with your approval, I conducted an interface review of the CASH system. The specific components reviewed were the following:

Presentation	Data entry screens
Conversation	Menu language Data input
Navigation	Navigating via menus Navigating between screens
Explanation	Error-handling

Recommendations. Attached please find six checklists, which show the results of the interface review. My findings and recommendations are as follows:

Presentation   No recommendations. The data entry screens meet all criteria but one for effective screen design; this is discussed under Navigation (item 4, below).

Conversation   1. The grammatical structures of menu items are not parallel.
For example, the CASH Main Menu lists all choices in the same syntax (Open Account, Close Account, and so on), while the System Administration Menu mixes syntax (Password Management, New User, How to Add a Printer). I would be happy to help you identify and resolve these inconsistencies.

2. Data entry would be easier, and errors would be reduced, if some data entry codes were modified.
For example, tellers should be able to enter "m" for "married" and "s" for "single." Currently, they must remember the codes "1" and "2" for these choices.

3. The requirement to enter the time in European format (dd/mm/yy) is causing many data entry errors. I realize the system was set up this way because it was developed in Canada. If the system could be modified to include a translation function, users could enter dates as mm/dd/yy and the system would convert the entry to dd/mm/yy. If this is not possible, the field-level error message should be modified to read "Dates must be entered as dd/mm/yy (22/6/92)."

Navigation   4. The Add New Customer function is composed of four screens. It would be easier for users to navigate between these screens if each page were titled and sequentially numbered.

5. Change the menu codes from numbers to mnemonics.
For example, the account management menu could read:

CASH MAIN MENU
O   Open a new account
U   Update an existing account
C   Close an account
Q   Quit

6. Because the CASH system is "deep" (it contains many levels of menus) rather than "broad" (containing fewer menus with more items on each), and because I have been informed by the programming staff that the database design cannot support a change to the menu structure, allow the users to enter menu mnemonics as a string on the command line.
For example, U C C *(Update, Checking, Change Account-Holder's Name) would bypass three menus and bring the user directly to a data entry screen.*

Explanation 7. When errors are detected in a data entry field, the cursor is always placed in the first field on the screen no matter which field the error is in. This increases the amount of time users need to find and correct errors because they first have to read the error message, then decide which field it applies to, and finally tab to that field. Can the system be modified to move the cursor to the field in error? If this is not possible, the field-level error message should be modified to include the field name: "STATUS: Codes are A(ctive), I(nactive), or P(ending)."

8. Some of the system error messages indicate that there is an error but do not indicate how the user can fix the error. I would be happy to work with you to identify and rewrite these messages.

Results and Benefits

Reality check: What actually got implemented

Based on Mort's memo, Blanche agreed to implement several of his recommendations the next time her department made a major upgrade to the CASH system. However, some redesigns were deemed either too costly or time-consuming to be approved by the organization. Here is what resulted from Mort's memo:

Recommendation 1. Resolve inconsistencies in menu grammar.

Blanche took Mort up on his offer to rewrite menu names. Because this could be accomplished without adding any new functions to the system, this redesign was implemented quickly, giving an immediate "new look" to the CASH system and assuring branch managers that their concerns were being heard.

Recommendation 2. Modify data entry codes.

Blanche promised that data entry codes would be modified within six months. As an interim solution, Mort designed a printed list of field names and their associated data input codes. The list is posted on each teller terminal and is explained during the teller training course.

Recommendation 3. Perform data translation for confusing date format.

Blanche said this seemingly trivial programming task would take more time and cost more money than Mort could possibly imagine. Mort is not happy, and he is continuing to pursue the matter. In the meantime, he has rewritten the error message to remind users of the correct date format (dd/mm/yy).

Recommendation 4. Title and number the screens in a multiscreen function.

Blanche promised that this would be done within the month; such a change requires little additional system functionality.

Recommendation 5. Change menu codes from numbers to mnemonics.

Blanche agreed to make this change immediately; it can be accomplished without adding new system functions.

Recommendation 6. Allow entry of menu mnemonics as a string.

Blanche said that this would be a major programming effort since the system currently has no facility for recognizing multiple command strings. She agreed to put it on her "future enhancements" list but made no promises.

Recommendation 7. Place cursor in erroneous data entry fields.

Blanche promised to make this change within twelve months. In the meantime, she agreed to modify the error messages to include the field name.

Recommendation 8. *Rewrite error messages.*

Blanche was delighted to let Mort rewrite the error messages as described in his memo. This required no additional system functionality so this redesign was implemented quickly, giving the CASH system a new "personality" and assuring branch managers that their concerns were being heard.

Benefits to the organization

Six months after Mort conducted the original interface review, all agreed-to changes were in place. Three months later, Mort followed up to determine the impact of these changes on teller performance. He administered the User Satisfaction Survey to a group that included both new and experienced users. He also interviewed the branch managers who had complained most bitterly about the quality of CASH training. The survey and interviews indicated the following:

- Branch managers were generally satisfied with the post-training skill level of tellers.

- All but three branches had eliminated on-the-job training of new tellers after their return to the branch.

- New and experienced tellers were making fewer data entry errors.

- Experienced tellers reported that they now preferred the CASH system to the old CAM system.

Exhibit 8.1. User Satisfaction Survey.

Part 1: Your experience		
How long have you worked on this system or application?	☐ Days	*40%*
	☐ Months	*35%*
	☐ Over a year	*25%*
How much time do you spend per week on this system or application?	☐ 1–5 hours	*0%*
	☐ 6–15 hours	*5%*
	☐ More than 15 hours	*95%*
How many other systems or applications have you worked with?	☐ None	*85%*
	☐ 1–3	*10%*
	☐ 4 or more	*5%*
How would you rate your general level of computer expertise?	☐ *Novice:* I'm just learning how to use computers.	*40%*
	☐ *Knowledgeable:* I can use computers to accomplish my work.	*45%*
	☐ *Expert:* I can solve problems and help others use computers.	*5%*
How would you rate your level of expertise on this system or application?	☐ *Novice:* I'm just learning how to use this system or application.	*40%*
	☐ *Knowledgeable:* I can use the system or application to do my work.	*30%*
	☐ *Expert:* I can solve problems and help others use the system or application.	*30%*
How familiar are you with the subject matter of this system or application? For example, if you are evaluating an accounting system, how much do you know about accounting practices?	☐ *Unfamiliar:* I don't really know much about the subject matter.	*40%*
	☐ *Familiar:* I am comfortable with the subject matter.	*60%*

Part 2: The big picture
What is your overall reaction to this system or application?

Question	Left label	1	2	3	4	5	6	7	8	9	Right label	NA
How easy was it to learn to use the system?	A struggle	12%	13%	19%	16%	18%	2%	5%	7%	8%	A breeze	0%
How easy is it to accomplish your work on this system?	Difficult	11%	14%	18%	14%	20%	2%	6%	7%	8%	Easy	0%
What is your typical feeling when you use the system?	Frustrated	18%	11%	14%	18%	16%	0%	8%	13%	2%	Satisfied	0%
If this system were a person, how would you characterize its "personality"?	Hostile	8%	8%	22%	17%	12%	8%	10%	6%	9%	Supportive	0%
May we interview you to learn more about your opinions of the system?	No thanks	66%	0%	0%	0%	0%	0%	0%	0%	34%	Sure	0%
May we observe you while you use the system?	No thanks	88%	0%	0%	0%	0%	0%	0%	0%	12%	Sure	0%

Part 3: Presentation
How does information appear on the screen?

Question	Left label	1	2	3	4	5	6	7	8	9	Right label	NA
What is your impression of the overall appearance of screen displays?	Unappealing	32%	5%	5%	1%	2%	3%	7%	40%	5%	Appealing	0%
Amount of information on each screen	Inadequate	28%	9%	0%	6%	5%	0%	12%	35%	5%	Adequate	0%
How information is arranged on each screen	Confusing	30%	7%	5%	1%	1%	4%	8%	39%	5%	Clear	0%
Finding the correct option on a menu	Difficult	2%	6%	2%	5%	0%	3%	2%	0%	80%	Easy	0%
Number of screens required to perform a single task	Inadequate	0%	0%	0%	15%	2%	1%	7%	1%	74%	Adequate	0%
Placement of system messages	Unpredictable	1%	1%	1%	12%	3%	0%	2%	9%	71%	Predictable	0%
Finding what you need on a screen	Difficult	52%	13%	1%	12%	2%	3%	10%	5%	2%	Easy	0%
Knowing where to enter data	Confusing	45%	13%	17%	10%	4%	2%	2%	1%	6%	Clear	0%
Use of color	Unpleasant	1%	1%	0%	13%	2%	1%	2%	11%	69%	Pleasant	0%
Tones, beeps, blinking, and so on	Annoying	2%	5%	3%	4%	1%	3%	2%	6%	74%	Helpful	0%

Exhibit 8.1. (Continued)

Question	Left anchor									Right anchor	NA
What is the general tone of system messages?	Unpleasant									Pleasant	NA
	2%	6%	2%	5%	0%	3%	2%	0%	80%		0%
Ability to control the amount of information you see in messages	Never									Always	NA
	0%	0%	0%	0%	0%	0%	0%	0%	0%		100%
Ability to "undo" an operation if you change your mind	Inadequate									Adequate	NA
	1%	1%	1%	12%	13%	1%	1%	8%	72%		0%
Explanations given in error messages	Ambiguous									Precise	NA
	51%	14%	0%	13%	2%	3%	11%	4%	2%		0%
The system tells you when you can start a new task	Rarely									Frequently	NA
	0%	2%	3%	10%	0%	1%	1%	33%	50%		0%
Speed of system operations	Sluggish									Just right	NA
	1%	7%	5%	2%	0%	2%	3%	12%	68%		0%
The system keeps you informed of what it is doing	Rarely									Frequently	NA
	2%	6%	2%	5%	0%	3%	2%	2%	78%		0%
Names of options on menus	Confusing									Helpful	NA
	52%	13%	1%	12%	2%	3%	10%	5%	2%		0%
The system warns you if you are about to take an action with serious consequences	Never									Always	NA
	1%	7%	2%	5%	0%	1%	4%	38%	52%		0%
Remembering names of commands	Difficult									Easy	NA
	50%	13%	3%	10%	4%	3%	11%	4%	2%		0%
Shortcuts for entering commands	Inadequate									Adequate	NA
	0%	0%	0%	0%	0%	0%	0%	0%	0%		100%
Commands used the same way in all parts of the system	Never									Always	NA
	0%	0%	0%	0%	0%	0%	0%	0%	0%		100%
Amount of information you have to type on data entry screens	Too much									Just right	NA
	49%	16%	1%	9%	2%	3%	13%	5%	2%		0%
Ability to save your work in the middle of a task	Inadequate									Adequate	NA
	8%	0%	2%	3%	2%	3%	2%	2%	78%		0%

Part 5: Navigation											
How easy is it for you to move around from one part of the system or application to another?											
Do you find that you get "lost" in the system?	Frequently								Rarely	NA	
	31%	6%	5%	1%	2%	3%	7%	38%	7%	0%	
Figuring out which menu contains the option you need	Puzzling								Obvious	NA	
	52%	13%	1%	12%	2%	3%	9%	6%	2%	0%	
Getting to where you want to go	Confusing								Clear	NA	
	48%	17%	7%	6%	4%	1%	10%	2%	5%	0%	
Getting back to where you were	Difficult								Easy	NA	
	42%	22%	2%	12%	2%	3%	8%	7%	2%	0%	
How the system responds to your actions	Unpredictable								Predictable	NA	
	0%	8%	7%	5%	0%	0%	0%	14%	66%	0%	
Availability of shortcuts to move around quickly	Inadequate								Adequate	NA	
	0%	0%	0%	0%	0%	0%	0%	0%	0%	100%	
Moving from one data entry field to another	Inconsistent								Consistent	NA	
	1%	1%	8%	4%	1%	3%	2%	19%	61%	0%	
Moving among multiple windows	Puzzling								Obvious	NA	
	0%	0%	0%	0%	0%	0%	0%	0%	0%	100%	
Function key assignments	Confusing								Clear	NA	
	0%	0%	0%	0%	0%	0%	0%	0%	0%	100%	
Arrangement of keys on the keyboard	Illogical								Logical	NA	
	2%	6%	2%	4%	1%	3%	2%	9%	71%	0%	

Exhibit 8.1. (Continued)

Question	Scale									NA
Does it warn you if you are about to make a serious mistake?	Never							Always		NA
	6%	2%	2%	5%	50%	3%	12%	0%	20%	0%
Does it explain how to correct your mistakes?	Never							Always		NA
	52%	13%	1%	12%	2%	3%	6%	9%	2%	0%
Can you change your mind and "undo" your last action?	Never							Always		NA
	0%	1%	9%	0%	5%	1%	1%	43%	40%	0%
Does it tell you which fields are optional on data entry screens?	Never							Always		NA
	0%	0%	0%	0%	0%	0%	0%	0%	0%	100%
Do error messages explain how to fix the problem?	Never							Always		NA
	42%	23%	3%	14%	2%	3%	8%	7%	2%	0%
How easy is it to use the on-line help facility?	Complicated							Simple		NA
	0%	0%	0%	0%	0%	0%	0%	0%	0%	100%
How helpful is the information in the on-line help facility?	Unhelpful							Helpful		NA
	0%	0%	0%	0%	0%	0%	0%	0%	0%	100%
Can you set up the system to match the way you want to work?	Never							Always		NA
	98%	2%	0%	0%	0%	0%	0%	0%	0%	0%

Part 7: Mousing around
Please rate these features only if you are using a system that has icons, windows, and uses a
mouse (for example, the Apple Macintosh or Microsoft Windows).

What is the overall appearance of the screen display?	Unattractive								Charming	NA
	0%	0%	0%	0%	0%	0%	0%	0%	0%	100%
Design of icons	Unappealing								Appealing	NA
	0%	0%	0%	0%	0%	0%	0%	0%	0%	100%
Deciding what the different icons mean	Puzzling								Easy	NA
	0%	0%	0%	0%	0%	0%	0%	0%	0%	100%
Using scroll bars	Confusing								Obvious	NA
	0%	0%	0%	0%	0%	0%	0%	0%	0%	100%
Moving between windows	Illogical								Logical	NA
	0%	0%	0%	0%	0%	0%	0%	0%	0%	100%
Rearranging, opening, and closing windows	Confusing								Clear	NA
	0%	0%	0%	0%	0%	0%	0%	0%	0%	100%
Finding, copying, deleting, moving files	Cumbersome								Easy	NA
	0%	0%	0%	0%	0%	0%	0%	0%	0%	100%
Keyboard shortcuts available	Never								Always	NA
	0%	0%	0%	0%	0%	0%	0%	0%	0%	100%
Knowing when you have selected an item on the screen	Confusing								Clear	NA
	0%	0%	0%	0%	0%	0%	0%	0%	0%	100%
Switching between the mouse and the keyboard	Distracting								Easy	NA
	0%	0%	0%	0%	0%	0%	0%	0%	0%	100%

Exhibit 8.2. Presentation Interface Checklist #4: Data Entry Screens.

# Review Checklist	yes	no	n/a
1. If users are working from hard copy, are the parts of the hard copy that go on-line marked?	☐	☐	☑
2. If users are working from hard copy, does the screen layout match the paper form?	☐	☐	☑
3. Does each data entry screen have a short, simple, clear, distinctive title?	☑	☐	☐
4. In multipage data entry screens, is each page labeled to show its relation to others?	☐	☑	☐
5. Is white space used to create symmetry and lead the eye in the appropriate direction?	☑	☐	☐
6. Have items been grouped into logical zones, and have headings been used to distinguish among zones?	☑	☐	☐
7. Are zones no more than twelve to fourteen characters wide and six to seven lines high?	☑	☐	☐
8. Have zones been separated by spaces, lines, color, letters, bold titles, ruled lines, or shaded areas?	☑	☐	☐
9. If the database includes groups of data, can users enter more than one group on a single screen?	☐	☐	☑
10. If users are experts, usage is frequent, or the system has a slow response time, are there fewer screens (more information per screen)?	☐	☐	☑
11. If users are novices, usage is infrequent, or the system has a fast response time, are there more screens (less information per screen)?	☑	☐	☐

# Review Checklist	yes	no	n/a
12. Are on-line instructions visually distinct?	☑	☐	☐
13. Do embedded field-level prompts appear to the right of the field label?	☐	☐	☑
14. Do on-line instructions appear in a consistent location across screens?	☑	☐	☐
15. Are field labels and fields distinguished typographically?	☑	☐	☐
16. Are field labels brief, familiar, and descriptive?	☑	☐	☐
17. Are field labels close to fields, but separated by at least one space?	☑	☐	☐
18. Are field labels consistent from one data entry screen to another?	☑	☐	☐
19. Are fields and labels left-justified for alpha lists, and right-justified for numeric lists?	☑	☐	☐
20. Are long columnar fields broken up into groups of five separated by a blank line?	☐	☐	☑
21. Are optional data entry fields clearly marked?	☐	☐	☑
22. Are symbols used to break long input strings into "chunks"?	☑	☐	☐
23. Do field labels appear to the left of single fields and above list fields?	☑	☐	☐
24. Do related and interdependent fields appear on the same screen?	☑	☐	☐
25. Have dots or underscores been used to indicate field length?	☑	☐	☐
26. If overtype and insert mode are both available, is there a visible indication of which one user is in?	☐	☐	☑
27. If pop-up windows are used to display error messages, do they allow the user to see the field in error?	☐	☐	☑

Exhibit 8.3. Conversation Interface Checklist #3: Menus.

# Review Checklist	yes	no	n/a
1. Do menu items fit logically into categories that have readily understood meanings?	☑	☐	☐
2. Is each lower-level menu choice associated with only one higher-level menu?	☑	☐	☐
3. Is the menu choice name on a higher-level menu used as the menu title of the lower-level menu?	☑	☐	☐
4. Do menu titles have consistent naming grammar?	☐	☑	☐
5. Are menu titles brief, yet long enough to communicate?	☐	☑	☐
6. Are menu choices logical, distinctive, and mutually exclusive?	☑	☐	☐
7. Is the first word of each menu choice the most important?	☐	☑	☐
8. Are menu choice names consistent, both within each menu and across the system, in grammatical style and terminology?	☐	☑	☐
9. Does the structure of menu choice names match their corresponding menu titles?	☑	☐	☐
10. Is the menu-naming terminology consistent with the user's task domain?	☑	☐	☐
11. If menu choices are ambiguous, does the system provide additional explanatory information when a choice is selected?	☐	☐	☑

Exhibit 8.4.   Conversation Interface Checklist #6: Data Input.

# Review Checklist	yes	no	n/a
1. For data entry screens with many fields or in which source documents can be incomplete, can users save a partially filled screen?	☐	☐	☑
2. Can users reduce data entry time by copying and modifying existing data?	☑	☐	☐
3. Does the system perform data translations for users?	☐	☑	☐
4. Are input data codes meaningful?	☐	☑	☐
5. Are input data codes distinctive?	☐	☑	☐
6. Have frequently confused data pairs been eliminated whenever possible?	☑	☐	☐
7. Have large strings of numbers or letters been broken up into chunks?	☑	☐	☐
8. Are data inputs case-blind whenever possible?	☑	☐	☐
9. Do field values avoid mixing alpha and numeric characters whenever possible?	☑	☐	☐
10. Have uncommon letter sequences been avoided whenever possible?	☑	☐	☐
11. Does the system automatically enter leading zeros?	☑	☐	☐
12. Does the system automatically enter leading or trailing spaces to align decimal points?	☑	☐	☐
13. Does the system automatically enter a dollar sign and decimal for monetary entries?	☑	☐	☐
14. Does the system automatically enter commas in numeric values greater than 9999?	☑	☐	☐
15. Are character edits allowed in data entry fields?	☑	☐	☐
16. Is the structure of a data entry value consistent from screen to screen?	☑	☐	☐
17. Are typing requirements minimal for question and answer interfaces?	☐	☐	☑

Exhibit 8.5. Navigation Interface Checklist #1: Navigating by Menus.

# Review Checklist	yes	no	n/a
1. If menu lists are short (seven items or fewer), can users select an item by moving the cursor?	☐	☐	☑
2. If menu lists are long (more than seven items), can users select an item either by moving the cursor or by typing a mnemonic code?	☐	☑	☐
3. If the system uses a pointing device, do users have the option of either clicking on menu items or using a keyboard shortcut?	☐	☐	☑
4. Are inactive menu items grayed out or omitted?	☑	☐	☐
5. Are there menu selection defaults?	☑	☐	☐
6. Are menus broad (many items on a menu) rather than deep (many menu levels)?	☐	☑	☐
7. If the system has deep (multilevel) menus, do users have the option of typing ahead?	☐	☑	☐
8. If the system uses a type-ahead strategy, do the menu items have mnemonic codes?	☐	☐	☑
9. If the system has many menu levels or complex menu levels, do users have access to an on-line spatial menu map?	☐	☐	☑
10. If the system has multiple menu levels, is there a mechanism that allows users to go back to previous menus?	☑	☐	☐
11. If users can go back to a previous menu, can they change their earlier menu choice?	☑	☐	☐
12. Do GUI menus offer affordance; that is, make obvious where selection is possible?	☐	☐	☑
13. Do GUI menus make obvious the item that has been selected?	☐	☐	☑
14. Do GUI menus make obvious whether deselection is possible?	☐	☐	☑
15. Do GUI menus offer activation: make obvious how to say "now do it"?	☐	☐	☑

Exhibit 8.6. Navigation Interface Checklist #3: Navigating Between Screens.

# Review Checklist	yes	no	n/a
1. If users must navigate between multiple screens, does the system use context labels, menu maps, and place markers as navigational aids?	☐	☑	☐
2. If the system has multipage data entry screens, do all pages have the same title?	☐	☑	☐
3. If the system has multipage data entry screens, does each page have a sequential page number?	☐	☑	☐
4. If the system has multipage data entry screens, can users move backward and forward among all the pages in the set?	☑	☐	☐
5. If the system uses a question and answer interface, can users go back to previous questions or skip forward to later questions?	☐	☐	☑
6. Does the system offer "find next" and "find previous" shortcuts for database searches?	☑	☐	☐

Exhibit 8.7. Explanation Interface Checklist #1: Error Handling.

# Review Checklist	yes	no	n/a
1. Does the system prevent users from making errors whenever possible?	☑	☐	☐
2. Does the system warn users if they are about to make a potentially serious error?	☑	☐	☐
3. Can users easily reverse their actions?	☑	☐	☐
4. If the system allows users to reverse their actions, is there a retracing mechanism to allow for multiple undos?	☐	☐	☑
5. If an error is detected in a data entry field, does the system place the cursor in that field and highlight the error?	☐	☑	☐
6. Do error messages inform the user of the error's severity?	☐	☑	☐
7. Do error messages suggest the cause of the problem?	☐	☑	☐
8. Do error messages provide appropriate semantic information?	☐	☑	☐
9. Do error messages provide appropriate syntactic information?	☐	☑	☐
10. Do error messages indicate what action the user needs to take to correct the error?	☐	☑	☐
11. If the system supports both novice and expert users, are multiple levels of error-message detail available?	☐	☐	☑

SECTION FOUR

RESOURCES

Overview

What is this section about?

Resources A through F contain blank surveys and checklists for the procedures in Section Two. Resource G is a glossary of all the special terms and acronyms that appear in the book.

How is this section organized?

Resource A: User Satisfaction Survey

Name: _____ System/application: _____

Part 1: Your experience	
How long have you worked on this system or application?	☐ Months ☐ Days ☐ Over a year
How much time do you spend per week on this system or application?	☐ 1–5 hours ☐ 6–15 hours ☐ More than 15 hours
How many other systems or applications have you worked with?	☐ None ☐ 1–3 ☐ 4 or more
How would you rate your general level of computer expertise?	☐ *Novice:* I'm just learning how to use computers. ☐ *Knowledgeable:* I can use computers to accomplish my work. ☐ *Expert:* I can solve problems and help others use computers.
How would you rate your level of expertise on this system or application?	☐ *Novice:* I'm just learning how to use this system or application. ☐ *Knowledgeable:* I can use the system or application to do my work. ☐ *Expert:* I can solve problems and help others use the system or application.
How familiar are you with the subject matter of this system or application? For example, if you are evaluating an accounting system, how much do you know about accounting practices?	☐ *Unfamiliar:* I don't really know much about the subject matter. ☐ *Familiar:* I am comfortable with the subject matter.

Resource A (Continued)

Part 2: The big picture
What is your overall reaction to this system or application?

How easy was it to learn to use the system?	A struggle A breeze 1 2 3 4 5 6 7 8 9	NA
How easy is it to accomplish your work on this system?	Difficult Easy 1 2 3 4 5 6 7 8 9	NA
What is your typical feeling when you use the system?	Frustrated Satisfied 1 2 3 4 5 6 7 8 9	NA
If this system were a person, how would you characterize its "personality"?	Hostile Supportive 1 2 3 4 5 6 7 8 9	NA
May we interview you to learn more about your opinions of the system?	No thanks Sure 1 2 3 4 5 6 7 8 9	NA
May we observe you while you use the system?	No thanks Sure 1 2 3 4 5 6 7 8 9	NA

Part 3: Presentation
How does information appear on the screen?

What is your impression of the overall appearance of screen displays?	Unappealing Appealing 1 2 3 4 5 6 7 8 9	NA
Amount of information on each screen	Inadequate Adequate 1 2 3 4 5 6 7 8 9	NA
How information is arranged on each screen	Confusing Clear 1 2 3 4 5 6 7 8 9	NA
Finding the correct option on a menu	Difficult Easy 1 2 3 4 5 6 7 8 9	NA
Number of screens required to perform a single task	Inadequate Adequate 1 2 3 4 5 6 7 8 9	NA
Placement of system messages	Unpredictable Predictable 1 2 3 4 5 6 7 8 9	NA
Finding what you need on a screen	Difficult Easy 1 2 3 4 5 6 7 8 9	NA
Knowing where to enter data	Confusing Clear 1 2 3 4 5 6 7 8 9	NA
Use of color	Unpleasant Pleasant 1 2 3 4 5 6 7 8 9	NA
Tones, beeps, blinking, and so on	Annoying Helpful 1 2 3 4 5 6 7 8 9	NA

Part 4: Conversation How easy is it for you to tell the system or application what you want to do next? How understandable are the system responses back to you?		
What is the general tone of system messages?	Unpleasant Pleasant 1 2 3 4 5 6 7 8 9	NA
Ability to control the amount of information you see in messages	Never Always 1 2 3 4 5 6 7 8 9	NA
Ability to "undo" an operation if you change your mind	Inadequate Adequate 1 2 3 4 5 6 7 8 9	NA
Explanations given in error messages	Ambiguous Precise 1 2 3 4 5 6 7 8 9	NA
The system tells you when you can start a new task	Rarely Frequently 1 2 3 4 5 6 7 8 9	NA
Speed of system operations	Sluggish Just right 1 2 3 4 5 6 7 8 9	NA
The system keeps you informed of what it is doing	Rarely Frequently 1 2 3 4 5 6 7 8 9	NA
Names of options on menus	Confusing Helpful 1 2 3 4 5 6 7 8 9	NA
The system warns you if you are about to take an action with serious consequences	Never Always 1 2 3 4 5 6 7 8 9	NA
Remembering names of commands	Difficult Easy 1 2 3 4 5 6 7 8 9	NA
Shortcuts for entering commands	Inadequate Adequate 1 2 3 4 5 6 7 8 9	NA
Commands used the same way in all parts of the system	Never Always 1 2 3 4 5 6 7 8 9	NA
Amount of information you have to type on data entry screens	Too much Just right 1 2 3 4 5 6 7 8 9	NA
Ability to save your work in the middle of a task	Inadequate Adequate 1 2 3 4 5 6 7 8 9	NA

Resource A   (Continued)

Part 5: Navigation
How easy is it for you to move around from one part of the system or application to another?

Do you find that you get "lost" in the system?	Frequently								Rarely				
		1	2	3	4	5	6	7	8	9			NA
Figuring out which menu contains the option you need	Puzzling								Obvious				
		1	2	3	4	5	6	7	8	9			NA
Getting to where you want to go	Confusing								Clear				
		1	2	3	4	5	6	7	8	9			NA
Getting back to where you were	Difficult								Easy				
		1	2	3	4	5	6	7	8	9			NA
How the system responds to your actions	Unpredictable								Predictable				
		1	2	3	4	5	6	7	8	9			NA
Availability of shortcuts to move around quickly	Inadequate								Adequate				
		1	2	3	4	5	6	7	8	9			NA
Moving from one data entry field to another	Inconsistent								Consistent				
		1	2	3	4	5	6	7	8	9			NA
Moving among multiple windows	Puzzling								Obvious				
		1	2	3	4	5	6	7	8	9			NA
Function key assignments	Confusing								Clear				
		1	2	3	4	5	6	7	8	9			NA
Arrangement of keys on the keyboard	Illogical								Logical				
		1	2	3	4	5	6	7	8	9			NA

Part 6: Explanation
Does the computer give you a helping hand when you need it?

Does it warn you if you are about to make a serious mistake?	Never									Always		
		1	2	3	4	5	6	7	8	9		NA
Does it explain how to correct your mistakes?	Never									Always		
		1	2	3	4	5	6	7	8	9		NA
Can you change your mind and "undo" your last action?	Never									Always		
		1	2	3	4	5	6	7	8	9		NA
Does it tell you which fields are optional on data entry screens?	Never									Always		
		1	2	3	4	5	6	7	8	9		NA
Do error messages explain how to fix the problem?	Never									Always		
		1	2	3	4	5	6	7	8	9		NA
How easy is it to use the on-line help facility?	Complicated									Simple		
		1	2	3	4	5	6	7	8	9		NA
How helpful is the information in the on-line help facility?	Unhelpful									Helpful		
		1	2	3	4	5	6	7	8	9		NA
Can you set up the system to match the way you want to work?	Never									Always		
		1	2	3	4	5	6	7	8	9		NA

Resource A   (Continued)

What is the overall appearance of the screen display?	Unattractive	Charming	
	1 2 3 4 5 6 7 8 9		NA
Design of icons	Unappealing	Appealing	
	1 2 3 4 5 6 7 8 9		NA
Deciding what the different icons mean	Puzzling	Easy	
	1 2 3 4 5 6 7 8 9		NA
Using scroll bars	Confusing	Obvious	
	1 2 3 4 5 6 7 8 9		NA
Moving between windows	Illogical	Logical	
	1 2 3 4 5 6 7 8 9		NA
Rearranging, opening, and closing windows	Confusing	Clear	
	1 2 3 4 5 6 7 8 9		NA
Finding, copying, deleting, moving files	Cumbersome	Easy	
	1 2 3 4 5 6 7 8 9		NA
Keyboard shortcuts available	Never	Always	
	1 2 3 4 5 6 7 8 9		NA
Knowing when you have selected an item on the screen	Confusing	Clear	
	1 2 3 4 5 6 7 8 9		NA
Switching between the mouse and the keyboard	Distracting	Easy	
	1 2 3 4 5 6 7 8 9		NA

Part 8: Additional comments
Is there anything else you want to tell us about the system or application?

_____

_____

_____

_____

_____

_____

_____

Resource B: Evaluation Task Selection Worksheet

System: _____ Date: _____

Source: _____

#	Initial Task List	core	frequent	high risk	n/a
1.	_____	☐	☐	☐	☐
2.	_____	☐	☐	☐	☐
3.	_____	☐	☐	☐	☐
4.	_____	☐	☐	☐	☐
5.	_____	☐	☐	☐	☐
6.	_____	☐	☐	☐	☐
7.	_____	☐	☐	☐	☐
8.	_____	☐	☐	☐	☐
9.	_____	☐	☐	☐	☐
10.	_____	☐	☐	☐	☐
11.	_____	☐	☐	☐	☐
12.	_____	☐	☐	☐	☐
13.	_____	☐	☐	☐	☐
14.	_____	☐	☐	☐	☐

Resource C: Presentation Interface Checklists

C.1. Presentation Interface Checklist #1: General Screen Design

Reviewer: _____ Date: _____

System: _____

Evaluation Task(s):

1. _____

2. _____

3. _____

4. _____

#	Review Checklist	yes	no	n/a
1.	For question and answer interfaces, are visual cues and white space used to distinguish questions, prompts, instructions, and user input?	☐	☐	☐
2.	Does the data display start in the upper-left corner of the screen?	☐	☐	☐
3.	Are multiword field labels placed horizontally (not stacked vertically)?	☐	☐	☐
4.	Have industry or company formatting standards been followed consistently in all screens within a system?	☐	☐	☐
5.	Is only (and all) information essential to decision making displayed on the screen?	☐	☐	☐
6.	Are all data a user needs on display at each step in a transaction sequence?	☐	☐	☐
7.	Are prompts, cues, and messages placed where the eye is likely to be looking on the screen?	☐	☐	☐
8.	Have prompts been formatted using white space, justification, and visual cues for easy scanning?	☐	☐	☐
9.	Does every display begin with a title or header that describes screen contents?	☐	☐	☐
10.	Has a heavy use of all uppercase letters on a screen been avoided?	☐	☐	☐
11.	Do abbreviations not include punctuation?	☐	☐	☐
12.	Do text areas have "breathing space" around them?	☐	☐	☐
13.	Are integers right-justified and real numbers decimal-aligned?	☐	☐	☐

Summary of Findings:

_____

_____

_____

_____

_____

_____

_____

_____

Side Issues:

_____

_____

_____

_____

_____

_____

_____

_____

_____

Resource C   (Continued)

C.2. Presentation Interface Checklist #2: GUI Screens

Reviewer: _____   Date: _____

System: _____

Evaluation Task(s):

1. _____

2. _____

3. _____

4. _____

#	Review Checklist	yes	no	n/a
1.	Is there a consistent icon design scheme and stylistic treatment across the system?	☐	☐	☐
2.	Is each individual icon a harmonious member of a family of icons?	☐	☐	☐
3.	Are icons concrete and familiar?	☐	☐	☐
4.	Are all icons in a set visually and conceptually distinct?	☐	☐	☐
5.	Has excessive detail in icon design been avoided?	☐	☐	☐
6.	Have large objects, bold lines, and simple areas been used to distinguish icons?	☐	☐	☐
7.	Has color been used with discretion?	☐	☐	☐
8.	Is a single, selected icon clearly visible when surrounded by unselected icons?	☐	☐	☐
9.	Does each icon stand out from its background?	☐	☐	☐
10.	Are icons labeled?	☐	☐	☐
11.	Are there no more than twelve to twenty icon types?	☐	☐	☐
12.	Can users choose between iconic and text display of information?	☐	☐	☐
13.	Are window operations easy to learn and use?	☐	☐	☐
14.	Has the amount of required window housekeeping been kept to a minimum?	☐	☐	☐
15.	Are there salient visual cues to identify the active window?	☐	☐	☐
16.	Does each window have a title?	☐	☐	☐
17.	Are vertical and horizontal scrolling possible in each window?	☐	☐	☐
18.	If setting up windows is a low-frequency task, is it particularly easy to remember?	☐	☐	☐
19.	In systems that use overlapping windows, is it easy for users to rearrange windows on the screen?	☐	☐	☐
20.	In systems that use overlapping windows, is it easy for users to switch between windows?	☐	☐	☐

Summary of Findings:

_____

_____

_____

_____

_____

_____

_____

Side Issues:

_____

_____

_____

_____

_____

_____

_____

Resource C   (Continued)
C.3. Presentation Interface Checklist #3: Menus

Reviewer: _____ Date: _____

System: _____

Evaluation Task(s):

1. _____

2. _____

3. _____

4. _____

#	Review Checklist	yes	no	n/a
1.	Does the menu structure match the task structure?	☐	☐	☐
2.	Have industry or company standards been established for menu design, and are they applied consistently on all menu screens in the system?	☐	☐	☐
3.	Are menu choice lists presented vertically?	☐	☐	☐
4.	Are menu choices ordered in the most logical way, given the user, the item names, and the task variables?	☐	☐	☐
5.	If there is a natural sequence to menu choices, has it been used?	☐	☐	☐
6.	If "exit" is a menu choice, does it always appear at the bottom of the list?	☐	☐	☐
7.	If the system uses a standard GUI interface where menu sequence has already been specified, do menus adhere to the specification whenever possible?	☐	☐	☐
8.	Are menu titles either centered or left-justified?	☐	☐	☐
9.	Are menu items left-justified, with the item number or mnemonic preceding the name?	☐	☐	☐
10.	Are meaningful groups of items separated by white space?	☐	☐	☐
11.	Do menu instructions, prompts, and error messages appear in the same place(s) on each menu?	☐	☐	☐
12.	Is there an obvious visual distinction made between "choose one" menus and "choose many" menus?	☐	☐	☐
13.	Have spatial relationships between soft function keys (on-screen cues) and keyboard function keys been preserved?	☐	☐	☐
14.	Does the system gray out or delete labels of currently inactive soft function keys?	☐	☐	☐

Summary of Findings:

_____
_____
_____
_____
_____
_____
_____
_____

Side Issues:

_____
_____
_____
_____
_____
_____
_____
_____

Resource C   *(Continued)*

C.4. Presentation Interface Checklist #4: Data Entry Screens

Reviewer: _____   Date: _____

System: _____

Evaluation Task(s):

1. _____

2. _____

3. _____

4. _____

#	Review Checklist	yes	no	n/a
1.	If users are working from hard copy, are the parts of the hard copy that go on-line marked?	☐	☐	☐
2.	If users are working from hard copy, does the screen layout match the paper form?	☐	☐	☐
3.	Does each data entry screen have a short, simple, clear, distinctive title?	☐	☐	☐
4.	In multipage data entry screens, is each page labeled to show its relation to others?	☐	☐	☐
5.	Is white space used to create symmetry and lead the eye in the appropriate direction?	☐	☐	☐
6.	Have items been grouped into logical zones, and have headings been used to distinguish between zones?	☐	☐	☐
7.	Are zones no more than twelve to fourteen characters wide and six to seven lines high?	☐	☐	☐
8.	Have zones been separated by spaces, lines, color, letters, bold titles, rules lines, or shaded areas?	☐	☐	☐
9.	If the database includes groups of data, can users enter more than one group on a single screen?	☐	☐	☐
10.	If users are experts, usage is frequent, or the system has a slow response time, are there fewer screens (more information per screen)?	☐	☐	☐
11.	If users are novices, usage is infrequent, or the system has a fast response time, are there more screens (less information per screen)?	☐	☐	☐
12.	Are on-line instructions visually distinct?	☐	☐	☐
13.	Do embedded field-level prompts appear to the right of the field label?	☐	☐	☐
14.	Do on-line instructions appear in a consistent location across screens?	☐	☐	☐

#	Review Checklist	yes	no	n/a
15.	Are field labels and fields distinguished typographically?	☐	☐	☐
16.	Are field labels brief, familiar, and descriptive?	☐	☐	☐
17.	Are field labels close to fields, but separated by at least one space?	☐	☐	☐
18.	Are field labels consistent from one data entry screen to another?	☐	☐	☐
19.	Are fields and labels left-justified for alpha lists and right-justified for numeric lists?	☐	☐	☐
20.	Are long columnar fields broken up into groups of five, separated by a blank line?	☐	☐	☐
21.	Are optional data entry fields clearly marked?	☐	☐	☐
22.	Are symbols used to break long input strings into "chunks"?	☐	☐	☐
23.	Do field labels appear to the left of single fields and above list fields?	☐	☐	☐
24.	Do related and interdependent fields appear on the same screen?	☐	☐	☐
25.	Have dots or underscores been used to indicate field length?	☐	☐	☐
26.	If overtype and insert mode are both available, is there a visible indication of which one the user is in?	☐	☐	☐
27.	If pop-up windows are used to display error messages, do they allow the user to see the field in error?	☐	☐	☐

Summary of Findings:

_____

_____

_____

_____

_____

_____

Side Issues:

_____

_____

_____

_____

_____

_____

_____

C.5. Presentation Interface Checklist #5: Attention-Getting Techniques

Reviewer: _____   Date: _____

System: _____

Evaluation Task(s):

1. _____

2. _____

3. _____

4. _____

#	Review Checklist	yes	no	n/a
1.	Is reverse video or color highlighting used to get the user's attention?	☐	☐	☐
2.	Is reverse video used to indicate that an item has been selected?	☐	☐	☐
3.	Are size, boldface, underlining, color, shading, or typography used to show relative quantity or importance of different screen items?	☐	☐	☐
4.	If shape is used as a visual cue, does it match cultural conventions?	☐	☐	☐
5.	Are borders used to identify meaningful groups?	☐	☐	☐
6.	Is sound used to signal an error?	☐	☐	☐
7.	Are attention-getting techniques used with care?			
	• Intensity: two levels only	☐	☐	☐
	• Size: up to four sizes	☐	☐	☐
	• Font: up to three	☐	☐	☐
	• Blink: two to four hertz	☐	☐	☐
	• Color: up to four (additional colors for occasional use only)	☐	☐	☐
	• Sound: soft tones for regular positive feedback, harsh for rare emergency conditions	☐	☐	☐
8.	Are attention-getting techniques used only for exceptional conditions or for time-dependent information?	☐	☐	☐

Summary of Findings:

_____

_____

_____

_____

_____

_____

Side Issues:

_____

_____

_____

_____

_____

_____

_____

_____

_____

C.6. Presentation Interface Checklist #6: Color

Reviewer: _____   Date: _____

System: _____

Evaluation Task(s):

1. _____

2. _____

3. _____

4. _____

#	Review Checklist	yes	no	n/a
1.	Are there no more than four to seven colors, and are they far apart along the visible spectrum?	☐	☐	☐
2.	Has color been used specifically to draw attention, communicate organization, indicate status changes, and establish relationships?	☐	☐	☐
3.	Has the same color been used to group related elements?	☐	☐	☐
4.	Is color coding consistent throughout the system?	☐	☐	☐
5.	Do the selected colors correspond to common expectations about color codes?	☐	☐	☐
6.	Does the system automatically color-code items, with little or no user effort?	☐	☐	☐
7.	Can users turn off automatic color coding if necessary?	☐	☐	☐
8.	Is color used in conjunction with some other redundant cue?	☐	☐	☐
9.	Is a legend provided if color codes are numerous or not obvious in meaning?	☐	☐	☐
10.	Are high-value, high-chroma colors used to attract attention?	☐	☐	☐
11.	Have pairings of high-chroma, spectrally extreme colors been avoided?	☐	☐	☐
12.	Are saturated blues avoided for text or other small, thin line symbols?	☐	☐	☐
13.	Is there good color and brightness contrast between image and background colors?	☐	☐	☐
14.	Have light, bright, saturated colors been used to emphasize data and have darker, duller, and desaturated colors been used to de-emphasize data?	☐	☐	☐

Summary of Findings:

_____

_____

_____

_____

_____

_____

_____

Side Issues:

_____

_____

_____

_____

_____

_____

_____

_____

Resource D: Conversation Interface Checklists

D.1. Conversation Interface Checklist #1: Prompts

Reviewer: _____ Date: _____

System: _____

Evaluation Task(s):

1. _____

2. _____

3. _____

4. _____

#	Review Checklist	yes	no	n/a
1.	Is the most important information placed at the beginning of the prompt?	☐	☐	☐
2.	Do the instructions follow the sequence of user actions?	☐	☐	☐
3.	When prompts imply a necessary action, are the words in the message consistent with that action?	☐	☐	☐
4.	Are user actions named consistently across all prompts in the system?	☐	☐	☐
5.	Are system objects named consistently across all prompts in the system?	☐	☐	☐
6.	Do keystroke references in prompts match actual key names?	☐	☐	☐
7.	On data entry screens, are tasks described in terminology familiar to users?	☐	☐	☐
8.	Are field-level prompts provided for data entry screens?	☐	☐	☐
9.	Do field-level prompts provide more information than a restatement of the field name?	☐	☐	☐
10.	For question and answer interfaces, are the valid inputs for a question listed?	☐	☐	☐
11.	For question and answer interfaces, are questions stated in clear, simple language?	☐	☐	☐
12.	Are prompts expressed in the affirmative, and do they use the active voice?	☐	☐	☐
13.	Are prompts stated constructively, without overt or implied criticism of the user?	☐	☐	☐
14.	Do prompts imply that the user is in control?	☐	☐	☐

#	Review Checklist	yes	no	n/a
15.	Are prompts brief and unambiguous?	☐	☐	☐
16.	If the system supports both novice and expert users, are multiple levels of detail available?	☐	☐	☐

Summary of Findings:

_____

_____

_____

_____

_____

_____

_____

_____

Side Issues:

_____

_____

_____

_____

_____

_____

_____

_____

Resource D (Continued)

D.2. Conversation Interface Checklist #2: Feedback

Reviewer: _____ Date: _____

System: _____

Evaluation Task(s):

1. _____

2. _____

3. _____

4. _____

#	Review Checklist	yes	no	n/a
1.	Is there some form of system feedback for every operator action?	☐	☐	☐
2.	After the user completes an action (or group of actions), does the feedback indicate that the next group of actions can be started?	☐	☐	☐
3.	Is there visual feedback in menus or dialog boxes about which choices are selectable?	☐	☐	☐
4.	Is there visual feedback in menus or dialog boxes about which choice the cursor is on now?	☐	☐	☐
5.	If multiple options can be selected in a menu or dialog box, is there visual feedback about which options are already selected?	☐	☐	☐
6.	Is there visual feedback when objects are selected or moved?	☐	☐	☐
7.	Is the current status of an icon clearly indicated?	☐	☐	☐
8.	Is there feedback when function keys are pressed?	☐	☐	☐
9.	Are error messages worded so that the system, not the user, takes the blame?	☐	☐	☐
10.	If humorous error messages are used, are they appropriate and inoffensive to the user population?	☐	☐	☐
11.	Are error messages grammatically correct?	☐	☐	☐
12.	Do error messages avoid the use of exclamation points?	☐	☐	☐
13.	Do error messages avoid the use of violent or hostile words?	☐	☐	☐
14.	Do error messages avoid an anthropomorphic tone?	☐	☐	☐
15.	Do all error messages in the system use consistent grammatical style, form, terminology, and abbreviations?	☐	☐	☐

#	Review Checklist	yes	no	n/a
16.	If the system supports both novice and expert users, are multiple levels of error message detail available?	☐	☐	☐
17.	If there are observable delays (greater than fifteen seconds) in the system's response time, is the user kept informed of the system's progress?	☐	☐	☐
18.	Are response times appropriate to the task?			
	• Typing, cursor motion, mouse selection: 50–150 milliseconds	☐	☐	☐
	• Simple, frequent tasks: less than 1 second	☐	☐	☐
	• Common tasks: 2–4 seconds	☐	☐	☐
	• Complex tasks: 8–12 seconds	☐	☐	☐
19.	Are response times appropriate to the user's cognitive processing?			
	• Continuity of thinking is required and information must be remembered throughout several responses: less than two seconds	☐	☐	☐
	• High levels of concentration aren't necessary and remembering information is not required: two to fifteen seconds	☐	☐	☐

Summary of Findings:

_____

_____

_____

_____

_____

_____

_____

_____

Side Issues:

_____

_____

_____

_____

_____

_____

_____

_____

_____

Resource D   (Continued)

D.3. Conversation Interface Checklist #3: Menus

Reviewer: _____   Date: _____

System: _____

Evaluation Task(s):

1. _____

2. _____

3. _____

4. _____

#	Review Checklist	yes	no	n/a
1.	Do menu choices fit logically into categories that have readily understood meanings?	☐	☐	☐
2.	Is each lower-level menu choice associated with only one higher-level menu?	☐	☐	☐
3.	Is the menu choice name on a higher-level menu used as the menu title of the lower-level menu?	☐	☐	☐
4.	Are menu titles parallel grammatically?	☐	☐	☐
5.	Are menu titles brief, yet long enough to communicate?	☐	☐	☐
6.	Are menu choices logical, distinctive, and mutually exclusive?	☐	☐	☐
7.	Is the first word of each menu choice the most important?	☐	☐	☐
8.	Are menu choice names consistent, both within each menu and across the system, in grammatical style and terminology?	☐	☐	☐
9.	Does the structure of menu choice names match their corresponding menu titles?	☐	☐	☐
10.	Is the menu-naming terminology consistent with the user's task domain?	☐	☐	☐
11.	If menu choices are ambiguous, does the system provide additional explanatory information when an item is selected?	☐	☐	☐

Summary of Findings:

_____

_____

_____

_____

_____

_____

_____

Side Issues:

_____

_____

_____

_____

_____

_____

_____

Resource D   (Continued)

D.4. Conversation Interface Checklist #4: Locus of Control

Reviewer: _____   Date: _____

System: _____

Evaluation Task(s):

1. _____

2. _____

3. _____

4. _____

#	Review Checklist	yes	no	n/a
1.	Are users the initiators of actions rather than the responders?	☐	☐	☐
2.	Do messages place users in control of the system?	☐	☐	☐
3.	Does the system provide *visibility*: that is, by looking, can the user tell the state of the system and the alternatives for action?	☐	☐	☐
4.	Does the system provide *mapping*: that is, are the relationships between controls and actions apparent to the user?	☐	☐	☐
5.	When a user's task is complete, does the system wait for a signal from the user before processing?	☐	☐	☐
6.	Can users type-ahead in a system with many nested menus?	☐	☐	☐
7.	Are users prompted to confirm commands that have drastic, destructive consequences?	☐	☐	☐
8.	Is there an "undo" function at the level of a single action, a data entry, and a complete group of actions?	☐	☐	☐
9.	Can users cancel out of operations in progress?	☐	☐	☐

Summary of Findings:

_____

_____

_____

_____

_____

_____

_____

_____

Side Issues:

_____

_____

_____

_____

_____

_____

_____

_____

Resource D   (Continued)

D.5. Conversation Interface Checklist #5: Commands

Reviewer: _____ Date: _____

System: _____

Evaluation Task(s):

1. _____

2. _____

3. _____

4. _____

#	Review Checklist	yes	no	n/a
1.	Are commands used the same way, and do they mean the same thing, in all parts of the system?	☐	☐	☐
2.	Does the command language have a consistent, natural, and mnemonic syntax?	☐	☐	☐
3.	Does the command language use normal action-object syntax?	☐	☐	☐
4.	Does the command language avoid arbitrary, non-English use of punctuation, except for symbols that users already know?	☐	☐	☐
5.	Does the system allow novices to use a keyword grammar and experts to use a positional grammar?	☐	☐	☐
6.	Does the command language employ user jargon and avoid computer jargon?	☐	☐	☐
7.	Are command names specific rather than general?	☐	☐	☐
8.	Does the command language allow both full names and abbreviations?	☐	☐	☐
9.	Do abbreviations follow a simple primary rule and, if necessary, a simple secondary rule for abbreviations that otherwise would be duplicates?	☐	☐	☐
10.	Is the secondary rule used only when necessary?	☐	☐	☐
11.	Are abbreviated words all the same length?	☐	☐	☐
12.	Can users define their own synonyms for commands?	☐	☐	☐
13.	Are character edits allowed in commands?	☐	☐	☐
14.	Does the system allow novice users to enter the simplest, most common form of each command, and allow expert users to add parameters?	☐	☐	☐
15.	Do expert users have the option of entering multiple commands in a single string?	☐	☐	☐
16.	Does the system provide function keys for high-frequency commands?	☐	☐	☐

Summary of Findings:

_____

_____

_____

_____

_____

_____

_____

_____

Side Issues:

_____

_____

_____

_____

_____

_____

_____

_____

Resource D   (Continued)

D.6. Conversation Interface Checklist #6: Data Input

Reviewer: _____ Date: _____

System: _____

Evaluation Task(s):

1. _____

2. _____

3. _____

4. _____

#	Review Checklist	yes	no	n/a
1.	For data entry screens with many fields or in which source documents may be incomplete, can users save a partially filled screen?	☐	☐	☐
2.	Can users reduce data entry time by copying and modifying existing data?	☐	☐	☐
3.	Does the system perform data translations for users?	☐	☐	☐
4.	Are input data codes meaningful?	☐	☐	☐
5.	Are input data codes distinctive?	☐	☐	☐
6.	Have frequently confused data pairs been eliminated whenever possible?	☐	☐	☐
7.	Have large strings of numbers or letters been broken into chunks?	☐	☐	☐
8.	Are data inputs case-blind whenever possible?	☐	☐	☐
9.	Do field values avoid mixing alpha and numeric characters whenever possible?	☐	☐	☐
10.	Have uncommon letter sequences been avoided whenever possible?	☐	☐	☐
11.	Does the system automatically enter leading zeros?	☐	☐	☐
12.	Does the system automatically enter leading or trailing spaces to align decimal points?	☐	☐	☐
13.	Does the system automatically enter a dollar sign and decimal for monetary entries?	☐	☐	☐
14.	Does the system automatically enter commas in numeric values greater than 9999?	☐	☐	☐
15.	Are character edits allowed in data entry fields?	☐	☐	☐
16.	Is the structure of a data entry value consistent from screen to screen?	☐	☐	☐
17.	Are typing requirements minimal for question and answer interfaces?	☐	☐	☐

Summary of Findings:

_____

_____

_____

_____

_____

_____

_____

_____

Side Issues:

_____

_____

_____

_____

_____

_____

_____

_____

Resource E: Navigation Interface Checklists

E.1. Navigation Interface Checklist #1: Navigating by Menus

Reviewer: _____ Date: _____

System: _____

Evaluation Task(s):

1. _____

2. _____

3. _____

4. _____

#	Review Checklist	yes	no	n/a
1.	If menu lists are short (seven items or fewer), can users select an item by moving the cursor?	☐	☐	☐
2.	If menu lists are long (more than seven items), can users select an item either by moving the cursor or by typing a mnemonic code?	☐	☐	☐
3.	If the system uses a pointing device, do users have the option of either clicking on menu items or using a keyboard shortcut?	☐	☐	☐
4.	Are inactive menu items grayed out or omitted?	☐	☐	☐
5.	Are there menu selection defaults?	☐	☐	☐
6.	Are menus broad (many items on a menu) rather than deep (many menu levels)?	☐	☐	☐
7.	If the system has deep (multilevel) menus, do users have the option of typing ahead?	☐	☐	☐
8.	If the system uses a type-ahead strategy, do the menu items have mnemonic codes?	☐	☐	☐
9.	If the system has many menu levels or complex menu levels, do users have access to an on-line spatial menu map?	☐	☐	☐
10.	If the system has multiple menu levels, is there a mechanism that allows users to go back to previous menus?	☐	☐	☐

#	Review Checklist	yes	no	n/a
11.	If users can go back to a previous menu, can they change their earlier menu choice?	☐	☐	☐
12.	Do GUI menus offer affordance: that is, make obvious where selection is possible?	☐	☐	☐
13.	Do GUI menus make obvious which item has been selected?	☐	☐	☐
14.	Do GUI menus make obvious whether deselection is possible?	☐	☐	☐
15.	Do GUI menus offer activation: that is, make obvious how to say ''now do it''?	☐	☐	☐

Summary of Findings:

_____

_____

_____

_____

_____

_____

_____

_____

_____

Side Issues:

_____

_____

_____

_____

_____

_____

_____

_____

Resource E *(Continued)*

E.2. Navigation Interface Checklist #2: Navigating in a Single Screen or Dialog Box

Reviewer: _____ Date: _____

System: _____

Evaluation Task(s):

1. _____

2. _____

3. _____

4. _____

#	Review Checklist	yes	no	n/a
1.	When the user enters a screen or dialog box, is the cursor already positioned in the field users are most likely to need?	☐	☐	☐
2.	Can users move forward and backward within a field?	☐	☐	☐
3.	Can users move forward and backward between fields or dialog box options?	☐	☐	☐
4.	Is the method for moving the cursor to the next or previous field both simple and visible?	☐	☐	☐
5.	Is the method for moving the cursor to the next or previous field consistent throughout the system?	☐	☐	☐
6.	If the system uses a pointing device, do users have the option of either clicking on fields or using a keyboard shortcut?	☐	☐	☐
7.	Has auto-tabbing been avoided except when fields have fixed lengths or users are experienced?	☐	☐	☐
8.	Are protected areas completely inaccessible?	☐	☐	☐

Summary of Findings:

_____

_____

_____

_____

_____

_____

_____

Side Issues:

_____

_____

_____

_____

_____

_____

_____

Resource E   (Continued)

E.3. Navigation Interface Checklist #3: Navigating Between Screens

Reviewer: _____   Date: _____

System: _____

Evaluation Task(s):

1. _____

2. _____

3. _____

4. _____

#	Review Checklist	yes	no	n/a
1.	If users must navigate between multiple screens, does the system use context labels, menu maps, and place markers as navigational aids?	☐	☐	☐
2.	If the system has multipage data entry screens, do all pages have the same title?	☐	☐	☐
3.	If the system has multipage data entry screens, does each page have a sequential page number?	☐	☐	☐
4.	If the system has multipage data entry screens, can users move backward and forward among all the pages in the set?	☐	☐	☐
5.	If the system uses a question and answer interface, can users go back to previous questions or skip forward to later questions?	☐	☐	☐
6.	Does the system offer "find next" and "find previous" shortcuts for database searches?	☐	☐	☐

Summary of Findings:

_____

_____

_____

_____

_____

_____

_____

_____

Side Issues:

_____

_____

_____

_____

_____

_____

_____

_____

Resource E   (Continued)
E.4. Navigation Interface Checklist #4: Navigating by Direct Manipulation

Reviewer: _____   Date: _____

System: _____

Evaluation Task(s):

1. _____

2. _____

3. _____

4. _____

#	Review Checklist	yes	no	n/a
1.	If the system displays multiple windows, is navigation between windows simple and visible?	☐	☐	☐
2.	Are there salient visual cues to identify the active window?	☐	☐	☐
3.	On data entry screens, do users have the option of either clicking directly on a field or using a keyboard shortcut?	☐	☐	☐
4.	On menus, do users have the option of either clicking directly on a menu item or using a keyboard shortcut?	☐	☐	☐
5.	In dialog boxes, do users have the option of either clicking directly on a dialog box option or using a keyboard shortcut?	☐	☐	☐
6.	Can expert users bypass nested dialog boxes with either type-ahead, user-defined macros, or keyboard shortcuts?	☐	☐	☐

Summary of Findings:

_____

_____

_____

_____

_____

Side Issues:

_____

_____

_____

_____

_____

E.5. Navigation Interface Checklist #5: Navigating with Input Devices

Reviewer: _____ Date: _____

System: _____

Evaluation Task(s):

1. _____

2. _____

3. _____

4. _____

#	Review Checklist	yes	no	n/a
1.	Do the selected input device(s) match user capabilities?	☐	☐	☐
2.	Do the selected input device(s) match environmental constraints?	☐	☐	☐
3.	If the system uses multiple input devices, has hand and eye movement between input devices been minimized?	☐	☐	☐
4.	If the system supports graphical tasks, has an alternative pointing device been provided?	☐	☐	☐
5.	Are cursor keys arranged in either an inverted T (best for experts) or a cross configuration (best for novices)?	☐	☐	☐
6.	Is the numeric keypad located to the right of the alpha key area?	☐	☐	☐
7.	Are important keys (for example, (ENTER), (TAB)) larger than other keys?	☐	☐	☐
8.	Has the system been designed so that keys with similar names do not perform opposite (and potentially dangerous) actions?	☐	☐	☐
9.	Are there enough function keys to support functionality, but not so many that scanning and finding are difficult?	☐	☐	☐
10.	Are function keys reserved for generic, high-frequency, important functions?	☐	☐	☐
11.	Does the system follow industry or company standards for function key assignments?	☐	☐	☐
12.	Are function keys arranged in logical groups?	☐	☐	☐
13.	Are the most frequently used function keys in the most accessible positions?	☐	☐	☐

Resource E   (Continued)

E.5. Navigation Interface Checklist #5   (Continued)

#	Review Checklist	yes	no	n/a
14.	Are the function keys that can cause the most serious consequences in hard-to-reach positions?	☐	☐	☐
15.	Are the function keys that can cause the most serious consequences located far away from low-consequence and high-use keys?	☐	☐	☐
16.	Do function keys that can cause serious consequences have an undo feature?	☐	☐	☐
17.	Has the use of qualifier keys been minimized?	☐	☐	☐
18.	If the system uses qualifier keys, are they used consistently throughout the system?	☐	☐	☐
19.	Are function keys labeled clearly and distinctively, even if this means breaking consistency rules?	☐	☐	☐
20.	Are function key assignments consistent across screens, subsystems, and related products?	☐	☐	☐

Summary of Findings:

_____

_____

_____

_____

_____

_____

Side Issues:

_____

_____

_____

_____

_____

_____

_____

_____

_____

Resource F: Explanation Interface Checklists

F.1. Explanation Interface Checklist #1: Error-Handling

Reviewer: _____ Date: _____

System: _____

Evaluation Task(s):

1. _____

2. _____

3. _____

4. _____

#	Review Checklist	yes	no	n/a
1.	Does the system prevent users from making errors whenever possible?	☐	☐	☐
2.	Does the system warn users if they are about to make a potentially serious error?	☐	☐	☐
3.	Can users easily reverse their actions?	☐	☐	☐
4.	If the system allows users to reverse their actions, is there a retracing mechanism to allow for multiple undos?	☐	☐	☐
5.	If an error is detected in a data entry field, does the system place the cursor in that field or highlight the error?	☐	☐	☐
6.	Do error messages inform the user of the error's severity?	☐	☐	☐
7.	Do error messages suggest the cause of the problem?	☐	☐	☐
8.	Do error messages provide appropriate semantic information?	☐	☐	☐
9.	Do error messages provide appropriate syntactic information?	☐	☐	☐
10.	Do error messages indicate what action the user needs to take to correct the error?	☐	☐	☐
11.	If the system supports both novice and expert users, are multiple levels of error-message detail available?	☐	☐	☐

Resource F (Continued)

F.1. Explanation Interface Checklist #1 (Continued)

Summary of Findings:

_____

_____

_____

_____

_____

Side Issues:

_____

_____

_____

_____

_____

_____

_____

F.2. Explanation Interface Checklist #2: Performance Support

Reviewer: _____ Date: _____

System: _____

Evaluation Task(s):

1. _____

2. _____

3. _____

4. _____

#	Review Checklist	yes	no	n/a
1.	Does the system intelligently interpret variations in user commands?	☐	☐	☐
2.	Do data entry screens and dialog boxes indicate the number of character spaces available in a field?	☐	☐	☐
3.	Do data entry screens and dialog boxes indicate when fields are optional?	☐	☐	☐
4.	Does the system complete unambiguous partial input on a data entry field?	☐	☐	☐
5.	Are there pop-up or pull-down menus within data entry fields that have many, but well-defined, entry options?	☐	☐	☐
6.	On data entry screens and dialog boxes, are dependent fields displayed only when necessary?	☐	☐	☐
7.	Do fields in data entry screens and dialog boxes contain default values when appropriate?	☐	☐	☐
8.	Can users set their own system, session, file, and screen defaults?	☐	☐	☐
9.	Are data entry screens and dialog boxes supported by navigation and completion instructions?	☐	☐	☐
10.	If menu items are ambiguous, does the system provide additional explanatory information when an item is selected?	☐	☐	☐
11.	Are there memory aids for commands, either through on-line quick reference or prompting?	☐	☐	☐
12.	Does the system correctly anticipate and prompt for the user's probable next activity?	☐	☐	☐

Resource F (Continued)

F.2. Explanation Interface Checklist #2 (Continued)

Summary of Findings:

_____

_____

_____

_____

_____

_____

_____

Side Issues:

_____

_____

_____

_____

_____

_____

_____

F.3. Explanation Interface Checklist #3: On-Line Help

Reviewer: _____ Date: _____

System: _____

Evaluation Task(s):

1. _____

2. _____

3. _____

4. _____

#	Review Checklist	yes	no	n/a
1.	Is the help function visible; for example, a key labeled HELP or a special menu?	☐	☐	☐
2.	Is the help system interface (navigation, presentation, and conversation) consistent with the navigation, presentation, and conversation interfaces of the application it supports?	☐	☐	☐
3.	Navigation: Is information easy to find?	☐	☐	☐
4.	Presentation: Is the visual layout well designed?	☐	☐	☐
5.	Conversation: Is the information accurate, complete, and understandable?	☐	☐	☐
6.	Is the information relevant?			
	• Goal-oriented (What can I do with this program?)	☐	☐	☐
	• Descriptive (What is this thing for?)	☐	☐	☐
	• Procedural (How do I do this task?)	☐	☐	☐
	• Interpretive (Why did that happen?)	☐	☐	☐
	• Navigational (Where am I?)	☐	☐	☐
7.	Is there context-sensitive help?	☐	☐	☐
8.	Can the user change the level of detail available?	☐	☐	☐
9.	Can users easily switch between help and their work?	☐	☐	☐
10.	Is it easy to access and return from the help system?	☐	☐	☐
11.	Can users resume work where they left off after accessing help?	☐	☐	☐

Resource F *(Continued)*

F.3. Explanation Interface Checklist #3 (Continued)

Summary of Findings:

_____

_____

_____

_____

_____

_____

Side Issues:

_____

_____

_____

_____

_____

_____

Resource G: Glossary

Active window   The window that is available for user manipulation. Several windows may be on the screen simultaneously, but the user can only manipulate the data in one at a time.

Alpha data   Input data that consist only of letters.
Example: Month: January.

Alphanumeric data   Input data that consist of both letters and numbers.
Example: Address: 33 Southern Road.

Auto-tabbing   Automatic movement of the cursor by the system after the user enters a character in the last position of a field (instead of the user pressing a key to move to the next data entry field). The purpose of auto-tab is to save keystrokes; however, some studies have shown that while auto-tab can may be appropriate for frequent users, it can actually slow performance for others.

Broad menus   A menu containing many choices (in contrast with *deep menus;* see entry following). Users are frequently able to move directly from a single menu to the screen they need.

Character edit   Allows a user to revise a command simply by typing over the incorrect characters rather than retyping the entire command.

Color coding   Assigning colors to system states or conditions (for example, the system clock is displayed in green when running in real time and in yellow when running batch processes).

Command   An instruction that can be interpreted and acted upon by the system.
Example: find region1

Command line   A single word or an instruction string (for example, "erase myletter.doc") that is typed by the user to select a system function or object.

Context-sensitivity   The content (and sometimes the structure) of the on-line help changes, depending on what the user is doing when help is requested.
Example: If a user is in a data entry field, pressing the (HELP) key displays instructions on what to type in the field. If a user is viewing a menu, pressing the (HELP) key displays information on each menu choice.

Controlling question   A question that breaks into the interviewee's response (for example, "Haven't we spent enough time on error messages? I have to get back to my list of questions or we'll never get done").

Conversation   The two-way communication from the system to the user (prompts, feedback, menus) and from the user to the system (locus of control, commands, data input).

Example: the wording of error messages is part of the conversation interface.

Data code   A short string of numbers or letters that represents a longer entry.

Example: The data entry code P may represent the status Pending.

Database   A data storage and retrieval system designed to capture data (*input*), manipulate (*process*), and report on it (*output*).

Deep menus   A menu containing only a few choices. When users select a choice, they are brought down to a lower menu level and the process continues until the required screen is reached. Deep menus are also called nested menus.

Default   A value that is assigned automatically by the system, and that remains in effect unless the user deliberately changes it.

Dependent field   A field in which information must be entered (for example, Spouse Name) after a particular value is entered in another field (for example, Marital Status = married).

Dialog box   A pop-up display that elicits one or more responses from a user.

Evaluation task   A core, frequent, or high-risk procedure that users perform on the system.

Explanation   The on-line performance support provided by the system to teach itself to users. For example, an on-line help system is part of the explanation interface.

Feedback   Describes the result of a user's action and informs the user of the system's current state.

Example: When the user issues a command to save a file to disk, the system responds, Unable to save file. Disk full.

Field   The part of the data entry screen into which the user enters information.

Field label   Identifies the kind of information that goes into a field.

Function keys   ''Shortcut'' keys that allow users to perform actions by pressing a key rather than by either entering a command or selecting an option from a menu. Function key labels on the keyboard can be *generic* ((F1), (F2), (F3)), *dedicated* ((ESC), (HOME), (DEL)), or a combination of the two.

Functions   The major activities the user can perform on a system, viewed from an external high-level perspective.

Example: Combine text and graphics, add a column of numbers in a table, or move a paragraph.

GUI   The acronym for graphical user interface. GUIs use icons to create the illusion that the system is composed of manipulatable objects.

High chroma   Bright saturated colors such as vivid reds, yellows, or oranges.

High contrast   A maximum difference in brightness between the light and dark areas of a high-contrast image.

Icon   A picture that represents an object (for example, an annual report) or a process (for example, setting up a printer).

Inactive item   A choice not currently available to the user, usually because of the system state. For example, in a word processor, if a document is not open, the "Save" choice is inactive because there is nothing for the system to save. Once a document is opened, the "Save" choice becomes active.

Intensity   The color level or shade of an object (for example, the selected menu choice might appear in a bold typeface, while the unselected menu choices are in plain text).

Leading question   A question phrased in a way that points to an answer (for example, "The menus seem fine . . . right?").

Leading zero   Used to fill in the blank spaces in fields that can accept numbers of different lengths.
Example: Quantity: 0037.

Lexicon   The specific names used in a command language.
Example: copy, find, delete, rename.

Loaded question   A loaded question requires an answer that poses a potential risk for the interviewee (for example, "Do you spend more time doing your work or reading the manual?").

Low contrast   A minimal difference in brightness between the light and dark areas of a low-contrast image.

Mapping   The relationship between a system control and a user's actions. For example, clicking on a menu name in a GUI interface (user action) pulls down the menu (system control).

Menu choices   The list of options available on a menu. Each menu offers multiple choices.

Menu level   A hierarchical structure frequently used by non-GUI systems to organize menus. Selecting an option from a high-level menu displays a lower-level menu and this progression continues until an option on the lowest-level menu is selected, allowing the user to accomplish a task.

Menu map   A graphic illustration of the menu hierarchy, often in the form of an organization chart. Users can display the menu map on the screen to determine where they are and where they can go next.

Menu title   The name of the menu. Each menu has a single title.

MIS   An acronym for management information systems.

MIS group   The organization that has primary responsibility for data processing within a company. In many companies, this group is responsible for developing and maintaining internal systems.

Multipage   Information that is too extensive to fit onto a single screen and spills over onto additional screens; because each screenful is usually called a "page," these entry screens are "multipage."

Navigation   The method or methods by which users move around from one part of the system to another. For example, selecting an item from a menu is part of the navigation interface.

Numeric data   Input data that consist only of numbers.
Example: Issue Date: 03/27/93.

Optional field   A data entry field that the user may leave blank. Many database systems require entry of some information (for example, social security number) and allow users the option of entering other information (for example, middle name).

Partial input   An incomplete value that is entered by the user, and completed by the system.
Example: Users can type jan and the system will record the entry as January.

Presentation   The design of individual screen elements and the arrangement of these elements on screens. For example, the placement of fields on a data entry screen is part of the presentation interface.

Productivity   A measure of the amount of output that can be produced in a given period of time.

Proficiency   A measure of the number of system functions being used by a representative sample of the user population.

Prompt   A system message that tells the user what to do next.
Example: After the user moves the cursor to a data entry field, the system responds with Enter status code (A, P, or R).

Pull-down menu   A permanent menu bar displayed at the top of many GUI system screens. To select options, users click on one of the menu titles in the menu bar, causing all of the choices available in that menu to appear. Thus, with GUI systems, all system options are visible at all times.

Qualifier key   A key that is pressed in combination with another key. Qualifier keys can increase the number of available keyboard shortcuts (for example, (F1), (ALT) (F1), and (SHIFT) (F1) can each perform a different function), but their overuse can make the interface confusing.

Quality   A measure of the degree to which output meets or exceeds an established standard.

Query   A search of the database to find a particular record or set of records. For example, a query might ask the system to display all customers with accounts that are more than three months overdue.

Record   A single instance of a collection of data in a database. For example, in a payroll database, an employee record contains the name, home address, and hourly wage for a particular employee.

Reverse video   A method of highlighting text information by placing a background behind the text and changing the text color; thus, while most on-screen text is yellow on a black background, the reverse video shows black text on a yellow background.

Saturation   The purity of the color in a scale from gray (low saturation) to the most vivid shade of the color (high saturation).

Scrolling   Used to bring a different part of a document into view when a window offers a view of only a portion of the document. GUI interfaces often have *scroll bars,* which can be manipulated on screen to scroll horizontally or vertically.

Semantics   The complete set of functions in a system and how they are driven by the command language.
Example: The four valid data entry codes for the Region: field are N,S,E,W.

Soft function keys   An on-screen display of the commands that correspond to function keys on the keyboard. They help users to remember the actions of generic function keys.

Spectrum   The range of available colors.

Syntax   The structure of a command language. Syntax rules govern the order of words and the use of punctuation.
Example: The syntax for the instruction "Change the name of this file from 1992report to 1993report" might be "rename 1992report 1993report" in one command language and "fnr 1992report : 1993report" in another.

Syntax-savvy user   A user who knows the specific details required to operate a specific system. For example, users of a specific word processor are syntax savvy if they know that (Ctrl) (Q) exits from this particular program and that (Ctrl) (N) opens a new file.

System requirements   A document, generally developed by the systems analysis or design group, that uses a combination of narratives and diagrams to describe how the system will operate. The *functional requirements* are the component of the system requirements that describe the business needs being met by the system.

System-savvy novice   A user who has had previous experience with computers but is new to a particular system or application. For example, a system-savvy novice may already know how to use a word processor but has never used a spreadsheet program.

Task-savvy novice A user who is new to the world of computers, but already knows how to do the work that must be accomplished on the computer. For example, a task-savvy novice already knows how to balance a checkbook but has never used a computer to perform this task.

Tiled windows A method of displaying several windows at once. Each window occupies its own portion of the screen, and there are no overlaps. Tiled windows are easy to find but displays may be small if a number of windows are open.

True novice A user who is new to the world of computers and has no prior experience with the work that must be accomplished on the computer.

Typing-ahead A method of bypassing nested menus. Each menu is assigned a code (generally a number or a letter); users enter a string of codes to jump directly to the desired menu level.

Undo An error-handling feature that allows users to "take back" their last action or set of actions. For example, select a block of text in a word processor. Select the Delete command by mistake (you meant to select the Cut command.) Select the Undo command, and the deleted text reappears. Some systems provide multiple levels of undo, where each individual action is reversed, working backwards one action at a time.

User guide A document, generally developed by the training or technical writing group, that describes how users interact with the system.

Visibility The user's ability to determine what actions are possible simply by looking at the system. For example, reverse video in a data entry field indicates that data can be typed into that field.

Window A view into a document. GUI interfaces are often characterized by the ability to display several windows on the screen at once, each containing a different type of data (for example, a letter, a spreadsheet, and a graph).

Zone An identifiable region of the data entry screen. Good screen design organizes related fields into zones in order to make them easier to find.

References

Andrus, G. R. "Human Interface User Analysis." *Performance & Instruction,* Jan. 1988, *27*(1), 5–6.

Apple Computer. *Macintosh Human Interface Guidelines.* Reading, Mass.: Addison-Wesley, 1992.

Asimov, I. "The Word Processor and I." *Popular Computing,* Feb. 1982, pp. 32–36.

Bailey, R. W. *Human Performance Engineering: A Guide for System Designers.* Englewood Cliffs, N.J.: Prentice-Hall, 1982.

Bailey, R. W. *Human Error in Computer Systems.* Englewood Cliffs, N.J.: Prentice-Hall, 1983.

Barnard, P. J., MacLean, A., and Hammond, N. V. "User Representations of Ordered Sequences of Command Operations." *Proceedings, Interact '84,* September 1984, *1,* 434–438.

Barrett, E. (ed.). *The Society of Text: Hypertext, Hypermedia, and the Social Construction of Information.* Cambridge, Mass.: MIT Press, 1991.

Bowen, D. "The Puny Payoff from Office Computers." In T. Forester (ed.), *Computers in the Human Context.* Cambridge, Mass.: MIT Press, 1989.

Bratton, B. "Getting Information from SMEs." *Performance & Instruction,* Aug. 1984, *23*(6), 25.

Brennan, S. "Conversation as Direct Manipulation: An Iconoclastic View." In B. Laurel (ed.), *The Art of Human-Computer Interface Design.* Reading, Mass: Addison-Wesley, 1990.

Brinkley, R. C. "Getting the Most from Client Interviews." *Performance & Instruction,* Apr. 1989, *28*(4), 5–8.

Bullock, D. *Training Consultant's Memo, 1*(1), pp. 3–8. Simpson Ville, Md.: D. Bullock, 1981.

Burgess, J. H. *Designing for Humans: The Human Factor in Engineering.* Princeton, N.J.: Petrocelli Books, 1986.

Burley-Allen, M. *Listening: The Forgotten Skill.* New York: Wiley, 1982.

Campbell, R. L. "Will the Real Scenario Please Stand Up?" *SIGCHI Bulletin,* Apr. 1992, *24*(2), 6–8.

Card, S. K., Moran, T. P., and Newell, A. *The Psychology of Human-Computer Interaction.* Hillsdale, N.J.: Erlbaum, 1983.

Carlisle, K. E. *Analyzing Jobs and Tasks.* Englewood Cliffs, N.J.: Educational Technology Publications, 1986.

Carr, C. "Performance Support Systems—The Next Step?" *Performance & Instruction,* Feb. 1992, *31*(2), 23–26.

Carroll, J. M. "The Adventure of Getting to Know a Computer." *IEEE Computer,* Nov. 1982, 49–58.

Carroll, J. M. *The Nurnberg Funnel: Designing Minimalist Instruction for Practical Computer Skill.* Cambridge, Mass.: MIT Press, 1990.

Chen, M., and Leahy, F. "A Design for Supporting New Input Devices." In B. Laurel (ed.), *The Art of Human-Computer Interface Design.* Reading, Mass.: Addison-Wesley, 1990.

Chin, J. P., Diehl, V. A., and Norman, K. L. "Development of an Instrument Measuring User Satisfaction of the Human-Computer Interface." *Proceedings of the CHI 1988 Conference on Human Factors in Computing Systems.* New York: Association for Computing Machinery, 1988, pp. 213–218.

Coe, J. B., and others. "Visual Display Units." *Report W/1/80.* Wellington: New Zealand Department of Health, 1980.

Downton, A. "Evaluation Techniques for Human-Computer Systems Design." In A. Downton (ed.), *Engineering the Human-Computer Interface.* New York: McGraw-Hill, 1991a.

Downton, A. "Dialog Styles: Basic Techniques and Guidelines." In A. Downton (ed.), *Engineering the Human-Computer Interface.* New York: McGraw-Hill, 1991b.

Downton, A., and Leedham, G. "Human Aspects of Human-Computer Interaction." In A. Downton (ed.), *Engineering the Human-Computer Interface.* New York: McGraw-Hill, 1991.

Duncan, J. B., and Powers, E. S. "The Politics of Intervening in Organizations." In H. Stolovitch and E. J. Keeps (eds.), *Handbook of Human Performance Technology.* San Francisco: Jossey-Bass, 1992.

Foshay, W. R., and Moller, L. "Advancing the Field Through Research." In H. D. Stolovich and E. J. Keeps (eds.), *Handbook of Human Performance Technology: A Comprehensive Guide for Analyzing and Solving Performance Problems in Organizations.* San Francisco: Jossey-Bass, 1992.

Foss, D. J., and DeRidder, M. "Technology Transfer." In J. M. Carroll (ed.), *Interfacing Thought: Cognitive Aspects of Human-Computer Interaction.* Cambridge, Mass.: MIT Press, 1987.

Freedman, D. P., and Weinberg, G. M. *Handbook of Walkthroughs, Inspections, and Technical Reviews: Evaluating Program, Projects, and Products.* New York: Dorset House, 1990.

Galitz, W. O. *User-Interface Screen Design.* Boston: QED Publishing Group, 1993.

Gause, D. C., and Weinberg, G. M. *Exploring Requirements: Quality Before Design.* New York: Dorset House, 1989.

Gery, G. *Electronic Performance Support Systems.* Boston: Weingarten Publications, 1991.

Gilbert, T. F. *Human Competence: Engineering Worthy Performance.* New York: McGraw-Hill, 1978.

Gilbert, W. S., and Sullivan, A. *The Mikado.* First performed by the D'Oyle Carte Opera Company in 1885. First published in Leipzig, Germany in 1898.

Grandjean, E. "Ergonomics Aspects of VDUs: Review of Present Knowledge." In E. Grandjean and E. Vigliani (eds.), *Ergonomic Aspects of Visual Display Terminals.* London: Taylor and Francis, 1980.

Grudin, J. "The Case Against User Interface Consistency." *Communications of the ACM,* Oct. 1989, *32*(10), 1164–1173.

Harmon, P., Maus, R., and Morrissey, W. *Expert Systems: Tools and Applications.* New York: Wiley, 1988.

Hartmanis, J. "Computing the Future." *Communications of the Association for Computer Machinery.* Nov. 1992, *35*(11), 30–40.

Hetzel, W. *The Complete Guide to Software Testing.* Wellesley, Mass.: QED Information Sciences, 1984.

Horn, R. E. *Mapping Hypertext.* Lexington, Mass.: Lexington Institute, 1989.

Horton, W. K. *Designing and Writing Online Documentation: Help Files to Hypertext.* New York: Wiley, 1990.

Horton, W. "The Wired Word: Designing Online Documentation." *Technical Communication,* May 1992, *39*(2), 258–263.

IBM Corporation. *Common User Access: Advanced Interface Design Reference* (Publication No. SC34-4290-00). 1991.

IBM Corporation. *Common User Access: Basic Interface Design Guide* (Publication No. SC26-4583-0). 1989.

Jackson, S. F., and Addison, R. M. "Planning and Managing Projects." In H. Stolovitch and E. J. Keeps (eds.), *Handbook of Human Performance Technology.* San Francisco: Jossey-Bass, 1992.

Jennings, K. *The Devouring Fungus: Tales of the Computer Age.* New York: W. W. Norton, 1990.

Jong, S. "Designing a Text Editor? The User Comes First." *Byte,* Apr. 1982, *7*(3), 284–300.

Karat, C., Campbell, R., and Fiegel, T. "Comparison of Empirical Testing and Walkthrough Methods in User Interface Evaluation." *Proceedings of the CHI 1992 Conference, Association for Computing Machinery,* Monterey, California, May 3–7, 1992, 397–404.

Kay, A. "User Interface: A Personal View." In B. Laurel (ed.), *The Art of Human-Computer Interface Design.* Reading, Mass.: Addison-Wesley, 1990.

Kearsley, G. *Online Help Systems: Design and Implementation.* Norwood, N.J.: Ablex, 1988.

Kemerer, C. "How the Learning Curve Affects CASE Tool Adoption." *IEEE Software,* May 1992, 23–28.

Kemerer, R. W., and Schmid, R. F. "How to Summarize Questionnaire Data and Extract Useful Information for Revisions." *Performance & Instruction,* July 1984, *23*(5), 9–10.

Laurel, B. "Interface Agents: Metaphors with Character." In B. Laurel (ed.), *The Art of Human-Computer Interface Design.* Reading, Mass.: Addison-Wesley, 1990.

Mack, R. L., Lewis, C. H., and Carroll, J. M. "Learning to Use Word Processors: Problems and Prospects." *ACM Transactions on Office Information Systems,* July 1983, *1*(3), 254–271.

Marcus, A. *Graphic Design for Electronic Documents and User Interfaces.* New York: ACM Press, 1992.

Mayhew, D. J. *Principles and Guidelines in Software User Interface Design.* Englewood Cliffs, N.J.: Prentice-Hall, 1992.

McConnell, V. C., and Koch, K. W. *Computerizing the Corporation: The Intimate Link Between People and Machines.* New York: Van Nostrand Reinhold, 1990.

Mcdonald, G. *The Education of Gregory Mcdonald.* New York: Warner Books, 1985.

Miller, J. R., and Jeffries, R. "Usability Evaluation: Science of Trade-Offs." *IEEE Software,* Sept. 1992, *9*(5), 97–102.

Moran, T. P. "Getting into a System: External-Internal Task Mapping Analysis." *Proceedings of the CHI 1983 Conference on Human Factors in Computing.* Boston, 1983, 45–49.

Nelson, T. E. "The Right Way to Think About Software Design." In B. Laurel (ed.), *The Art of Human-Computer Interface Design.* Reading, Mass.: Addison-Wesley, 1990.

Nielsen, J. "The Usability Engineering Life Cycle." *IEEE Computer,* Mar. 1992, *25*(3), 12–22.

Nielsen, J., and Molich, R. "Heuristic Evaluation of User Interfaces." *CHI '90 Proceedings,* Apr., 1990, 249–256.

Norman, D. A. *The Psychology of Everyday Things.* New York: Basic Books, 1988.

Oborne, D. J. "Ergonomics and Information Technology." In T. Forester (ed.), *Computers in the Human Context.* Cambridge, Mass.: MIT Press, 1989.

"Office Computer Use Continues to Increase." *IEEE Computer,* Oct. 1988, p. 64.

Peddie, J. *Graphical User Interfaces and Graphic Standards.* New York: McGraw-Hill, 1992.

Pipe, P. "Ergonomic Performance Aids." In H. Stolovitch and E. J. Keeps (eds.), *Handbook of Human Performance Technology.* San Francisco: Jossey-Bass, 1992.

Polson, P. G. "Cognitive Walkthroughs: A Method for Theory-Based Evaluation of User Interfaces." *International Journal of Man-Machine Studies,* May 1992.

Polson, P. G., and Kieras, D. E. "A Formal Description of Users' Knowledge of How to Operate a Device on User Complexity." *Behavior Research Methods and Instruments, and Computers,* 1984, *16*(2), 249–255.

Powell, J. E. *Designing User Interfaces.* San Marcos, Calif.: Microtrend Books, 1990.

Puterbaugh, G., Rosenberg, M., and Sofman, R. "Performance Support Tools: A Step Beyond Training." *Performance & Instruction,* Nov./Dec., 1989, *28*(10), 1–5.

Rettig, M. "A Succotash of Projections and Insights." *Communications of the ACM,* May 1992, *35*(5), 25–30.

Rheingold, H. "An Interview with Don Norman." In B. Laurel (ed.), *The Art of Human-Computer Interface Design.* Reading, Mass.: Addison-Wesley, 1990.

Ridgway, L. "Read My Mind: What Users Want from Online Information." *IEEE Transactions on Professional Communication,* June 1987, *30*(2), 87–90.

Rossett, A. "Analysis of Human Performance Problems." In H. Stolovitch and E. J. Keeps (eds.), *Handbook of Human Performance Technology.* San Francisco: Jossey-Bass, 1992.

Rossett, A., and Gautier-Downes, J. *A Handbook of Job Aids.* San Diego: Pfeiffer, 1990.

Rosson, M. B. "Effects of Experience on Learning, Using, and Evaluating a Text Editor." *Human Factors,* 1984, *26*(4), 463–475.

Rouse, W. B., and Morris, N. M. "On Looking into the Black Box: Prospects and Limits in the Search for Mental Models." *Psychological Bulletin,* 1986, *100*(3), 349–363.

Rowley, D. E., and Rhoades, D. G. "The Cognitive Jogthrough: A Fast-Paced User Interface Evaluation Procedure." *Proceedings of the Association for Computer Machinery, CHI 1992,* Monterey, California, May 3–7, 1992, 389–395.

Rubenstein, R., and Hersh, H. M. *The Human Factor: Designing Computer Systems for People.* Bedford, Mass.: Digital Press, 1984.

Rummler, G. A., and Brache, A. P. *Improving Performance: How to Manage the White Space on the Organization Chart.* San Francisco: Jossey-Bass, 1990.

Rummler, G. A., and Brache, A. P. "Transforming Organizations Through Human Performance Technology." In H. Stolovitch and E. J. Keeps (eds.), *Handbook of Human Performance Technology.* San Francisco: Jossey-Bass, 1992.

Salomon, G. "New Uses for Color." In B. Laurel (ed.), *The Art of Human-Computer Interface Design.* Reading, Mass.: Addison-Wesley, 1990.

Sellen, A., and Nichol, A. "Building User-Centered On-Line Help." In B. Laurel (ed.), *The Art of Human-Computer Interface Design.* Reading, Mass.: Addison-Wesley, 1990.

Shneiderman, B. *Designing the User Interface: Strategies for Effective Human-Computer Interaction.* Reading, Mass.: Addison-Wesley, 1992.

Shore, J. *The Sachertorte Algorithm.* New York: Viking Penguin, 1985.

Silber, K. H. "Intervening at Different Levels in Organizations." In H. Stolovitch and E. J. Keeps (eds.), *Handbook of Human Performance Technology.* San Francisco: Jossey-Bass, 1992.

Simpson, H. "A Human-Factors Style Guide for Program Design." *Byte,* Apr. 1982, *7*(3), 108–132.

Smith, B. R. *Soft Words for a Hard Technology: Humane Computerization.* Englewood Cliffs, N.J.: Prentice-Hall, 1984.

Stepich, D. "From Novice to Expert: Implications for Instructional Design." *Performance and Instruction,* July 1991, *30*(6), 13–17.

Stolovitch, H. D., and Keeps, E. J. (eds.). *Handbook of Human Performance Technology.* San Francisco: Jossey-Bass, 1992a.

Stolovitch, H. D., and Keeps, E. J. "What Is Human Performance Technology?" In H. D. Stolovitch and E. J. Keeps (eds.), *Handbook of Human Performance Technology,* San Francisco, Calif.: Jossey-Bass, 1992b.

Swanson, R. A. "Demonstrating Financial Benefits to Clients." In H. Stolovitch and E. J. Keeps (eds.), *Handbook of Human Performance Technology.* San Francisco: Jossey-Bass, 1992.

Tiemann, P. W., and Markle, S. M. "On Getting Expertise into an Expert System." *Performance & Instruction,* Nov. 1984, *23*(9), 25–29.

Tognazzini, B. "Consistency." In B. Laurel (ed.), *The Art of Human-Computer Interface Design.* Reading, Mass.: Addison-Wesley, 1990.

Tognazzini, B. *TOG on Interface.* Reading, Mass.: Addison-Wesley, 1992.

Tosti, D., and Jackson, S. F. "Influencing Others to Act." In H. Stolovitch and E. J. Keeps (eds.), *Handbook of Human Performance Technology.* San Francisco: Jossey-Bass, 1992.

Tufte, E. R. *The Visual Display of Quantitative Information.* Cheshire, Conn.: Graphics Press, 1983.

Tufte, E. R. *Envisioning Information.* Cheshire, Conn.: Graphics Press, 1990.

van Steenis, H. *How to Plan, Develop, and Use Information Systems: A Guide to Human Qualities and Productivity.* New York: Dorset House, 1990.

Weinberg, G. M. *Rethinking Systems Analysis and Design.* New York: Dorset House, 1988.

Weiss, E. "Improving Performance in the Automated Office." *Performance & Instruction,* July 1989, *28*(6), 29–33.

Wharton, C., Bradford, J., Jeffries, R., and Franzke, M. "Applying Cognitive Walkthroughs to More Complex User Interfaces: Experiences, Issues, and Recommendations." *Proceedings of the CHI 1992 Conference, Association for Computer Machinery,* Monterey, California, May 3–7, 1992, 381–388.

White, E. B. *Essays of E. B. White.* New York: HarperCollins, 1977.

Wilson, R. *Help! The Art of Computer Technical Support.* Berkeley, Calif.: Peachpit Press, 1991.

Wurman, R. S. *Information Anxiety.* New York: Doubleday, 1989.

Yang, Y. "Undo Support Models." *International Journal of Man-Machine Studies,* 1988, *28,* 457–481.

Index

A

Active window, 63, 152
Addison, R. M., 7
Alpha data, 125
Alphanumeric data, 125
Andrus, G. R., 37
Apple Computer, 22, 23, 25, 26, 57, 132
Asimov, I., 17
Association for Computing Machinery, 4
Attention-getting techniques: alternatives to redesign of, 85; evaluation of, 82-84; redesign of, 84
Auto-tabbing, 142

B

Bailey, R. W., 22, 23, 26, 37, 95, 162
Barnard, P. J., 20
Barrett, E., 166
Bowen, D., 4
Bradford, J., 14
Bratton, B., 37
Brennan, S., 26
Brinkley, R. C., 38, 184
Burgess, J. H., 18
Burley-Allen, M., 38, 184

C

Campbell, R., 22, 23, 26, 38
Card, S. K., 20
Carlisle, K. E., 38
Carr, C., 166
Carroll, J. M., 9, 17, 20, 48, 163, 166
Case study, flawed user-interface, 195-203

Character edit, 120
Chen, M., 26
Chin, J. P., 38
Coe, J. B., 24
Cognitive walkthroughs, and user interface review, 13, 14
Color coding, 86
Color displays: alternatives to redesign of, 89; evaluation of, 86-88; redesign of, 89
Command, 120
Command interface: alternatives to redesign of, 123; evaluation of, 93, 119-122; redesign of, 123
Command line, 46
Context sensitivity, 179
Conversation interface, 11, 32, 36, 39, 91-128; easy-to-learn features of, 22; easy-to-use features of, 26
Conversation Interface Checklist #1: Prompts, 98-100
Conversation Interface Checklist #2: Feedback, 103-105
Conversation Interface Checklist #3: Menus, 111-113, 212
Conversation Interface Checklist #4: Locus of Control, 116-117
Conversation Interface Checklist #5: Commands, 121-122
Conversation Interface Checklist #6: Data Input, 126-127, 213
Cost savings, and accessible user interface, 10

D

Data code, 125
Data entry screen displays, 54, 75, 142; alternatives to redesign of, 81; evaluation of, 75-81; redesign of, 34, 80-81